THE MURDER OF NAPOLEON

THE MURDER OF NAPOLEON

BEN WEIDER
AND DAVID HAPGOOD

CONGDON & LATTÈS, INC.

New York

Library of Congress Cataloging in Publication Data

Weider, Ben, 1923–
The murder of Napoleon.

1. Napoleon I, Emperor of the French, 1769–1821—
Death and burial. 2. France—Kings and rulers—Biography.
I. Hapgood, David. II. Title.
DC212.W44   944.05′092′4 [B]   81-17315
ISBN 0-86553-035-1   AACR2
ISBN 0-312-92548-4 (St. Martin's Press)

Published by Congdon & Lattès, Inc.
Empire State Building, New York, N.Y. 10001

Distributed by St. Martin's Press
175 Fifth Avenue, New York, N.Y. 10010

Published simultaneously in Canada by Thomas Nelson & Sons Limited
81 Curlew Drive, Don Mills, Ontario M3A 2R1

Designed by Irving Perkins

First Edition

AUTHORS' NOTE

Our account of Sten Forshufvud's quest is based on interviews and conversations conducted over a number of years. Our account of Napoleon's life and death at St. Helena is drawn from the ample contemporary documentation, both eyewitness testimony and secondary accounts. All four of the officers Napoleon took into exile with him wrote their memoirs. These are, with the date of their first publication: Emmanuel de las Cases, *Mémorial de Sainte-Hélène*, 1823; Charles-Tristan de Montholon, *Histoire de Sainte-Hélène*, 1846; Gaspard Gourgaud, *Journal de Sainte-Hélène*, 1899, and Henri-Gratien Bertrand, *Cahiers de Sainte-Hélène*, 1949–59. Both of Napoleon's physicians wrote memoirs: Barry O'Meara, *Napoleon in Exile*, 1822; and Francesco Antommarchi, *Les Derniers Moments de Napoléon*, 1825. So did two of Napoleon's valets: Louis-Etienne Saint-Denis (Ali), *Souvenir du Mamelouke Ali sur l'Empereur Napoléon*, 1922; and Louis Marchand, *Mémoires de Marchand*, vol. II, 1955. Napoleon's stay at the Briars is described by Betsy Balcombe, writing as Mrs. Abell, in her *Recollections of the Emperor Napoleon*, 1844. Among the many third-person accounts of those years, the most recent are Octave Aubry, *Sainte-Hélène*, 1935; Paul Ganière, *Napoléon à Sainte-Hélène*, 1956; and Ralph Korngold, *The Last Years of Napoleon*, 1959. The island itself is described in Gilbert Martineau's *La Vie Quotidienne à Saint-Hélène au Temps de Napoléon*, 1966. Events in France while Napoleon was in exile are described in Jean Lucas-Dubreton, *Le Culte de Napoléon*, 1960.

Major Characters
═ AT ST. HELENA ═

Antommarchi, Francesco (1789–1838). Napoleon's personal physician at Longwood House from September 1819 to May 1821.

Arnott, Alexander (1771–1855). English military doctor. Attended Napoleon in the last weeks of his life.

Balcombe, Betsy (1800–1873). Daughter of William Balcombe.

Balcombe, William (1779–1829). English naval agent at St. Helena; food purveyor for Longwood House 1815–1818.

Balmain, Alexander (1779–1848). Russian commissioner at St. Helena.

Bertrand, Fanny Dillon. Wife of Henri-Gratien Bertrand.

Bertrand, Henri-Gratien (1773–1844). Military engineer; grand marshal of Napoleon's palace at les Tuileries; at St. Helena 1815–1821.

Cipriani, Franceschi (1757–1818). Napoleon's agent and majordomo of Longwood House.

Cockburn, George (1772–1853). Rear-admiral; commanded Napoleon's escort to St. Helena; acting governor 1815-1816.

Gorrequer, Gideon (1781–1841). Adjutant to Governor Hudson Lowe.

Gourgaud, Gaspard (1783-1852). Artillery officer; at St. Helena 1815–1818.

Las Cases, Emmanuel (1766–1842). Count of the old aristocracy and author; at St. Helena 1815–1816.

Lowe, Hudson (1769–1844). Governor of St. Helena from 1816 to 1821.

Malcolm, Pulteney (1768–1838). Rear-admiral commanding St. Helena squadron, 1816–1817.

Marchand, Louis (1791–1876). Napoleon's chief valet; at St. Helena 1815–1821.

Montchenu, Claude Marin Henri. Commissioner of the Bourbon government at St. Helena.

Montholon, Albine de (1780?–1848). Wife of Charles-Tristan de Montholon.

Montholon, Charles-Tristan de (1783–1853). Count of the old aristocracy; major general; at St. Helena 1815–1821.

Noverraz, Abram. Valet to Napoleon.

O'Meara, Barry (1786–1836). Irish-born; English officer; physician to Napoleon; resident at Longwood House 1815–1818.

Pierron. Chef at Longwood House; at St. Helena 1815–1821.

Reade, Thomas (1785–1849). Lieutenant-colonel; chief of police at St. Helena.

Saint-Denis, Etienne (1788–1856). Valet to Napoleon. Known as Ali.

Stokoe, John (1775–1852). English military doctor; attended Napoleon briefly in 1818.

Sturmer, Barthelemy (1787–1853). Austrian commissioner at St. Helena.

Theed, John. Captain of the *Leveret*; called at Longwood House, January 14, 1816.

Wilks, Mark. Governor of St. Helena, 1815.

THE MURDER OF NAPOLEON

After my death, which cannot be far off, I want you to open my body. . . . I want you to remove my heart, which you will put in spirits of wine and take to Parma, to my dear Marie-Louise. . . . I recommend that you examine my stomach particularly carefully; make a precise, detailed report on it, and give it to my son. . . . I charge you to overlook nothing in this examination. . . . I bequeath to all the ruling families the horror and shame of my last moments.

—NAPOLEON TO HIS DOCTOR,
SIX DAYS BEFORE HIS DEATH

CHAPTER ONE

The tall, slender man with the bold cheekbones and the flowing gray-blond hair settled himself in his armchair and opened the book. It was the last of the memoirs to be published. He had been reading it with great interest, especially now that he had reached the account of the last days, for there still were questions in his mind about what had happened a century and a half ago on that distant island.

MAY 1821
LONGWOOD HOUSE, ST. HELENA

At dusk, they heard the cannon of the British garrison sound retreat, and the sun vanished in a burst of light. The Emperor sighed, and one doctor, his eyes on his watch, counted the time until he would sigh again. Fifteen seconds passed, then thirty, then a minute. The Emperor's eyes opened suddenly, and another doctor, who was standing by the Emperor's head, immediately closed them. The eyes rolled up under the lids. The pulse disappeared. It was eleven minutes before six. Napoleon was no more.

The melancholy duties of death fell first of all on Louis

Marchand. Marchand had been Napoleon's chief valet for the five-and-a-half years of exile at St. Helena. Now thirty years old, the sturdy Marchand had served Napoleon all his adult life. He was utterly devoted to his master, whom he considered the greatest man of his time, if not of all time. During the long, slow years of exile, Marchand had stayed aloof from the quarrels within the French colony living in isolation at Longwood House, and he had never sought a pretext for going home before the end. In the terrible last months, Marchand had spent almost every waking moment at his master's bedside. The dying Napoleon had rewarded his faithful valet by making him an executor of his estate, along with his two remaining officers. Now the loyal Marchand, who had cared for Napoleon in life, was charged with caring for him in death.

With his assistant valets, Marchand washed the Emperor's body with eau de cologne and carried it to the bedroom from the parlor that had served as the sickroom. They laid it on his iron campaign cot, the one that had accompanied him from battlefield to battlefield. The little room had been arranged as a mortuary chapel: the walls were draped in black, and candles lit an altar. A priest was reciting prayers. Gazing at his master's face, Marchand thought Napoleon in death looked twenty years younger than he had during the last months of his slow and painful dying.

"After my death, which cannot be far off," Napoleon had instructed his own doctor, "I want you to open my body. . . . I charge you to overlook nothing in this examination." Autopsy had become an obsession with Napoleon, as his body slowly succumbed to its mysterious ailment. "You won't know what's wrong with me," he told the doctor three weeks before he died, "until you cut me open." An autopsy was scheduled, therefore, at two o'clock the next afternoon, and Louis Marchand spent the morning preparing for it. He set up the trestle table, the one on which Napoleon used to spread out his beloved maps and refight his campaigns, in the billiard room. The room had been chosen because it was the largest and best lit of the twenty-three rooms

4

in Longwood House, the sprawling, gloomy building that had housed Napoleon and his entourage for all but the first months of their exile. Napoleon's bare body was carried in and placed on a sheet spread over the trestle table.

Shortly before two o'clock the participants and observers began quietly filing into the billiard room. Among the seventeen people present were Louis Marchand and his fellow servants; the two French officers, Montholon and Bertrand; representatives of the English governor of St. Helena; and seven doctors.

The autopsy that was about to begin would be an intensely political event: everyone in attendance knew that. Already the English governor, Sir Hudson Lowe, had arranged for one of his officers to take the first fast ship and carry the news of Napoleon's death to England, two months' sail away. It was the news for which the crowned heads of Europe, from England to Russia, from Spain to Sweden, had been waiting and hoping for six long years. Now they could rest easy on their thrones.

None had more cause to be relieved than Louis XVIII of France, the weak, unpopular monarch who had been put back on his family's throne by foreign armies after Napoleon's final defeat at Waterloo. For two decades Napoleon had terrorized the ruling aristocracies of Europe, first as the flaming young general of the French Revolution and then as the Emperor of the French and master of the Continent. During those years he had led his incomparable soldiers all over Europe, smashing the armies of the kings and carrying with him the seeds of the Revolution. Now at last he was dead, and the kings could hope that the Revolution was buried with him.

Napoleon was dead, but how and why? Why had a man whose physical vigor and stamina were legendary died at the early age of fifty-one? Napoleon had grown steadily weaker during his years in exile, and the cause of his poor health had become a bitter issue between the French at Longwood and their English guardians. The exiles blamed the climate of St. Helena and accused the English government of deliberately sending Napoleon there to

5

die. Napoleon's two resident doctors had diagnosed a "disease of the climate" as the cause of his illness and death. Hudson Lowe, the English governor, was so fearful of anything that might be blamed on himself or his government that he had court-martialed an English military doctor for diagnosing Napoleon as suffering from hepatitis because it was a disease that could be attributed to the island's environment. All this was known to the seventeen people now gathered in the billiard room and waiting for the autopsy to begin.

Of the seven doctors, six were English, all military, all subject to the discipline of Hudson Lowe, all aware of the political implications of their findings. The seventh, Francesco Antommarchi, was a thirty-year-old Corsican, trained in pathology, who had been Napoleon's personal physician for the last eighteen months of his life. Antommarchi, at Napoleon's request, was to perform the autopsy; the English doctors would observe. While the others in the room watched in silence, the young Corsican doctor went to work on Napoleon's body. He cut open the chest cavity to expose the vital organs for the doctors' inspection. He removed the heart, and it was sealed in an alcohol-filled silver jar; Napoleon had ordered that his heart be sent to his widow, Marie-Louise (but the English governor later ordered it buried with the body). Antommarchi removed the stomach, by general agreement the organ that was the seat of Napoleon's fatal illness, and opened it for the others to examine. At one point Antommarchi suggested examining the brain because, he said, "the state of that organ in a man like the Emperor would be of the greatest interest." The executors angrily denied him permission, saying the body should not be mutilated any more than necessary to determine the cause of death. Once the doctors had finished examining the organs, the chest cavity was washed out with an aromatic liquor—embalming materials were not available to preserve the corpse. With a surgical needle Antommarchi sutured up the incision he had made.

Everyone left the billiard room except Antommarchi and Marchand. The doctor asked the chief valet to help him take the

6

body's measurements and to record his findings. Then Marchand, who had so often dressed Napoleon in life, set about the sad ceremonial task of clothing his body for the last time. With the help of another servant, Marchand, as he later recounted in his memoirs, dressed him "in the full uniform of the light cavalry of the Imperial Guard; we put a white shirt on him, a white muslin cravat and over it a black silk collar, fastened in back by a buckle; white silk stockings; knee breeches of white Kenseymere, a vest of the same material, the green uniform with red trimming of the Guard cavalry, decorated with the orders of the Legion of Honor" —which Napoleon had founded—"of the Iron Crown, of Réunion; riding boots and his hat with the tricolor cockade."

At four o'clock, two hours after the autopsy had begun, Marchand and the other servants carried the Emperor's body back to his bedroom, and laid it on the iron cot in which he had died. Marchand and the others cut up as relics the blood-stained parts of the sheet on which the body had lain during the autopsy.

At the end the doctors had not been able to agree on a single written report on the cause of death. The seven doctors handed in four separate reports. They did agree that there was an ulcer in the stomach near the pylorus, the opening from stomach to intestine. Antommarchi called it a "cancerous ulcer"; the English doctors found "scirrhous portions leading to cancer." This led to the commonly accepted belief that Napoleon died of cancer of the stomach or pylorus, the latter having been the cause of his father's death, though none of the doctors reported an actual cancer. Such a verdict would relieve Hudson Lowe and the English of all responsibility: Napoleon would be seen to have died of a possibly hereditary ailment that had nothing to do with what happened at St. Helena.

But one of the English doctors, Thomas Shortt, also found the liver to be "enlarged." That was just what Hudson Lowe, suspicious even in his better moments, did not want to hear—a diseased liver would support the theory that Napoleon died of liver trouble caused by health conditions on St. Helena. The

7

Governor called Dr. Shortt to his office and ordered him to take the offending statement out of his report. Shortt reluctantly complied, but recorded what had happened once he was safely off the island. Antommarchi, like Shortt, had found the liver abnormally large though not visibly diseased. Antommarchi believed the English were responsible for Napoleon's death, because of the climate, and he said so. There was nothing Hudson Lowe could do to silence Napoleon's own doctor.

Three days later, on May 9, Napoleon was buried in a valley on St. Helena. On May 27 his followers embarked for England aboard the English ship *Camel*. They were returning after almost six years of exile in the South Atlantic to a world they had never known—a Europe without Napoleon.

On July 25, the fifty-ninth day at sea, Louis Marchand was summoned to the cabin of Count Charles-Tristan de Montholon. The captain of the *Camel* had just told Montholon the ship was in European waters: it was the time Napoleon had fixed for the reading of his will. In Montholon's cramped quarters Marchand joined his two fellow executors, Henri-Gratien Bertrand, the onetime grand marshal of Napoleon's palace, and Montholon. With them was the priest, Angelo Vignali, who had witnessed the signing of the will.

Montholon and Bertrand were the only officers who had remained with Napoleon through the exile. During those difficult years, the two had been rivals for Napoleon's favor. In the last months Montholon, a handsome, polished aristocrat, had won out over the quiet, retiring Bertrand, even though Bertrand had spent many more years in Napoleon's service. Montholon had been made first executor and entrusted with the will itself. Now his triumph was complete: he would read the will while his rival sat in silence.

Montholon broke the wax seals on the document he was holding and began to read aloud in his smooth courtier's voice. As Louis Marchand listened to his master's words, his mind went back to the agonizing days and nights, four months ago, when the dying Napoleon was struggling to commit his will to paper. During those last few months, Marchand had been at Napoleon's bedside almost without interruption. More than anyone else in the little exile colony, he knew day by day how Napoleon had suffered. Marchand remembered Napoleon propped up in his sickbed covering sheet after sheet in his almost illegible scrawl. His writing was interrupted repeatedly by terrible convulsions; the bedsheets were stained with vomit and ink; Napoleon fought to master his failing body and keep on writing. He had to get his last message out to those around him—and to the distant continent of Europe that he had once dominated.

The document Montholon was reading to the three men in the little cabin was what they could expect of the man who wrote it. Even on his deathbed, Napoleon was a master of detail. In the will he provided for those who had been with him, distributing all his personal possessions as mementos, and reaching far back in his memory to recognize with smaller bequests people who had served him in the early days of his career. Louis Marchand felt a sense of profound gratitude as he listened to what Napoleon had provided for him. He had left Marchand enough, in money and jewels, so that the young valet would never have to be anyone's servant again. Most important to Marchand was the one line in which Napoleon wrote of his valet: "His services to me were those of a friend." To be called friend by the great man was an honor beyond price. Another line in the will must have made the handsome, curly-haired Marchand smile. Certainly, given Napoleon's willingness to order the lives of those around him, it could come as no surprise when Montholon read the instructions to Marchand "to marry a widow, sister or daughter of an officer or soldier of my Old Guard."

Louis Marchand was determined that he would not fail in the duties that were being assigned to him. He would obey Napoleon in death as he had in life. Already, in the two months' sail that had brought the *Camel* to European waters, the young valet had ample reason to worry about his new responsibilities. He was in charge of three sealed mahogany trunks, packed with Napoleon's personal possessions and including locks of his hair, that he was to distribute to the immediate family and other relatives once he reached Europe. He also had mementos of his own that he was able to keep in his tiny cabin—fortunately, since a storm a few days earlier had wrecked or swept overboard many of the exiles' possessions. During the storm Marchand had lost his bottles of Napoleon's wine and, a personal treasure, the glass from which he served Napoleon during his final illness. Most painful to Marchand, the storm had swept overboard his last living relic of St. Helena: the branch he had picked, the day before they left, from one of the three weeping willows under which the man who had filled Marchand's life lay buried.

The will that Montholon read was also a weapon aimed at public opinion in the world Napoleon had left behind when he was sent into exile. The throne he once occupied was lost, the armies no longer his to command; but Napoleon was always a genius at contriving to use the weapons at hand. So, with his last weapon, the will, Napoleon aimed a shaft at those who sent him to die on that lonely island in the South Atlantic, and at his detested jailer, the English governor Hudson Lowe:

> I die prematurely, murdered by the English oligarchy and its hired assassin.

Napoleon's last accusation was to reverberate across Europe, just as its author had intended.

The *Camel* dropped anchor off Portsmouth on August 2, a week after Montholon had read the will to his fellow executors. By the time the ship arrived, Louis Marchand noted, its supply of fresh meat was down to two sheep. The news of Napoleon's death had arrived a month ahead of them, on the faster ship. In the harbor, while they awaited permission to land, Marchand saw —as in a bad dream—the *Northumberland,* the English ship that had taken them to St. Helena six years before.

When allowed to land, Marchand, unloading his three lead-sealed trunks of souvenirs, was met by friendly crowds who plied him avidly with questions about St. Helena. Marchand was surprised and moved by the reception he was getting from the English; he concluded that these people must have disapproved of the way their government had treated Napoleon. In fact, even during the years that Napoleon was fighting his gigantic duel against England, there had been an undercurrent among English liberals of admiration for Napoleon as the embodiment of the French Revolution; and now that he was dead it was safe to praise him (but the value of English government bonds had risen when the news arrived from St. Helena).

Marchand was soon given permission to go to France, and ten days after his arrival in England he was on the boat to Calais with his trunks and three of his fellow servants from St. Helena. Marchand was worried about how his precious relics would be treated at French customs. The customs chief picked a trunk at random and ordered Marchand to open it. It was the trunk containing Napoleon's clothes, and, Marchand wrote in his memoirs, "Everyone could see, in the open trunk, the Emperor's hat with the tricolor cockade of the Revolution, lying on a uniform of the Imperial Guard, on which could be seen the decoration of the Legion of Honor." Two employees started to ferret among the clothes, to Marchand's dismay, but the customs chief stopped them. "These are things that must be left to rest in peace," he told Marchand. Three days later Marchand was in Paris with his family, happy to find them all alive.

The exiles returning to their native land found a silent France. It was not for want of emotion: here, in the nation that he brought to the pinnacle of glory and then to defeat in the extraordinary fifteen years of his rule, passions about Napoleon were feverish. But little could be expressed in public under the Bourbon Restoration of Louis XVIII. The Bourbon rulers had ample reason to know how strong was Napoleon's hold on the French imagination and how weak was their own. It was only six years since Napoleon had effortlessly overthrown them when he

11

returned from his first exile in Elba. While he lived it could happen again; and during the St. Helena years the Bourbons had been constantly searching out Bonapartist conspiracies, most of which proved to exist only in their own fantasies. Now his death seemed at last to guarantee their rule. As one of Napoleon's veterans, Colonel Fantin des Odoards, wrote: "It is only from this moment that they can consider themselves firmly seated on the throne, for even when chained in the middle of the ocean, the Giant who made them tremble for so long was still a bugbear, an endless nightmare."

Whatever their private feelings of relief, the Bourbons did not rejoice in public. The government paper, *Le Moniteur*, had printed an item in its second column following trivial court news: "The English papers announce the death of Buonaparte" (as usual giving the original Italian spelling of his family name in an effort to deny him to France). The affable, sickly King Louis XVIII was silent; so was his fanatical brother and eventual successor, the Count d'Artois. D'Artois had spent much of his time during his own long years in exile in mounting plots on Napoleon's life. D'Artois was as bullheaded as he was sinister; but even he knew enough not to gloat openly over his great enemy's death.

Fear kept the French people from expressing their feelings except to their friends. Those who showed public sympathy for Napoleon got in trouble. A jeweler named Collier got three months in jail for selling a trinket bearing an inscription: "Weep, Frenchman, the great man is no more"; his improbable defense was that the "great man" was the Duke de Berry, the King's nephew assassinated (by a Bonapartist) more than a year earlier. Many people, especially in the countryside, just did not believe the news. There had been so many false rumors over those six years: Napoleon is dead—shot, strangled, smothered, pushed off a cliff; he has escaped from St. Helena, he is in America, he is leading an army of Turks against France . . . A year later, in a remote corner of rural France, Napoleon was believed to be living in a nearby monastery; peasants reported seeing him ride by on horseback dressed as a monk. From London the news of his death spread in less than a week across Europe, bring relief to the crowned rulers Napoleon had so many times defeated in battle, and sorrow to people whose hopes of change at home rested with "the Revolution concentrated in one man." In Parma, Marie-Louise, the Austrian princess Napoleon married for political reasons after he divorced Josephine, learned of her husband's death from a newspaper; Metternich, the Austrian minister of foreign affairs who had arranged her marriage, had not bothered to inform her. Marie-Louise, dominated by her Austrian royal relatives, had not sought to join her husband either in his first brief exile at Elba or at St. Helena. Now she decided to stage a funeral, but she did not argue when her lover, Count Neipperg, ordered that the name of the deceased was not to be pronounced during the service. She gave birth to Neipperg's child on August 15, the day Napoleon would have been fifty-two. Napoleon's ten-year-old son and heir, known as l'Aiglon, the eaglet, wept quietly at the news of his father's demise.

In Rome, Napoleon's mother, the formidable Madame Mère, refused at first to believe the reports. Some years earlier she had been persuaded by a clairvoyant that her son was not at St. Helena at all—he had been spirited away to an unknown destination. Finally convinced he was dead, she fainted, remained silent for two weeks, then wrote the British foreign minister, Lord Castlereagh, asking for her son's body. Castlereagh did not reply. Napoleon's favorite sister, the beautiful and wanton Pauline, was also in Rome. Only five days before she heard of the death, Pauline had written the British asking for permission to go to St. Helena to "join the Emperor and receive his last sigh." Her letter was dated July 11; her brother had been dead for more than two months.

Once they had returned to France, the exiles of St. Helena tried to pick up the threads of their lives. The Bertrand family went to their home in Chateauroux where, watched by the police,

Bertrand saw few people. Montholon went to Brussels to join his wife and children, who had left St. Helena two years earlier, then came back to Paris. Doctor Antommarchi went around Europe trying, unsuccessfully, to collect money he claimed was owing to him from the Bonapartes.

Louis Marchand settled in the town of Auxerre. The Emperor's valet still had duties to perform for his master. In his trunks was a supply of hair that had been shaved from Napoleon's head after his death. From this hair, on Napoleon's instructions, Marchand had made a bracelet for Marie-Louise and a watch chain for his son. He also enclosed locks of hair in gold medallions which he sent to the many members of the Bonaparte clan: mother and uncle, brothers and sisters, nieces and nephews. To make sure that no other hair was substituted for Napoleon's, Marchand had all the work done at his home. Then he set about a different task left to him by Napoleon: the Emperor's order in his will to "marry a widow, sister or daughter of an officer or soldier of my Old Guard." Marchand would not think to disobey, any more than he thought to disobey when, on St. Helena, Napoleon forbade him to marry a fellow servant who was carrying his child. Two years after his return to France he married Michelle-Mathilde Brayer, whose father had been a general of the Guard.

Louis Marchand did not use all the hair shaved from Napoleon's head in the keepsakes he made for the family. He kept one lock of hair for himself, and in time he left it with his unpublished memoirs to the daughter he had by the woman Napoleon had told him to marry.

CHAPTER TWO

AUTUMN 1955
GÖTEBORG, SWEDEN

========================= THE SEAPORT of Göteborg is Sweden's window on the world. This city of half a million people on the southwest coast looks out over the Kattegat strait to Denmark and the mainland of Europe. Many of the port's seventeenth-century settlers came from the Netherlands, and the canals they laid out give the old city an unmistakable Dutch appearance.

The outskirts of Göteborg, though, are largely made up of postwar development housing, the standard suburbia found all over the Western world. A visitor to number 9 Ulveliden would have found the three-story house hard to distinguish from its similarly mass-produced neighbors. Not so the man who now sat reading in the living room, for he was as distinctive as his dwelling was commonplace. Sten Forshufvud came off no one's assembly line.

Sten Forshufvud was a tall spare man, who then, in the autumn of 1955, was in his early fifties. The erect frame, the abundant blond hair, now graying, the strong brow over piercing blue eyes and high cheekbones: all were as Scandinavian as the name Forshufvud (pronounced for-*shoo*-fut). In manner, Forshufvud was courteous, almost courtly, and his speech, in any of his several languages, had an old-fashioned turn to it; it was easy to miss the occasional deadpan humor behind the apparently solemn exterior. He had the air of a European gentleman from the era that died in two world wars.

Despite this conventional manner, Forshufvud had spent a lifetime dissenting from the established wisdom in his chosen fields of endeavor. He had divided his working career between the practice of dentistry, at which he earned his living, and research in serology, the study of blood, and a related field, toxicology, the study of poison. His research led him to the conclusion that dental enamel is not dead but living tissue and is nourished by minute blood plasma vessels that he called ultracapillaries; if this were so, he reasoned, dental decay in children could be cured by proper nutrition. Forshufvud's opinions ran contrary to established opinion in his profession—a fact that did not disturb him in the least. Forshufvud's dissenting views were known only to those who read his articles in publications with names like *Acta Odontologica* and *Annales d'Anatomie Pathologique.* He was not known to the public at large.

That Sten Forshufvud had an interest beyond his scientific work would be immediately evident to anyone entering his home. Napoleon dominated the Forshufvud living room. Above the mantelpiece was a portrait made in porcelain of the Emperor in his coronation gown. On a huge, antique, gold-plated mirror was carved a gilt bust of the young, long-haired Napoleon as First Consul. A statuette of Napoleon on horseback stood on the table clock, and in the cupboard was a set of china decorated with the bee, Napoleon's personal symbol. The framed etchings on the walls were all of Napoleonic scenes. The largest of these was of the famous moment in the courtyard of the palace at Fontainebleau when Napoleon, leaving for exile in Elba, says farewell to his Imperial Guard. It was, Forshufvud's son Lennart later recalled, a "picture that made a child dream." Forshufvud's study

16

on the third floor was crammed with well-thumbed books on Napoleon and his time. Forshufvud got both his interest in Napoleon and his unorthodox views of science from his father. He had grown up, as his own three sons were to grow up, in a home where Napoleon was a revered presence. He remembered as a child reciting Napoleon's sayings for his father, and at fourteen he wrote his high school entrance essay on Napoleon; in it he described his subject as "one of the greatest personalities of world history." That year he also dropped out of school to go to sea, announcing to his father: "I have sat at my desk for too long." His father said: "I understand you."

Young Forshufvud got a ship going to the Black Sea, where he was briefly held prisoner by Bolshevik guerrillas fighting in the Russian Civil War. But he found that a maritime career was not really what he wanted, and he reluctantly decided he had to go back to school and learn a profession. His father was a physician, and the young man asked if he could follow in his footsteps. "No," his father said decisively, "there's enough humbug in this family already." Though he respected the science of medicine, the older Forshufvud had little use for many of his profession's practices, especially the use of chemical drugs, which he very rarely prescribed. In this, his opinions paralleled those of his idol: Napoleon promoted science generally and pioneered the use of military ambulances, but he distrusted doctors' prescriptions to the point that he once considered banning *all* drugs.

Rebuffed in his first choice, young Forshufvud asked if he might become a dentist instead. "Yes," his father pronounced. "A dentist is a craftsman, and a craftsman always earns his pay." Much later Forshufvud was to conclude that there was plenty of humbug in his profession too.

That evening in the autumn of 1955, Sten Forshufvud was sitting in his living room, under the eyes of the several Napoleons, and reading the memoirs of Louis Marchand. The memoirs of Napoleon's chief valet were the last of the eyewitness accounts of life at St. Helena to be published. Marchand had written his memoirs only for his daughter, in order, he said, "to show you—and later your children—what the Emperor was for me." Not until well into this century did Marchand's grandson, his daughter's only child, give permission for the memoirs to be published. The second volume, covering the years at St. Helena, had just come out in France.

Forshufvud had been especially looking forward to Marchand's account of Napoleon's last illness. The faithful valet had spent much more time at Napoleon's bedside than anyone else, and he had stayed aloof from the petty vendettas with which the exiles had filled their empty days. Marchand had no scores to settle in his memoirs, which in any event he did not intend to be published. For all these reasons, Forshufvud had reason to hope that Marchand's testimony might shed some light on the cause of Napoleon's death.

Forshufvud had always believed Napoleon's fall from power and premature death to be one of the great tragedies of all time. Napoleon was only forty-five when he went into exile; he could have ruled France—and Europe—for another two decades. He could have carried out his dream of a united Europe, a dream that he once put in these words: "My destiny is not yet accomplished. I want to complete what has only been sketched out. I want a European Code, a European Court of Appeals, the same currency, the same weights and measures, the same laws. I must make all the nations of Europe one nation. . . ." It was a dream that would not be realized, and then only in part, for another century and a half. If Napoleon had succeeded in that dream, Europe would have been spared the two terrible wars that drenched the Continent with blood during Forshufvud's lifetime. If Napoleon had only lived to do that—what a difference!

Accordingly, Forshufvud had followed with particular interest the continuing, unresolved debates among specialists over how and why Napoleon died. Physicians as well as historians were still putting forth restatements of a dozen theories: all were based on their varying interpretations of the same autopsy reports and eyewitness accounts. Forshufvud found them all unconvincing. He did not believe Napoleon had died of cancer, but he had not seen a conclusive case made for any other of the several explanations that had been argued. In Forshufvud's opinion, no one knew what killed Napoleon. But perhaps Marchand could offer some new evidence.

That evening Forshufvud had come to Marchand's detailed, day-by-day account of January to May of 1821, the last months of Napoleon's life. As he read, Forshufvud came across details he had not found in the other accounts. Marchand was providing glimpses of Napoleon's last ordeal, and of his own suffering at the approaching death of the man he worshipped. Touching as these passages were to Forshufvud, who had always admired the strength of character the young valet showed in the last days, what he reported did not at first seem to alter the known events of Napoleon's dying.

Marchand was adding detail to a well-known chronology. He told, with a convincing simplicity, how Napoleon was feeling on a given day; how the patient himself described his symptoms; what he ate on that date, *exactly* what he ate and how he reacted to it; how Napoleon responded to the medicines he was given, usually against his will; how Napoleon's body appeared to Marchand. And the valet described all this as the person—the only person—who in those last months had spent most of every twenty-four hours at Napoleon's bedside.

As he read on, Forshufvud began to sense that there was some kind of pattern in the details Marchand was reporting. Taken together, this information must mean something, but on the first reading Forshufvud could not tell what it was. Marchand described Napoleon alternating between somnolence and insomnia; how his feet were swollen and he complained that "my legs don't hold me up"; he observed that Napoleon had lost all the hair on his body—except on his head. Then, in the very last days, Marchand described the dying man's response to the sequence of drugs he was given.

As he pondered these facts, something tugged at Forshufvud's memory from his own studies of poison. Could Napoleon

19

after all have been poisoned? It seemed it could not have been done by a single lethal dose: the evidence of that would surely have shown up either in the autopsy or in the eyewitness descriptions of his last moments. But what about a slow killing, stretched out over months or even years, by repeated small doses of poison —of which, in Napoleon's time, the most likely was surely arsenic?

Now Forshufvud could see the pattern in Marchand's information. The alternating somnolence and insomnia; the swollen feet; the loss of body hair: all these Forshufvud knew to be symptoms of a chronic poisoning (or intoxication, as it is often called) by arsenic. Forshufvud remembered now that at the autopsy Napoleon's doctor, Antommarchi (and the British doctor Shortt, before he was overruled), found the liver enlarged but not visibly diseased: that was how an arsenic victim's liver would look.

Arsenic: Forshufvud knew that this poison had been around since time out of mind. It was particularly popular in France in the centuries just before Napoleon, when it was known as the "inheritance powder" because it was so often used to speed up the settlement of an estate. In many ways arsenic was the ideal poisoner's tool. Used as a pesticide, and even in tiny doses as a drug, it was always available. Odorless and bland, it is easily disguised by almost any food or drink. A fifth of a gram is enough to kill within twenty-four hours, but it was also common, with repeated small doses, to kill the victim slowly, over months or years. The advantage of the slow method was that, until well after Napoleon's time, it was virtually impossible to diagnose chronic arsenic poisoning because its symptoms are similar to those of many common illnesses. If certain other drugs—notably tartar emetic and calomel—were administered, death would be brought on while no trace of arsenic would be visible in the victim's stomach should the body be autopsied. Thus, since doctors at that time tended to prescribe those two drugs for almost any complaint, it was possible for the killer to get the doctor himself to finish off

20

the victim and destroy the evidence at the same time—the perfect crime.

It all made sense to Forshufvud as, with growing excitement, he put Marchand's testimony together with what he already knew about the circumstances of Napoleon's death. The doctors treating him would have no reason to diagnosis, or even suspect, arsenic because his symptoms could be explained, or so it would have seemed, by other ailments. Poison, in any event, was not an explanation the English doctors wanted to think about. And, at the autopsy, the seven doctors who examined the stomach would have seen no trace of arsenic because Napoleon had been given tartar emetic and calomel in the last days.

Forshufvud realized, also, that the arsenic theory would answer the most baffling of the many questions about Napoleon's death. The problem with the most common theory—cancer of the stomach—was that cancer victims grow emaciated as the disease progresses, while Napoleon got fatter and fatter almost to the end. But obesity is the rule among victims of slow arsenic poisoning.

Forshufvud turned to his wife, Ullabritta, in their living room and said in an abrupt, urgent tone that was unusual for him: "That's how they did it! They poisoned him with arsenic. Can you imagine that? The greatest crime of modern times! The evidence is right here in Marchand." And he slapped the book in his lap as if congratulating its long-dead author.

Forshufvud's wife was surprised at her austere, self-disciplined husband's excited manner. She could not help knowing quite a bit about Napoleon, and now she began to question him about the theory he had so suddenly announced. As he framed his answers, Forshufvud became even more convinced that the theory fit all the known facts. After a while she asked: "Do you know who did it?" Forshufvud shook his head; he had not begun to think about that. And then his wife asked: "Will you write about it?"

No, Forshufvud decided, he would not write about what he

21

had learned. It was not, after all, his line of work: he was a scientist, not a detective. Besides, the answer must be obvious to others. "Any pathologist, any toxicologist is bound to see it," he told his wife.

Forshufvud was wrong about that. But four years were to pass before the search for Napoleon's killer became the most important thing in Sten Forshufvud's life—a search that began with the day Napoleon and his little band of faithful followers were sent into exile at St. Helena.

CHAPTER THREE

JULY 1815
ABOARD THE *BELLEROPHON*

IT WAS Napoleon's most desperate gamble. Escaping from France after the disaster at Waterloo five weeks earlier, he had thrown himself on the mercy of the enemy he had fought for twenty years—the English. Now, on the morning of July 31, he was in their custody, waiting off Plymouth on board an English warship, the *Bellerophon,* to learn what they were going to do with him.

Napoleon and his entourage of close to one hundred people —officers, servants, wives, and children—had the freedom of the ship, and so they were able to see what a tourist attraction the fallen Emperor had become. The flood of tourists had begun a few days earlier, when the *Bellerophon* had anchored for a week off the town of Torbay, its first English landfall after it had been boarded by Napoleon. When word got out that he was on board, English notables besieged the Admiralty—without success—for permission to visit the ship. The docks were packed with people hoping for a glimpse of the fabled "Boney," the Corsican Ogre. Midshipman George Home, stepping ashore, was plied with questions by a group of young girls: "What was he like? Is he really a man? Were his hands and clothes all over blood when he came on board? Aren't you afraid of him?" People arrived on foot, on horseback, from as far away as London; all the rooms in the inns of Torbay were full. On the dock a woman asked, "Are they going to show him to us? Is he in chains?" Soon the ship was surrounded by rented boats filled with tourists. The sailors on the *Bellerophon* kept the tourists informed by hanging out a board on which they had chalked the news: "He's gone to breakfast." "He's gone back to his cabin."

The same scene was repeated on a much larger scale when the *Bellerophon* moved on to Plymouth, where Napoleon was now waiting to learn his fate. The bay was literally covered with boats, Midshipman Home recalled; people were paying as much as sixty pounds—a year's rent on a house—to rent a rowboat. In the boats, bands played popular French tunes in an effort to attract Napoleon's attention. By July 30, reported Frederick Maitland, captain of the *Bellerophon,* "the number of boats was greater than I had yet seen. I am sure I do not exaggerate by saying that there were over a thousand, with an average of eight persons in each." When guard boats tried to disperse the water-borne crowd, one boat was upset and a man drowned. Louis Marchand, Napoleon's valet, commented disapprovingly on the "revolting brutality" of this action.

Napoleon, evidently pleased at the attention, much of it friendly, he was getting from his foes, did not deny the tourists what they were looking forward to. Each day, whatever his anxiety about his own future, Napoleon went out on the deck of the *Bellerophon,* sometimes for an hour or more. None of what went on in the boats "escaped the eagle eye of Napoleon," Midshipman Home recalled. "He showed no disinclination to satisfy the eager spectators." Dressed in the green uniform of a colonel in his Imperial Guard, Napoleon strolled the deck, gazing down at the tourists staring up at him, and at times he smiled and tipped his famous cocked hat to the ladies. "What pretty women," he murmured occasionally. To Captain Maitland the fallen Emperor observed that the English seemed to have more than the usual dose of curiosity in their makeup.

If the tourists were crowding the harbor, it was because Napoleon Bonaparte was already a legendary figure all over Europe. His squat figure and broad brooding face, with the single lock of hair across the forehead above his piercing eyes, dominated the imagination of Europeans as he had dominated the Continent itself. No man was so loved, no man so hated and feared; no man's name had ever been so widely known in his lifetime. Everyone knew the incredible story of the obscure Corsican youth who, in his twenties, became the most successful general of the French Revolution; led a spectacular expedition to Egypt; made himself at thirty First Consul and master of France; in four brilliant years settled the conflicts of the Revolution, laid the foundations of a new France—the Napoleonic Code, the university and the schools, the administration—and brought the French people more personal opportunity and a greater, more widely shared prosperity than the people of any European nation had ever enjoyed; defeated on dozens of battlefields the combined armies of the crowned heads of Europe; made himself Emperor of the French; then, reaching beyond his grasp in his endless struggle against the English, lost his empire in the mountains of Spain and the snows of Russia; won it back for a hundred days, and lost it again at Waterloo. He was not yet forty-six years old.

Now, as he waited on board the *Bellerophon* for England's verdict, it seemed his meteoric career must be over. But Napoleon had been in tight corners before; that was when he was at his best. His life had been a series of brilliantly planned gambles. In a time when rank was determined by birth, only daring and an aspiration that denied all limits could have carried the young adventurer from nowhere to the mastery of Europe. Always against the odds, outnumbered in most of his battles, Napoleon studied his opponent carefully—then made the bold, unexpected move that won the day.

His decision to give himself up to the English was typical of

25

the man. He had considered other possibilities. In the confusion following his abdication, Napoleon had left Paris, riding out past his unfinished Arch of Triumph, and had gone to the Atlantic port of Rochefort with a few faithful followers. On the way, just outside Paris, he stopped at Malmaison, the palace he shared with Josephine before he divorced her. He lingered alone in the room where she had died a year earlier. Then he said his farewells to his mother, Madame Mère, and other relatives, including his two illegitimate sons, and went on his way.

France was in chaos. The Bourbon King Louis XVIII, ousted by Napoleon when he returned from Elba three months earlier, was waiting for the foreign conquerors to put him back on his throne. The French army was sullen and leaderless. Napoleon knew he had to leave France before the Bourbons were back in control if he was not to fall into the hands of those who had repeatedly conspired to have him killed. He toyed with a ship captain's offer to try to run the English blockade and get Napoleon to America. The new nation over there, the United States, had also been fighting the English; he could hope for welcome and, perhaps, a new world open to his talents. His brother Joseph, who resembled him, offered to impersonate Napoleon to give him a little more time for his getaway. The ship was ready, but still Napoleon, who never hesitated on the battlefield, could not make up his mind. Suppose the English captured him hidden in the hold of a ship running the blockade. What a humiliating end to his story!

By now Napoleon and his followers were holed up on the island of Aix, in the estuary of the Gironde River on the Atlantic coast. Napoleon was staying in a grim, gray house he had ordered built some years earlier for the local naval commander. Events were closing in on him. From his second-floor bedroom he could see the *Bellerophon*, the English ship of the line leading the blockade, patrolling off the harbor. Paris had fallen to the Allies and the Bourbons were back in France; Napoleon angrily threw to the floor the paper bringing him the news. Outside he heard the *Bellerophon* firing its cannon to celebrate the capture of Paris. Soon his enemies would reach his island refuge with orders to turn him over to the English as a prisoner of war. Napoleon listened silently to the desperate advice of his intimates: try America, try England, fight it out in France. As usual he told no one what he was thinking. At last, close to midnight, he reached his solitary decision. He ordered word sent to the captain of the blockade runner that he would not be coming aboard: America was out. Instead, he would stake his future on a dramatic appeal to the English. On July 14—Bastille Day in France—he sent emissaries out to the *Bellerophon* to tell its captain that Napoleon would surrender to him. On the following day Napoleon himself, dressed in full uniform, came on board followed by his entourage. With him he had a message for the Prince Regent of England:

Pursued by the factions which divide my country and by the hostility of the Powers of Europe, I have finished my political career, and I come, like Themistocles, to sit at the hearth of the British people. I put myself under the protection of the laws which I claim from Your Royal Highness as the most powerful, constant, and generous of my enemies.

The reference to Themistocles was calculated to appeal to what Napoleon knew about the English character. The Greek general forced into political exile after he had defeated the Persians was granted asylum by his enemies: would the English be less generous than the Persians?

During his first days on the *Bellerophon*, where he was treated as an honored guest, Napoleon had elaborated on his plans, or at least what he said were his plans. He wanted, he said, to take a pseudonym—perhaps Colonel Duroc or Colonel Muiron, the names of two aides killed in battle by his side—and live quietly in the country "ten or twelve leagues" from London. In fact, it seemed doubtful that Napoleon really wanted to live the

27

placid life of an English country squire. He had lived in the white heat of combat, on the battlefields of war and politics, ever since he was twenty-five. He had made one comeback, from Elba, only three months before. He was robust and energetic. Would he end his fabulous career at forty-five?

Whatever Napoleon may have been thinking and hoping, hardly anyone else believed in his role as country squire. His request for asylum had put the English government in a touchy situation. The English had all too much reason to fear Napoleon. In the years of their long struggle he had almost brought England to its knees, and at Waterloo, only six weeks earlier, he had almost won against huge odds; leading a hastily assembled army against much larger numbers of English and Prussians, Napoleon had once more outmaneuvered the opposing commanders, and might well have emerged victorious if the commander of his secondary army had not sat out the battle a few miles away. A man such as Napoleon had to be put away, and this time for good. Not in a nearby place like Elba, an island just off the northwestern coast of Italy; and certainly not in America, where he was bound to be warmly greeted by the former colonials who had gone to war with England in 1812, while Napoleon was in Russia. He could cause all sorts of trouble over there. Nor could they let him live in England. Like Elba, it was too close to the European scene. As Lord Liverpool, the Prime Minister, observed, if he stayed in England "he would become an object of curiosity immediately, and possibly of compassion within a few months."

In the brief two weeks he had been in their custody, the English had seen all too much evidence of Napoleon's magnetic personality: in the tourist boats clustering around the *Bellerophon* as the government deliberated his fate and, perhaps even more, in the remarkable impact he had had on the ship itself. Within days Napoleon had come to dominate life on the *Bellerophon.* Master of politics as well as war, he had set out to show the English that the Corsican Ogre was in fact very much human. He was unfailingly courteous to all, and maintained an outward show of good spirits (though on the day the ship left French waters he sat on the deck from dawn to noon, silent and motionless, staring at the receding shore of the empire he had lost). Shipboard schedules were arranged to suit him; Captain Maitland tried to provide him with French cuisine, although in fact Napoleon had little interest in food. He spent his days roaming the ship, inspecting its equipment, including even—one officer noted with surprise—the storerooms and sick bay, and talking with its people about, as one of them said, "anything and everything." His curiosity was insatiable. He questioned the officers about their war experiences, and especially about English ways, observing that "I'll have to learn to conform because I'll probably spend the rest of my life in England." He watched the ship's personnel at work, asked them about their duties, and commented on the differences between English and French practices; Captain Maitland was impressed by his knowledge of naval affairs. Language was no barrier. Many of the English spoke some French or Italian, Napoleon's two languages, and if not it did not seem to matter: a young midshipman would recall with delight years later how, when he gaped at the Emperor, "the great Napoleon" smiled at him, cuffed his head lightly, and pinched his ear.

The men Napoleon treated with a casual familiarity they never got from their own remote aristocratic officers. Napoleon knew the lives of soldiers better than any man in Europe. If French soldiers followed him with blind devotion, it was in large measure because he cared for their basic needs—water and food and clothing—better than any other commander, he shared their hardships on the campaign marches, and, when the fateful day came, Napoleon was on the battlefield with them while the enemy general was safely ensconced behind a hill. Now he spoke as confidently and easily with the English troops as he had once sat and talked with his own men around the campfires on the eve of battle. He asked about their years of service, the combat they had seen. To a surgeon he would say: "How many arms have you cut off?" And to a paymaster: "How much do you steal?" When he commented disapprovingly about the years one grizzled veteran had gone without promotion, he touched on a raw nerve, for many of the English were well aware that a man could rise by merit among the French, while among their own military only birth mattered. At a shipboard review of the troops, Napoleon suddenly plunged into the ranks, pushing aside bayonets with his bare hands, seized a startled soldier's musket, and demonstrated how to present arms in the proper French manner.

Incidents like this so endeared Napoleon to the troops that given a few more weeks, it seemed, they would follow him as loyally as his own Imperial Guard. Indeed, Napoleon had observed to one of his officers about the English troops: "What couldn't I do with two hundred thousand good men like these!" When he heard that, Midshipman Home mused to himself: "So you might well say, my most redoubtable Emperor, for give you two hundred thousand such fine fellows as these and allow you to land once more at Rochefort, and I shall be sworn for it that in three short weeks you would put Wellington and the Holy Allies flying before you in every direction . . . but it could not be."

No, a man who inspired that sort of admiration among their own soldiers was far too dangerous to be allowed to stay in England. Napoleon must somehow be put out of the way, and this time for good and all. Still, it was not in the English style to execute an opponent who, if implacable, had always been honorable in combat and, moreover, had the sympathy of a good number among the English who supported the goals of the Revolution. Nor was it good politics, for today's winner could always lose tomorrow; mindful of this, the rulers who sent men to die in battle protected their own lives by guaranteeing those of the opposing rulers. No less a figure than the Duke of Wellington, Napoleon's conqueror at Waterloo, dismissed the idea of shooting him as a "foul business." Hoping someone else would do the deed, the Prime Minister wrote that "we wish that the King of France would hang or shoot Buonaparte, as the best termination of the business."

But Louis XVIII was not prepared to do it either. True, he devoutly wished the threat of Napoleon permanently out of the way, but he could hardly afford to order his execution. Louis was a weak man in a weak position. The Bourbons were so unpopular in France that Louis could not even return to Paris except behind the guns of foreign armies. They had ample evidence that the French army was still loyal to the man who led it to glory before he led it to defeat; the soldiers would have torn France to pieces if the Bourbons had begun their second restoration by putting their hero to death. Louis made it clear he wanted the English to dispose of his enemy for him. That left only one solution: an exile from which the Corsican Ogre could not return. St. Helena —the remote, easily defended island in the South Atlantic—fit the bill perfectly.

On the morning of July 31, in his cabin, Napoleon heard the news that his desperate gamble had failed. An English admiral, Lord Keith, came on board the *Bellerophon* with an aide who, in halting French, translated the text of the decree banishing the Emperor to St. Helena. It was a particularly embarrassing job for Keith; his wounded nephew's life had been saved at Waterloo by Napoleon's personal intervention. Napoleon listened in silence to the decree. Then he burst out in anger: "It's worse than Tamerlane's cage of iron. . . . I'd rather be handed over to the Bourbons. . . . I put myself under the protection of the laws of your country. . . . The government is violating the sacred right of hospitality. . . . Might as well have signed my death sentence. . . ."

Despite the anger he professed, the news cannot have come as a surprise. Napoleon was above all a realist, and if, as he always did, he analyzed his opponent's situation, he certainly saw that the English would not give him the opportunity for another comeback. Even when he was on Elba, reports had reached him that his enemies, meeting in Vienna, were considering exiling him to a more distant island; St. Helena was one of those mentioned. There was a special irony in the choice of that island. In 1804, at the height of his power, Napoleon had briefly considered sending a naval expedition to capture St. Helena. "This objective would require from 1,200 to 1,500 men," he observed. The English were to send twice that number to guard a single man.

After his outburst Napoleon quickly regained his self-control. He left his cabin and, to Maitland's astonishment, he joined the captain on the bridge and made his usual appearance for the tourist boats as if nothing had happened. Then he went to his cabin. His valet, Louis Marchand, entering the cabin, "found the curtains drawn over the portholes; they were of red silk which gave the room a mysterious light. The Emperor had already taken off his uniform, saying he wanted to rest a little. Continuing to undress, he told me to go on reading to him from Plutarch's *Lives*, which was on the table, where the place was marked." Napoleon got in the bed and drew its green taffeta curtains, so Marchand could not see him. Marchand was worried, knowing that the Emperor—he would always be "the Emperor" to his faithful valet —"had on him the means to escape his enemies." Marchand recalled that "a thought of destruction came to me like lightning; I had a moment of inexpressible anguish . . . about what might take place before my eyes, when the Emperor without opening the curtains of the bed told me: 'Read.' I took the book and read in a firm enough voice to hide what I had been suspecting. After a half hour of reading that ended with the death of Cato, the Emperor came out from behind the curtains with a calm that made all my fears evaporate, and put on his bathrobe." After a time he sent Marchand to get one of his officers, Henri-Gratien Bertrand.

There was work to be done, and Napoleon, a voracious worker, set to it in his little cabin with Bertrand, without a word of disappointment about the failure of his gamble on the English or of regret about the American gamble he had passed up. The English had told Napoleon he could take into exile with him a maximum of three officers and a dozen servants. The exile could no longer choose among his many loyal followers in France; for this journey, his companions had to be culled from those who had hastily gone on board the *Bellerophon* with him two weeks earlier. Among the officers one choice was obvious: Bertrand. He was a dark-haired, slender man, a military engineer who had managed the imperial palace at les Tuileries with the rank of grand marshal. Bertrand was quiet, almost withdrawn, often irritatingly meticulous, and he was utterly loyal to Napoleon, whom he had served ever since the Egyptian campaign, when they were both in their twenties. He had followed his chief into his first exile at Elba, and he was ready to go into exile once again. His wife, Fanny, was not so ready. This tall, dark-eyed blonde was English on her father's side, and, after losing a child at Elba, she was looking forward to finding in England—where Bertrand had already transferred his substantial fortune—something like the glamorous social life she had enjoyed at the palace in Paris. When Fanny Bertrand heard about St. Helena, she burst into Napoleon's cabin unannounced, threw herself at his feet, screamed, and pleaded for her husband to be allowed to stay. Napoleon said only that Bertrand was free to do as he chose. The loyal Bertrand of course would go. In desperation his wife tried to throw herself out a porthole; Napoleon, with a smile, asked: "Do you think she really tried?" So the Bertrands went to St. Helena with their three children: there never really had been any doubt about it.

The other officers Napoleon picked were not such easy choices. None had been with him on Elba: during that first exile, two of those he chose had tried to land positions with the Bourbon rulers in Paris. Two were from the old pre-Revolutionary aristocracy. Count Charles-Tristan de Montholon had only been on the fringes of Napoleon's orbit; Napoleon barely knew him. Montholon was a handsome thirty-two-year-old with curly sideburns and the polished appearance of a courtier. Thanks to his family connections, he had held a series of military and diplomatic posts under Napoleon, and had distinguished himself in none of them. Although he held the rank of general, he had managed in those years of almost constant warfare never to see combat. Three years earlier, in 1812, when he was minister plenipotentiary to the

Grand Duke of Würzburg, Montholon married one Albine de Vassal, who had just divorced her second husband, without the Emperor's permission. Napoleon was then in Moscow, but the fact that he was in the middle of a desperate campaign did not stop him from running his empire with his usual attention to detail. He fired Montholon for a marriage which Napoleon considered "incompatible" with his diplomatic functions. Montholon reappeared after Waterloo, in the uniform of a court chamberlain, proclaiming his loyalty to Napoleon. He and the wife of whom Napoleon had once disapproved succeeded in ingratiating themselves with the Emperor on the *Bellerophon*. They went to St. Helena with their one child.

Las Cases—Emmanuel August Dieudonné Marius Joseph, Marquis de las Cases, to be exact—was also a latecomer, also from the old nobility. He had two useful assets: he was fluent in English, and he was a successful author. Las Cases told Napoleon that together they would write the history Napoleon had made; the opportunity to record that history seemed to be his motive for wanting to accompany the fallen Emperor into exile. He had the further distinction among the officers of being the only one who was both shorter (by an inch) and older (by four years) than Napoleon. Las Cases went to St. Helena with his fifteen-year-old son.

That made the quota of three officers, but now Gourgaud was heard from. Gaspard Gourgaud, thirty-two, an artillery officer like Napoleon, was a brave soldier who had saved Napoleon's life in Russia—so at least he said—and had fought at Waterloo. When he heard he was left off the list, Gourgaud stormed and wept and ranted. Unable on shipboard to escape the clamor of Gourgaud's entreaties, Napoleon agreed to make room for him by arranging to have Las Cases listed as a secretary. Gourgaud went to St. Helena without family.

Louis Marchand, the chief valet, held a position of the utmost trust. Napoleon's life was literally in his hands. He was in effect his chief bodyguard, and on shipboard Marchand slept on a mattress in Napoleon's cabin. He was twenty-four and single and knew no other occupation than serving Napoleon. He went to St. Helena as chief of the servants.

Among those listed as servants was a dark, silent man who in fact was much more than that. Franceschi Cipriani went back further with Napoleon than anyone else on board: as a youth he had been a hanger-on at the Buonaparte household in Corsica. Cipriani's role around Napoleon had always been mysterious, and not only because no one could understand the two of them when they spoke their Corsican dialect. From Elba, Napoleon had sent him to the mainland to spy on his enemies, and Cipriani's report that the Allies were considering sending Napoleon to a more remote place of exile was largely responsible for Napoleon's decision to make his dramatic return that ended at Waterloo. Cipriani went to St. Helena, and, like Louis Marchand, he went without family.

Napoleon was also allowed to take a physician. On the *Bellerophon* he had gotten on well with the ship's doctor, twenty-nine-year-old Barry O'Meara, an Irish Protestant who was fluent in Napoleon's native Italian and had served in Egypt after Napoleon was there. O'Meara accepted Napoleon's invitation to go to St. Helena. The English were pleased: the doctor might serve as a spy in the exile's household.

The English did not offer, nor did Napoleon ask, for his wife and four-year-old son to accompany him. Marie-Louise, the Austrian princess he married in an effort to legitimize his crown, had left him with their son before Elba and refused to join him in his brief return to power. None of the Bonapartes offered to join him either, though most of that numerous clan had been given wealth and position by their successful relative.

On August 7, Napoleon led his shrunken and oddly assorted little band of twenty-seven from the *Bellerophon* to a newer ship, the *Northumberland.* Louis Marchand had just time to write a brief note to his parents in France, whom he thought he might well not see again, before he went to work setting up Napoleon's iron campaign cot in the little cabin he had been given. Two days later the *Northumberland* set sail for the long voyage south to St. Helena.

CHAPTER FOUR

NOVEMBER 1959
GÖTEBORG

====================== **Y**EARS LATER Sten Forshufvud would recall as a landmark event the day in the Göteborg Library when he discovered Hamilton Smith. It was in November of 1959, several months after Forshufvud had decided somewhat reluctantly that he was going to devote a great deal of his time to solving the mystery of Napoleon's premature death.

Four years had passed since the evening on which Forshufvud had found, in the memoirs of Louis Marchand, what he believed to be evidence that Napoleon had died of arsenic poisoning. At that time, Forshufvud had assumed that someone in the coterie of Napoleon specialists would read Marchand's evidence as he had; it was not an outsider's job to point out the obvious to the experts. So during those years Forshufvud had devoted himself as always to his laboratory research and to his practice of dentistry, though, being the dissenting scientist that he was, that practice could not be a conventional one: Forshufvud limited himself to repairing the damage done by other practitioners' errors. "That still leaves me plenty of work," he was fond of saying. He followed the abundant flow of writing about Napoleon, from scholarly articles to popular biographies, watching for the inevitable revelation.

The revelation did not come, yet Forshufvud still resisted the idea of devoting himself to proving what he believed about the death of Napoleon. There was so much he could be doing in his laboratory. He had conducted pioneering research on blood and poison, and there was much more to be done. If he were to plunge into the Napoleon project—Forshufvud knew he would not go into it halfway, he was not that kind of man—it would take him away from his familiar laboratory, and surely it would cut into the time he could spend with his family. Besides, it was rather late in life—he was then in his late fifties—to enter this unknown territory. He would feel foolish if he failed. Yes, the arguments against it were compelling.

And yet Forshufvud was a dreamer and a dissenter as well as a scientist. He had gone to sea at fourteen because he refused to stay within the confines of school. In his research work, he had refused to stay within the bounds of established opinion, and that was what made his research valuable: he had pursued a dream and proved it in the laboratory. More than once, in his times of reflection, Forshufvud's thoughts turned to the man who was the subject of the project he was considering. That man was a gambler who followed his dream wherever it led him. Had he been anything less, the name Napoleon Bonaparte would be unknown except perhaps in an occasional thick history text where he might make a fleeting appearance as a minor French officer or as a Corsican politician named Napoleone Buonaparte. Forshufvud knew beyond any possible doubt what Napoleon would have done in his place.

What convinced Forshufvud at last that it *was* his job—that if the truth were ever to be known he would have to tell it—were two articles on Napoleon's death that appeared in Swedish publications. To Forshufvud's disgust, neither author mentioned the possibility of arsenic or discussed Marchand's new evidence; it was as if the memoirs of Napoleon's valet had never seen the light of day. The articles simply rehashed the old theories—cancer, hepatitis, a dozen others—that had been around for more than a century. "That settles it," Forshufvud announced one day to his family. "I'm going to have to do it myself." His wife, Ullabritta, prepared herself to see less of her husband: she had lived with him long enough to know that once he set himself an objective he would never relax in its pursuit.

Forshufvud began to spend all the time he could spare up in his third-floor study, working on what he was now calling "the Napoleon case." Trained in the disciplines of science, he went about this new kind of investigation in his usual methodical way. He reviewed the vast literature on arsenic, both its symptoms in the victim and its uses, legal and murderous, in Napoleon's day. He read and reread the accounts of eyewitnesses and the doctors' reports on the autopsy, studying them from his new perspective and comparing their testimony on details that had suddenly gained new meaning. He found himself living on familiar terms with people long dead in a world far separated in space and time from his comfortable Swedish home: the strange, unhappy world of Longwood House, set on that plateau on the lonely rock of St. Helena, surrounded by English soldiers and, beyond them, imprisoned by the empty South Atlantic ocean, where the exiled Emperor lay dying in the spring of 1821. Forshufvud watched those around Napoleon, his own entourage and their English jailers, playing out their roles in those last days. If Forshufvud was right, one of them had plotted and was now carrying out an historic murder. Which one? But Forshufvud with his usual self-discipline put that question out of his mind. He had not yet proved that Napoleon was poisoned, and without a crime there could be no point in searching for a criminal. There would be time for that later—if he was right. The scientific method was to prove one thing at a time and Forshufvud was always the scientist.

As he sifted through the records of Napoleon's last agonized months, Forshufvud became ever more firmly convinced that he was on the right track. The intuition that had come to him when reading Louis Marchand four years earlier was indeed the explanation of Napoleon's death. It was not an easy conclusion to reach, for arsenic poisoning is particularly baffling to diagnose. Its symptoms duplicate those of many common diseases. To complicate the diagnosis still more, some of the symptoms appear to be contradictory. Somnolence alternates with insomnia; general loss of appetite will be followed by a period when the victim is unusually hungry. One or even several symptoms cannot therefore be conclusive. But the evidence Forshufvud accumulated was overwhelming. Putting together the record of the autopsy, the casebook of Francesco Antommarchi, Napoleon's doctor, and Louis Marchand's detailed day-by-day description of the patient's condition, Forshufvud found that Napoleon in his last days showed no less that twenty-two of the thirty recognized symptoms of arsenic poisoning. That none of the witnesses who recorded those symptoms was thinking about the possibility of poison made their testimony all the more persuasive.

Equally important, there was nothing in the record to contradict the arsenic thesis. If all this was not seen by others who had read Marchand's testimony, it was because they were not looking for it: they were only trying to prove their own shopworn theories. Forshufvud was not surprised: his own years of experience in science and medicine had left him with little respect for most of their practitioners. Nor were historians any better. They all followed the herd.

Yet Forshufvud also knew, even after months of toil in his study, that he was a long way from being able to prove his theory, much less determine whether the poisoning was accidental or deliberate. There was, in fact, no physical evidence at all. The obvious way to get that evidence was to test Napoleon's remains for arsenic. Napoleon's body had been brought back to Paris nineteen years after his death, and now was lying in state in the great dramatic tomb of Les Invalides—under thirty-five tons of highly polished porphyry in the unusual colors of alizarin and burnt sienna. Forshufvud had to laugh as he pictured himself asking the French authorities to please move aside that huge slab so an unknown investigator, a foreigner at that, could test the body of the nation's hero for poison. Not a likely prospect: Forshufvud could not hope to call the victim's body as a witness. There was, Forshufvud thought, one other chance, though literally a slim one: Napoleon's hair. The body might be buried under a gigantic slab, but there was an excellent chance that some of Napoleon's hair was still in existence and outside the tomb. In Napoleon's day the lock of hair was a common souvenir of prominent people, the equivalent of the signed photographs that politicians hand out in modern times. Napoleon was known to have given away many locks of his hair. In his memoirs, Louis Marchand reported that he had brought back to France a quantity of hair shaved from his master's head right after his death; the valet had distributed most of the hair to the Bonaparte family, but one lock he left to his daughter. Forshufvud had learned also in his methodical research that hair was known to be an excellent place to measure the arsenic content of the body: the body tries to expel the poison through the hair. The method of analyzing hair for arsenic had been known and practiced for generations. So, if Napoleon's body would not bear witness to his death, perhaps his hair could.

But there was still another, seemingly insuperable obstacle. The current method of analysis required a comparatively large amount of hair—five grams, or approximately five thousand strands. That Forshufvud could find, somewhere in the world, a lock or two of Napoleon's hair seemed to him possible, even likely. That he could lay his hands on five thousand strands of that hair seemed as impossible a task as laying his hands on the thirty-five-ton slab of the tomb and pushing it off the Emperor's body. Physical evidence of arsenic seemed as remote as ever. It was a discouraging prospect, but Forshufvud was not a man to be easily discouraged, and he had kept on with his work, hoping, as a scientists so often do, for a break from some source as yet unknown.

That break came on the day in November when Forshufvud took the streetcar down to the Göteborg Library, as he regularly did, to check the latest issues of the scientific journals for something of interest to him. He found what he was looking for in an article in the journal *Analytical Chemistry*, reporting on a new method of testing hair for arsenic, a method moreover that required only a single strand. Forshufvud was as excited, sitting that day in the library's periodical room, as he had been in his living room four years earlier when he discovered the original evidence in Louis Marchand's memoirs. This was the break he had hoped for—if only he could obtain that single strand of hair, and he was sure that somehow he could. Forshufvud was sure, also, that day in the library, that he would not abandon the quest he had undertaken. He did not know where that quest would take him, or how long, but he would follow it to the end. He had come too far to stop.

The inventor of the new method of testing, the author of the article in the chemistry journal, was Dr. Hamilton Smith, a scientist in the department of forensic medicine at the University of Glasgow in Scotland. Hamilton Smith was a highly respected figure in the specialized field of toxicology, the study of poison. He had become interested in arsenic testing through a concern for the environmental effects of the poison, specifically in relation to lung cancer, for arsenic was then widely used as an insecticide on tobacco plants. Smith had sought a sensitive and reliable way of testing a small quantity of hair, and he had found it in a by-product of war: the research uses of nuclear energy. Working with the Harwell Atomic Research Center near London, Smith had developed a procedure in which the nuclear bombardment of a single strand of hair activates the arsenic in it in such a way that it can be accurately measured.

As he walked out of the library, Sten Forshufvud was both elated and relieved at what he had learned there. He was sure he could persuade Hamilton Smith to analyze a strand of hair for him. First, of course, he had to find the hair itself. The place to start this next stage of his quest was in Paris. Forshufvud decided he would write to the man known as Prince Napoleon, descendant of the Emperor's younger brother, Jerome, and the current representative of the Bonaparte clan.

CHAPTER FIVE
OCTOBER 1815
ST. HELENA

DINNER HAD just been served when the lookout gave the traditional and long-awaited cry of "Land!" The Admiral led Napoleon and his officers from the officers' lounge up to the bridge deck. It was seventy-one days since the *Northumberland* had sailed from Plymouth. The exiles strained to see the island to which they were being exiled. Through his spyglass Napoleon could make out the faint outline of a jagged mountain. "Diana's Peak," the Admiral said. Soon darkness fell and they could see no more. For one more night the exiles could see St. Helena not as it was but as they had variously pictured it during the long journey to the South Atlantic.

The exiles' life on the English warship, a seventy-four-gun ship of the line, had been a kind of dress rehearsal for St. Helena. The French lived in a strange half-world between freedom and prison. Neither guarded nor locked in their quarters at night, they had the freedom of the ship; yet at every turn, on deck or below, they confronted the red coats and the muskets of several hundred English soldiers stationed on board to prevent their escape. When they looked out over the ocean, they were likely to glimpse one of the nine other ships carrying still more soldiers to St. Helena. The lives of all on board the *Northumberland*, both French and English, revolved around the ambiguous figure of Napoleon —half a prisoner, still an Emperor. The English government, puzzled over how they should treat the one-time master of Europe, had finally decided to classify him for protocol purposes as a general without assignment—"General Buonaparte." It was a title Napoleon bitterly resented, and this seemingly petty issue became a never-ending source of conflict between French and English. Not that Napoleon cared about titles as such. He was too much of a realist for that. In his years of power he had dangled empty designations to make people do his will, had gotten men to die for a piece of ribbon, and when these were called baubles, he had answered: "Mankind is governed by such baubles." But his crown was different: it had been voted to him by the people of France in a referendum in 1804. He was, therefore, the only legitimate monarch in Europe. The man who believed above all in "the career open to talent," of which his own career was the most spectacular of examples, despised those who held power by the mere accident of birth. The Bourbon kings of France had first been given their title not by the people but by "a few bishops and priests," and none of the other monarchs who fought Napoleon had ever won his right to rule by the vote of his people. Such men might imprison him, kill him even, but they could not deprive him of his crown. Only the people of France could do that. So, to himself and to his followers, he would never be "General Buonaparte," always "the Emperor," even when, as now, his empire consisted of just twenty-seven men, women, and children.

Now, on the *Northumberland*, Napoleon had fallen into a routine far different from his sixteen-hour workdays at the Tuileries palace in Paris. He had been given the starboard of two small cabins on the poop deck just aft of the mizzenmast; the other was occupied by Admiral George Cockburn, commander of the flotilla sailing to St. Helena. These were the best quarters on the ship—the others on board, French and English alike, were piled into tiny, airless cabins—but on a warship the best was none too good. Louis Marchand, Napoleon's chief valet, had replaced the bed with one of the two iron cots with green taffeta curtains that accompanied Napoleon on every campaign. The rest of the furnishings consisted of a dressing table with washstand, a table and armchair, and some paintings that Marchand, himself an amateur painter, had hung on the walls in an effort to add some cheer to his master's glum lodgings. Marchand slept on a mattress on the floor of the cabin. Often his sleep was interrupted by a restless Napoleon demanding a candlestick, a book, pen and ink and paper. The valet would get a book from the collection he had hastily made up to replace the "campaign library," the six hundred volumes, packed in six mahogany chests that, like the iron cot, had always accompanied Napoleon when he went to war. Propped up on his cot, Napoleon read and made notes by candlelight, while the young valet lay sleepless on his mattress. During those long hours of the night, Napoleon seldom spoke except to give Marchand an order.

At dawn, Marchand brought Napoleon coffee, and about ten o'clock, a breakfast of meat and claret. Napoleon stayed in his tiny cabin most of the day. Often he would send Marchand to summon one of his officers. Usually it was Emmanuel de Las Cases, the English-speaking aristocrat and author who had joined Napoleon in the very last days in the apparent hope of becoming his historian. Las Cases was a self-important little man, much disliked by the other officers, who called him "the Jesuit" and were jealous of the newcomer who was getting so much of Napoleon's attention. With Las Cases, Napoleon began what was to be his last campaign: justifying himself before the judgment of history. Still in his dressing gown, he paced the few steps of his cabin, back and forth like a caged tiger, dictating from his prodigious memory his account of the years of war and power. "The Emperor dictates very fast, almost as fast as he speaks," Las Cases recalled. "I was therefore obliged to invent a kind of hieroglyphic writing; and I in turn dictated to my son." The next day Las Cases read back what he and his fifteen-year-old son had produced in the evening, and Napoleon revised it, doing a passage over as many as ten times until it was the way he wanted it.

In midafternoon, Marchand got out the familiar green colonel's uniform, and Napoleon dressed and went into the adjoining officers' lounge. There he played chess lackadaisically for a couple of hours with one of his officers. The master strategist was a mediocre chess player and he usually lost; his thoughts, whatever they were, appeared to be elsewhere. Dinner was at five in another room on the same deck. Napoleon presided at the large square table; two servants stood behind his chair to serve him. At his right sat Fanny Bertrand, the tall, blonde wife of his senior officer; on his left was the Admiral; the other officers, both French and English, and Albine de Montholon, were distributed around the table according to rank. By the Admiral's orders, the dinner conversation was in French, with Las Cases interpreting when needed, and was accompanied—to the displeasure of the French —by the music of the 53rd regimental band. Napoleon said little at table and, as had always been his habit, bolted his food, eating mostly with his fingers, and left while the English stayed on to drink and talk.

One night at dinner Napoleon saw a new face: Captain Wright, commander of a brig accompanying the *Northumberland.* "Are you related to the Captain Wright whom your libelers accused me of having strangled?" he demanded. "Yes, sire," the Captain answered. "I should be curious to know, sire, how the poor devil killed himself, for I never believed you had him hanged without reason." "Well, I will tell you," Napoleon began. He said that the other Captain Wright had commanded an English ship that landed on the French coast accomplices of those in the "infernal machine plot"—an assassination attempt in 1800 by French royalist emigrés that failed only because the bomb went off after Napoleon's carriage had passed. "I was weary of all these intrigues and resolved to put an end to them," Napoleon went on. He had Wright arrested and "I would have kept him in prison till the peace, but grief and remorse overwhelmed him—he committed suicide; and you English ought to be less astonished than any other people at such an occurrence because amongst you suicide is almost a national habit." With that pronouncement, Napoleon abruptly got up and left the table.

After dinner Napoleon would go up and pace the ship's deck in the company of one of his officers or, often, the Admiral himself. The fallen Emperor, short and now paunchy, and his tall jailer made an odd couple as they walked the deck, arm in arm, talking over their military adventures. Rear Admiral Sir George Cockburn, four years younger than Napoleon, was a spare, severe man, jealous of his authority but known for his fairness. He had fought the French at Toulon, where Napoleon won his first victory, and had commanded the English forces that captured Washington, D.C., during the War of 1812. Cockburn had started the voyage to St. Helena determined not to let England's prisoner "play the Emperor," but he had soon come to respect Napoleon's patience and good spirits in adversity. By the end of the journey, Cockburn's main concern was that Napoleon was becoming too popular, on this ship as on the *Bellerophon* a few weeks earlier, especially with the younger officers who goggled at him and mounted guard around him when he sat on the cannon they called the Emperor's gun.

After the evening walk on the deck, Napoleon went back to the officers' lounge and played cards with a group that usually included Cockburn, some of Napoleon's officers, and the wives of two of those officers, Fanny Bertrand and Albine de Montholon. They played whist or *vingt-et-un,* and the coins they wagered symbolized the recent history of France: the napoleon and the louis. Napoleon played mechanically, as if gambling a coin on the turn of a card were of little interest to the man who had gambled nations on the turn of a battle. He usually lost, except on August 15, which was his forty-sixth birthday. The occasion was marked only by a few toasts, none of the pomp of happier birthdays, and a winning night at *vingt-et-un.* When he retired to his cabin,

Napoleon said to Marchand: "My luck was such that I won eighty napoleons." Marchand found this remarkable since on most mornings he had to put a few napoleons in his master's purse to replace those lost the night before.

Such distractions were few and time hung heavy on the exiles' hands as the ship plowed slowly toward its destination. They crossed the equator: the familiar guidepost of the North Star disappeared from the night sky, replaced by the kite-shaped Southern Cross they had never seen. The exiles would remember the details that made one slow day different from another: the day they saw the flying fish; the day the man was lost overboard; the day Napoleon came on deck to see the live shark the sailors had caught and was splattered by its blood. Marchand got a box of watercolors—"to distract myself at St. Helena"—from a sailor allowed to go ashore at Madeira. He watched a flogging and wondered how human beings could tolerate such barbaric treatment which, he thought, must make them thereafter unable to "feel any sense of honor."

Most of the time the exiles were simply bored and, being bored, they quarreled. Fanny Bertrand, strong-willed and proper, quarreled with Albine de Montholon, once a beauty, now somewhat faded but still coquettish. Gourgaud, the tempestuous young artillery officer, who was single and did not like it, quarreled during dinner with Montholon, the elegant courtier, and took to his diary to write his catty observations about Albine. He did not think the dark-haired Albine was as beautiful as, in his opinion, she thought she was, and her habit of scratching her neck and smirking exasperated him. Nobody liked Las Cases, but the little historian loved himself enough to make up the difference. And they complained about the ways of the English—"so different from our own tastes!" Las Cases wrote.

The French knew little about what might await them at their remote destination, but they had cause to hope their exile would not be forever. A year ago Napoleon had been on Elba—Marchand and the Bertrands were with him there—and that exile had lasted only ten months. It could happen again. Perhaps France would throw out the Bourbons and call the Emperor back to his rightful place in the Tuileries palace. Perhaps they would be rescued: in the first days at sea, they saw some French ships passing and the rumor briefly flew that it was a rescue squadron. Or, at worst, the English would decide to let them spend their exile someplace closer to home. Most of all they hoped this endless journey would be over. "As for me," Louis Marchand wrote, "I was so tired of this floating house, so weary of these titles of General and Excellency given to the Emperor, that no matter what sort of place we had to live, as long as we were alone I would prefer it to the *Northumberland.*" And now at last, after more than two months at sea, they had arrived. In the morning they would see St. Helena.

The next morning the *Northumberland* dropped anchor off Jamestown, the island's only port. Napoleon dressed quickly and, accompanied by Marchand, went up on the bridge. There he and his followers gazed out at the place that was to be their home. They saw a great barren wall of basalt, unrelieved by any greenery, rising like a natural fortress to two equally desolate, slate-gray peaks. Directly in front of them, huddled in a cleft between two cliffs bristling with artillery, were the few houses, pale against the dark volcanic rock, of the tiny port of Jamestown. It was a hostile, forbidding landscape, far, far from the lush, green fields of France and the darker beauty of Napoleon's native Corsica. The French were appalled. "The devil must have shit this island as he flew from one world to the other," one of the women murmured. Even the English on board were repelled by a place that one of them, army surgeon Walter Henry, described as "the ugliest and most dismal rock conceivable, of rugged and splintered surface, rising like an enormous black wart from the face of the deep." To Marchand the island looked like a tomb. Napoleon stared in silence and—Marchand recalled—"after a few moments' examination, he went back to his cabin making no comment and giving no sign as to what was in his heart." A short while later, in his cabin, Napoleon said to Gourgaud: "It is not an attractive place. I would have done better to stay in Egypt. I would be Emperor of the Orient." Then he sent for Las Cases and went to work as usual.

Admiral Cockburn went ashore first, and a few hours later he brought the island's governor, Colonel Mark Wilks, to call on Napoleon in the officers' lounge. Wilks was a distinguished man of fifty-five, with abundant, curly gray locks over bushy black eyebrows, a scholar as well as an officer; his manner was easy and gracious. Since he was being replaced by Cockburn as governor, Wilks could talk freely. The two men got on well, and soon Napoleon was questioning Wilks in his usual rapid-fire way about the island he had governed for two years. He heard the full measure of his isolation: St. Helena, discovered in 1502 by the Portuguese and owned now by the English East India Company, lay 1,750 miles from Capetown in South Africa, 1,800 miles from South America, 4,000 miles from England; the nearest land, 700 miles away, Ascension Island, was just another English-owned volcanic speck in the empty ocean. Neither man had to state the obvious: its isolation was why the English had chosen St. Helena for Napoleon's second exile.

Who lived there? Wilks explained that the little island—only ten miles long by seven wide—had a population of four thousand, including a garrison of one thousand, now to be tripled thanks to Napoleon's presence. Of the civilians, fewer than eight hundred were European. The rest were blacks, Chinese, and Lascars, and three-quarters of the blacks were slaves. After each answer, Napoleon nodded and fired his next question at Wilks. The local people, known as Yamstocks after the staple of their diet, lived on the maritime trade brought by the island's location on the sea route from England to South Africa and India. Ships bound to and from the Orient called at St. Helena for water and a few days ashore in the grog shops that were the main business of Jamestown. Fuel, manufactured goods, meat, all had to be imported, and so the cost of living was very high.

51

The Yamstocks themselves were going wild on shore even as Wilks and Napoleon were discussing them in the ship's lounge. Normally what happened in the distant world outside mattered little to these insular people. It was three months before they heard the news, and it rarely affected them anyway. The local gossip was far more important. But now the islanders were getting ready for the biggest news in the history of St. Helena. They had learned about it five days earlier with the arrival of the brig *Icarus*, one of Cockburn's flotilla that had been separated from the *Northumberland* during a storm off Madeira. In fact, St. Helena heard about all of the great events of the last few months at that same time: Napoleon had left Elba and won back his throne, had lost it again after a hundred days at the Battle of Waterloo, and now, incredibly, he was about to arrive on their island.

Excitement had mounted day by day as the islanders waited for the *Northumberland*. Fear was mingled with their curiosity, for the Napoleon whose fame had reached them as a distant echo was a legendary, terrifying figure of more than mortal dimensions; he was the "Boney" that nurses told children would get them if they misbehaved. Betsy Balcombe, then fourteen, recalled that "the earliest idea I had of Napoleon was that of a huge ogre or giant, with one large flaming red eye in the middle of his forehead, and long teeth protruding from his mouth, with which he tore to pieces and devoured naughty little girls, especially those who did not know their lessons." Each day the islanders crowded onto the dock of Jamestown waiting to see the giant in chains come ashore. Two days later Napoleon at last came in on a small boat and stepped ashore on the stone steps of the small quay. But soldiers with fixed bayonets pushed the crowd back, and it was dusk. The islanders held up their lanterns and strained to see; Betsy Balcombe and her family were among them. They were disappointed. "It was too dark to distinguish his features," Betsy recalled. "He walked up the lines between the Admiral and General Bertrand, and enveloped as he was in his surtout, I could see little but the gleam of a diamond star which he wore on his heart.

... We returned to the Briars that night to talk and dream of Napoleon."

The *Record Book* of St. Helena on that date, October 17, 1815, reports the arrival on the *Northumberland* of "General Napoleon Buonaparte and certain individuals as state prisoners." That was the reality of their situation.

CHAPTER SIX
MAY 1960
PARIS

══════════════════ W<small>HEN</small> C<small>OMMANDANT</small> Lachouque agreed to see him, Sten Forshufvud decided his luck had
taken a turn for the better. It was about time.

Until the telephone call to Lachouque, Forshufvud's visit to
Paris had been a fiasco. He had come with his wife almost a week
ago, on the weekend before the Feast of the Assumption, expect-
ing to see Prince Napoleon—Napoleon Louis Jerome Victor
Bonaparte, the current heir of the Emperor's line. Forshufvud
had written Prince Napoleon from Göteborg, and the Prince had
replied inviting him to call if he were in Paris. Forshufvud had
come in the hope that Prince Napoleon could lead him to a lock
of Napoleon's hair which could then be tested for the presence
of arsenic.

Forshufvud had telephoned Prince Napoleon from his hotel
room the Monday after his arrival. He had reached the secretary
of the secretary of the Prince. The secretary of the secretary had
assured him that the secretary—one "Monsieur Fleury"—would
return Forshufvud's call. Forshufvud waited all day in his room,
while his wife went out to see Paris: it was her first visit. The

secretary did not call, and at 7:30 that evening Forshufvud decided he could safely leave his room to get something to eat. The next morning Forshufvud called again, and the secretary of the secretary expressed surprise that the secretary had not called; surely he would call Forshufvud today. Another long day of fruitless waiting in the hotel room dragged by. The next day, a Wednesday, Forshufvud made the same call, got the same reply, and again the secretary did not call.

Tomorrow would be Holy Thursday, the Feast of the Ascension and a major holiday. The silence at the other end of the telephone had convinced Forshufvud that Prince Napoleon did not want to see this stranger from Sweden who wanted to reopen the case of his illustrious ancestor's death. Now that he thought about it, Forshufvud could understand the Prince's reluctance to see the question raised. A Bonaparte—particularly the one viewed as the pretender to the first Napoleon's crown—had to walk carefully in France even in the mid-twentieth century. It was not so very long ago that the name Bonaparte evoked terror in many French hearts, and it was only ten years since the French government had abrogated the law barring the Bonapartes from residence on French soil. Raising the possibility that Napoleon had been poisoned could create a political storm that might endanger the Bonapartes' acceptance in France. The Prince had good reason to want the Emperor's bones to lie in peace. Forshufvud would get no help from that source.

While he had sat cooped up in the hotel room through those long days of fruitless waiting, Forshufvud had ample time to reflect on the quest that had brought him to Paris. He was beginning to feel uncomfortable, if not downright silly, in his new role of amateur detective. The face that looked back at him in the hotel mirror was that of a dignified, middle-aged gentleman: he did not look in the least like Sam Spade or any of the other fictional detectives who were Forshufvud's only experience of the world of crime and its detection. Not only was he out of place in this new role but, judging from his experience so far, he was a failure at it. He had made no progress in his quest and, come to think of it, he had scarcely even seen Paris, the city he had loved as a youth, except for the one street he now saw out the hotel window. He was a scientist, he had good work to do in Göteborg, work that he understood. Maybe it was time to go home. He came close during those days to giving it up, but Forshufvud was a stubborn man, and in the last few months he had invested a lot of himself in the search for the evidence that would prove his theory about the death of Napoleon. He would give it a few days more.

Shaking off his depression, Forshufvud cast around for another way to proceed. He wondered why he had not made an alternate plan in case he had no luck with Prince Napoleon. Well, it could not be helped now; he would have to improvise. He remembered then that the notes to Louis Marchand's memoirs referred to a "Madame Sylvestre" as possessing a lock of Napoleon's hair. The notes had been written within the last few years: it was worth a try. Forshufvud pulled out the hotel's Paris telephone directory, but soon found himself baffled again: there were at least fifty listings under "Sylvestre" and no way of knowing where to begin, or, for that matter, if "Madame Sylvestre" were alive and living in Paris.

Was there someone else he could try? Yes: Forshufvud turned to "Lachouque" and found to his relief that there was only one listing that could be *the* Commandant Henry Lachouque. This Lachouque was a leading member of the Paris circle of Napoleon experts, had been director of the army museum at Les Invalides, and had helped edit Marchand's memoirs. Lachouque could help him if he wanted to. Forshufvud dialed the number and reached Commandant Lachouque on the first try. He asked if he might call on him to discuss Napoleon. The voice at the other end of the line was cordial. They made an appointment for the following afternoon. Forshufvud decided things were looking up: at least someone in Paris would see him.

The man who ushered Forshufvud and his wife into his

56

living room in his Montmartre home proved to be a stocky, balding Frenchman of "a certain age," as the French say, and, like his guest, very much a gentleman of the old school. He was courteous to Forshufvud and with his wife he was gallant in the Gallic style—so much so, in fact, that Forshufvud thought perhaps the Frenchman had fallen in love at first sight. At Lachouque's invitation, Forshufvud outlined his theory, based on Louis Marchand's memoirs, that Napoleon was poisoned with arsenic. He told Lachouque how he had learned, only a few months earlier, of the procedure devised by Dr. Hamilton Smith of the University of Glasgow that made it possible to test a single strand of hair for arsenic. "That is what brings me here," Forshufvud concluded. "I am looking for a strand of the Emperor's hair."

"The Emperor's hair? I have some," Lachouque said. "Come with me." Sten Forshufvud is not a man to clap his hands and shout, but that was what he felt like doing as he followed Lachouque and Ullabritta out of the living room. At that moment it seemed to him the end of his quest was in sight.

The room they entered was Lachouque's private museum, a room filled with relics of the Emperor. Swords and sabers hung on the walls in fan-shaped arrangements. In one corner was a sort of shrine set off with drapes hanging from the ceiling. In the shrine a replica in white plaster of Napoleon's death mask—"The last face of the Emperor," Lachouque said—lay on a table draped in black velvet. There, too, was what had brought Forshufvud to Paris: Louis Marchand's *reliquaire,* the small wooden box in which the valet had left his mementos of the years at St. Helena. In the box were the sketches Marchand had made of the burial service, and the playing card on which he had scrawled, in the dark sick room one evening a week before the end, the last testamentary instructions of the dying Napoleon.

Also in the *reliquaire* was a small white envelope marked, in Marchand's handwriting, *"Les Cheveux de l'Empereur."* It contained a lock of hair shaved from the head the day after Napoleon died. Forshufvud gazed in silence at the lock—it was reddish-

57

brown and exceptionally silky—that had come from St. Helena and, after more than a century, was about to give up its secret. Commandant Lachouque took the envelope from the *reliquaire* and, in the grave manner of a man performing a ceremony, offered it to Forshufvud's wife. Forshufvud handed her a tweezer he had brought from Sweden. With skilled hands—she had been Forshufvud's dental assistant before she became his wife—Ullabritta Forshufvud carefully extracted a single hair from the several dozen that made up the lock and placed it in the small metal container held out by her husband. *"Allez-y, Madame:* take more!" Lachouque urged. But she politely declined, and her husband did not insist—a circumstance he would later have cause to regret. Forshufvud carefully closed the lid of the container over the strand of hair. That single strand could prove—or disprove— his theory.

Lachouque then asked: "Perhaps Madame would like a bee?" Forshufvud quickly said that Madame would be delighted. The Frenchman produced a representation of a bee, about four by six inches, woven of thick-spun gold thread; it had adorned Napoleon's coronation gown. Napoleon had chosen the bee as his personal symbol—his eagle represented the Empire—and Forshufvud had always thought it a particularly apt symbol for the man whose capacity for work was legendary. Another thought came to Forshufvud as he gazed at the golden bee in his palm. It was once common, he knew, for a ruler to give a symbol of himself to a person he was sending on a mission. Forshufvud was not prone to mysticism, but to be given this golden bee, this symbol of the Emperor, along with that crucial strand of hair, made him feel as if Napoleon himself had commanded him to solve the mystery of his death. There could be no greater honor than to be entrusted with such a mission by the man he admired above all others.

As Forshufvud and his wife left, he said to Lachouque: "This is the happiest day of my life."

CHAPTER SEVEN

DECEMBER 1815
THE BRIARS, ST. HELENA

BETSY BALCOMBE ran to her room and cried the day Napoleon left the Briars. Life on St. Helena could be boring for a fourteen-year-old girl, particularly a smart, mischievous one, but these last two months, since Napoleon came, had been full of marvelous fun. After all, not every girl can have the master of the world as her playmate.

Betsy and her sister, Jane, two years older, had returned the previous year from schooling in England, where they had studied French. Their father, William Balcombe, was naval agent and purveyor for the East India Company, a lucrative job that put the family in the small upper class of St. Helena. The family of six Balcombes lived comfortably, with servants and slaves, in a cottage in the hills of the island, a little more than a mile from the small port of Jamestown. They had a guesthouse fifty yards from the cottage. The Briars itself was unremarkable, "but"—Betsy later wrote—"surrounded, as this verdant spot was, by barren mountains, it looked a perfect little paradise—an Eden blooming in the midst of desolation. A beautiful avenue of banyan trees led up to it, and either side was flanked by evergreen and gigantic lacos, interspersed with pomegranate and myrtle, and a profusion of large white roses, much resembling our sweetbriar, from which, indeed, the place derived its name. A walk, shaded by pomegranate trees, thirty or forty feet in height, conducted to the garden."

Napoleon had ridden down that avenue of banyan trees the day after his arrival at St. Helena. He was returning from a visit to Longwood House, the property farther up in the interior chosen by the English as his residence. He had found Longwood far from ready to be occupied, and was returning unwillingly to Jamestown when he passed the entrance to the Briars. Napoleon detested his lodgings in town because the curious locals could stare in at him through his first-floor window. Perhaps, he suggested to Admiral Cockburn, who was in charge of arranging his residence, he could stay at the Balcombes' guesthouse until Longwood was ready.

Years later in London, after "the bright dreams and hopes of my early youth were withered and destroyed," Betsy Balcombe wrote about the memorable days at the Briars when she was fourteen and Napoleon was their guest. It was a strange, touching interlude in Napoleon's turbulent career, and the picture Betsy draws of him is unlike any other:

> How vividly I recollect my feelings of dread mingled with admiration, as I now first looked upon him whom I had learned to fear so much. His appearance on horseback was noble and imposing. The animal he rode was a superb one; his colour jet black; and as he proudly stepped up the avenue, arching his neck and champing his bit, I thought he looked worthy to be the bearer of him who was once the ruler of nearly the whole European world! . . .
>
> He seated himself on one of our cottage chairs, and after scanning our little apartment with his eagle glance, he complimented mamma on the pretty situation of the Briars. When once he began to speak, his fascinating smile and kind manner removed every vestige of the fear with which I had hitherto regarded him.

While he was talking to mamma, I had an opportunity of scrutinizing his features, which I did with the keenest interest; and certainly I have never seen any one with so remarkable and striking a physiognomy. The portraits of him give a good general idea of his features; but his smile, and the expression of his eyes, could not be transmitted to canvas, and these constituted Napoleon's chief charm.

The girl Napoleon saw was a pretty, rosy-cheeked blonde whose skinny adolescent's body was just beginning to round into womanhood. She wore a sunbonnet over unruly hair, a blouse with lace collar, flat shoes, and a short skirt over pantaloons down to the ankles—a fashion Napoleon so disliked, he later told her, that he would ban it were he governor of the island. The look in the girl's blue eyes was as direct and searching as Napoleon's own. He invited her to sit next to him:

which I did with a beating heart. He then said, "You speak French": I replied that I did, and he asked me who had taught me. I informed him, and he put several questions to me about my studies, and more particularly concerning geography. He inquired the capitals of the different countries of Europe. "What is the capital of France?" "Paris." "Of Italy?" "Rome." "Of Russia?" "Petersburg now," I replied; "Moscow formerly." On my saying this, he turned abruptly round, and, fixing his piercing eyes full in my face, he demanded sternly, *"Qui l'a brûlé?"* When I saw the expression of his eye, and heard his changed voice, all my former terror of him returned, and I was unable to utter a syllable.

I had often heard the burning of Moscow talked of, and had been present at discussions as to whether the French or or Russians were the authors of that dreadful conflagration. I therefore feared to offend him by alluding to it. He repeated the question, and I stammered, "I do not know, sir." *"Oui, oui,"* he replied, laughing violently: *"Vous savez très bien, c'est moi qui l'a brûlé."* On seeing him laugh, I gained

61

a little courage, and said, "I believe, sir, the Russians burnt it to get rid of the French." He again laughed and seemed pleased to find that I knew anything about the matter.

A remarkable friendship quickly grew up between the fallen ruler, only four months away from Waterloo, and the teenaged island girl. For the first time in his adult life, Napoleon had time on his hands: no empire to manage, no army to lead. Now he seemed to find with Betsy the adolescent he had never been. He had been hurled without transition from child to adult when, at the age of only nine, he was sent from his Corsican family home to the French military school in which each day was a struggle for survival for a scrawny Italian boy with poor French and no family connections. Across the gulf of age and nationality, Napoleon and Betsy quickly found they shared a rough-and-ready sense of fun. Their pranks were often at the expense of others:

> Shortly after his arrival, a little girl, Miss Legg, the daughter of a friend, came to visit us at the Briars. The poor child had heard such terrific stories of Bonaparte, that when I told her he was coming up the lawn, she clung to me in an agony of terror. Forgetting my own former fears, I was cruel enough to run out and tell Napoleon of the child's fright, begging him to come into the house. He walked up to her, and, brushing up his hair with his hand, shook his head, making horrible faces, and giving a sort of savage howl. The little girl screamed so violently, that mamma was afraid she would go into hysterics, and took her out of the room. Napoleon laughed a good deal at the idea of his being such a bugbear, and would hardly believe me when I told him that I had stood in the same dismay of him. When I made this confession, he tried to frighten me as he had poor little Miss Legg, by brushing up his hair, and distorting his features; but he looked more grotesque than horrible and I only laughed at him. He then (as a last resource) tried the howl, but was

equally unsuccessful, and seemed, I thought, a little provoked that he could not frighten me. He said the howl was Cossack, and it certainly was barbarous enough for anything.

Betsy's combative spirit delighted Napoleon, and she was happy to find an adult who enjoyed her mischief instead of punishing it, as her father did. She made it a point of honor not to let one of his jokes or pranks go by without seeking a way to pay him back. Napoleon found he could provoke her by threatening to marry her to the son of Las Cases, a quiet boy her age but, in her eyes, much too young:

Nothing enraged me so much; I could not bear to be considered such a child, and particularly at that moment, for there was a ball in prospect, to which I had great hopes papa would allow me to go, and I knew that his objection would be founded on my being too young. Napoleon, seeing my annoyance, desired young Las Cases to kiss me, and he held both my hands whilst the little page saluted me. I did all in my power to escape, but in vain. The moment, however, that my hands were at liberty, I boxed *le petit* Las Cases' ears most thoroughly. But I determined to be revenged on Napoleon, and in descending to the cottage to play whist, an opportunity presented itself which I did not allow to escape. There was no internal communication between the part occupied by the emperor and the rest of the house, and the path leading down was very steep and very narrow. There being barely room for one person to pass at a time, Napoleon walked first, Las Cases next, then his son, and, lastly, my sister Jane. I allowed the party to proceed very quietly until I was left about ten yards behind; and then I ran with all my force on my sister Jane—she fell with extended hands on the little page, he was thrown upon his father, and the grand chamberlain, to his dismay, was pushed against the emperor, who, although the shock was somewhat diminished by the time it reached him, had still some difficulty, from the steepness of the path, in preserving his footing. I was in ecstasies at the confusion I had created, and exulted in the revenge I had taken for the kiss; but I was soon obliged to change my note of triumph. Las Cases was thunderstruck at the insult offered to the emperor, and became perfectly furious at my uncontrollable laughter. He seized me by the shoulders, and pushed me violently on the rocky bank. It was now my turn to be enraged. I burst into tears of passion, and, turning to Napoleon, cried out, "Oh! sir, he has hurt me." "Never mind," replied the emperor, *"ne pleurs pas*—I will hold him while you punish him." And a good punishing he got; I boxed the little man's ears until he begged for mercy; but I would show him none; and at length Napoleon let him go, telling him to run, and that if he could not run faster than I, he deserved to be beaten again. He immediately started off as fast as he could, and I after him, Napoleon clapping his hands and laughing immoderately at our race round the lawn. Las Cases never liked me after this adventure, and used to call me a rude hoyden.

Las Cases and the other French officers had ample reason to resent, perhaps envy, the free-spirited English girl in their midst. Their relations with Napoleon were defined by rigid imperial protocol. The officer could not enter Napoleon's presence unless summoned by a valet; he could not speak to him, or even sit down, unless invited to do so—and the invitation to sit might be long in coming; and, of course, the person he addressed was *"vôtre Majesté."* None of these rules applied to Betsy. Her friend's name was Boney and, while no one else was allowed to enter the garden where he worked:

From this prohibition, however, I was exempt, at the emperor's own desire. I was considered a privileged person. Even when he was in the act of dictating a sentence to Las

Cases he would come and answer my call, "Come and unlock the garden door," and I was always admitted and welcomed with a smile.

Las Cases was the officer most often caught in the middle of Napoleon and Betsy's games, and the one most likely to resent it. At fifty, this rather pompous aristocrat was the only officer older than Napoleon. He fancied himself a historian, and was enormously flattered to be the one officer staying at the Briars: "I found myself alone, tête-à-tête in this desert, almost on familiar terms with the man who had governed the world! with Napoleon at last!!!" Now this unruly girl was forever getting in the way. Evidently the tiny, birdlike Las Cases was horrified by the following typically rough incident, set off when Napoleon showed Betsy an elegant sword:

I requested Napoleon to allow me to examine it more closely; and then a circumstance which had occurred in the morning, in which I had been much piqued at the emperor's conduct, flashed across me. The temptation was irresistible, and I determined to punish him for what he had done. I drew the blade out quickly from the scabbard, and began to flourish it over his head, making passes at him, the emperor retreating, until at last I fairly pinned him up in the corner; I kept telling him all the time that he had better say his prayers, for I was going to kill him. My exulting cries at last brought my sister to Napoleon's assistance. She scolded me violently, and said she would inform my father if I did not instantly desist; but I only laughed at her, and maintained my post, keeping the emperor at bay until my arm dropped from sheer exhaustion. I can fancy I see the figure of the grand chamberlain [Las Cases] now, with his spare form and parchment visage, glowing with fear for the emperor's safety, and indignation at the insult I was offering him. He looked as if he could have annihilated me on the spot, but he had felt the weight of my hand before on his ears, and prudence dictated to him to let me alone.

When I resigned my sword, Napoleon took hold of my ear, which had been bored only the day before, and pinched it, giving me great pain. I called out, and he then took hold of my nose, which he pulled heartily, but quite in fun; his good humour never left him during the whole scene.

The following was the circumstance which had excited my ire in the morning. My father was very strict in enforcing our doing a French translation every day, and Napoleon would often condescend to look over them and correct their faults. One morning I felt more than usually averse to performing this task, and when Napoleon arrived at the cottage, and asked whether the translation was ready for him, I had not even begun it. When he saw this, he took up the paper and walked down the lawn with it to my father, who was preparing to mount his horse to ride to the valley, exclaiming as he approached, *"Balcombe, voilà le thème de Mademoiselle Betsee. Qu'elle a bien travaillé";* holding up at the same time the blank sheet of paper. My father comprehended imperfectly, but saw by the sheet of paper, and my name being mentioned by the laughing emperor, that he wished me to be scolded, and entering into the plot he pretended to be very angry, and threatened if I did not finish my translation before he returned to dinner, I should be severely punished. He then rode off, and Napoleon left me, laughing at my sullen and mortified air, and it was the recollection of this which made me try and frighten him with the sword.

The incident of the sword soon became known even in Europe, where people eagerly gleaned the few scraps of news about the fallen Emperor in his distant exile. The Marquis de Montchenu, who came to St. Helena a few months later as the Bourbons' representative, wrote in his journal about first meeting the Balcombe family: "The two girls speak French, the younger, called Betzi, is quite extraordinary and says whatever passes through her head. She is the one Bonaparte is courting, if rumors circulating in Europe are to be believed." What came into Betsy's head that day was to boast to Montchenu that she had frightened Napoleon with his own sword; when Montchenu asked if she had wanted to kill Napoleon, she explained: "Not really, just puncture him slightly for fun." While there is no evidence that Napoleon was indeed courting Betsy, on occasion he showed off for her like a boy trying to impress his adolescent girl friend:

He one day asked me whether I thought he rode well. I told him, and with the greatest truth, that I thought he looked better on horseback than any one I had ever seen. He appeared pleased, and calling for his horse, he mounted and rode several times at speed around the lawn, making the animal wheel in a very narrow circle, and showing the most complete mastery over him.

One day, Archambault, his groom, was breaking in a beautiful young Arab, which had been bought for the emperor's riding. The colt was plunging and rearing in the most frightful manner, and could not be induced to pass a white cloth which had been purposely spread on the lawn to break him from shying. I told Napoleon it was impossible that he could ever ride that horse, it was so vicious. He smiled, and beckoning to Archambault, desired him to dismount; and then, to my great terror, he himself got on the animal, and soon succeeded in making him not only pass the cloth, but put his feet upon it; and then rode him over and over it several times.

"You could have been a horse-breaker," Betsy said, and Napoleon answered: "Men and horses have a similar mentality." Their games were played according to unwritten rules the two players instinctively understood. On Napoleon's side, there was an obligation never to show resentment over even the most irritating of Betsy's mischief:

Napoleon had some very beautiful seals and rare coins, from which he good-naturedly employed himself in taking off impressions in sealing-wax. Whilst he was thus engaged, I once mischievously jogged his elbow, and caused him to drop the hot wax on his fingers. It was very painful, and raised a large blister; but he was so very good-natured about it, that I told him I was quite sorry for what I had done; whereas, had he been cross, I should have rejoiced.

The rules of the game allowed Napoleon to retaliate with some adolescent mischief of his own. When Betsy accused him of cheating in a card game on the eve of her first dance—to which she was being allowed to go only because Napoleon had interceded with her father—the Emperor took her gown and locked himself with it in his room. Betsy cried and sent messages to him all through the following day, but he sent word he was unwell and could not see her—and returned the dress just in time for her to attend the dance. He played on her adolescent fears in the case of the man known as Old Huff, who had tutored one of Betsy's younger brothers (there being no school on the island). After Napoleon's arrival, the old man's mind had become unhinged; he told people he was destined to rescue the Emperor from his exile. Huff committed suicide and was ordered buried at the nearest intersection of three roads, which was on the way to the Briars:

I had amongst many other follies a terror of ghosts, and this weakness was well known to the emperor, who, for a considerable time after the suicide of poor Huff, used to frighten me nearly into fits. Every night, just before my hour of retiring to my room, he would call out, "Miss Betsee, ole Huff, ole Huff." The misery of those nights I shall never forget; I used generally to fly out of my bed during the night, and scramble into my mother's room, and remain there till morning's light dispelled the terrors of darkness.

One evening, when my mother, my sister, and myself were quietly sitting in the porch of the cottage, enjoying the coolness of the night breeze, suddenly we heard a noise, and turning round beheld a figure in white—how I screamed. We were then greeted with a low gruff laugh, which my mother instantly knew to be the emperor's. She turned the white covering, and underneath appeared the black visage of a little servant of ours, whom Napoleon had instigated to frighten Miss Betsee, while he was himself a spectator of the effect of his trick.

The adult Betsy recounted with frank relish most of her childish escapades with Napoleon. On one occasion she knew in retrospect she had acted heedlessly, though her punishment came not from the target himself but from her father:

I recollect exhibiting to Napoleon a caricature of him in the act of climbing a ladder, each step he ascended represented some vanquished country; at length he was seated astride upon the world. It was a famous toy, and by a dexterous trick Napoleon appeared on the contrary side tumbling down head over heels, and after a perilous descent, alighting on St. Helena. I ought not to have shown him this burlesque on his misfortunes, but at that time I was guilty of every description of mad action, though without any intention of being unkind; still I fear they were often deeply felt. My father, of whom I always stood in awe, heard of my rudeness, and desired me to consider myself under arrest for at least a week, and I was transferred from the drawing-room to a dark cellar, and there left to solitude and repentance. I did not soon forget that punishment, for the excavation swarmed with rats that leaped about me on all sides. . . . The emperor expressed regret at my severe punishment for so

69

trifling an offense, but was much amused by my relation of the battle with the rats; he said, he had been startled by observing a huge one jumping out of his hat, as he was in the act of putting it on.

On a subsequent occasion, I was confined during the day in the same prison that had been the scene of my nocturnal encounter. Having excited my father's ire for some mischievous trick, and for which, in spite of Napoleon's remonstrances, I was to be condemned to a week's imprisonment, I was taken to my cell every morning, and released at night only to go to bed. The emperor's great amusement during that time was to converse with me through my grated window, and he generally succeeded in making me laugh, by mimicking my dolorous countenance.

Napoleon said: "You see, we are both prisoners and you cry. I don't cry."

"You have cried."

"Yes, I have, but the prison remains nevertheless, so it is better to be occupied and cheerful."

While at the Briars, Napoleon befriended the Balcombe's gardener, an old Malay slave named Toby who had been captured, taken on an English ship, and sold in St. Helena many years ago. When strolling in the garden, Napoleon liked to stop and talk with Toby. The slave, leaning on his shovel and smiling at this unusual attention, would answer the rapid questions Napoleon put to him, with Las Cases interpreting, about his distant country of origin and his life in slavery. At Betsy's insistence, Napoleon asked William Balcombe if he might buy the old man's freedom; the English governor refused because "it is not Toby alone that General Bonaparte wants to liberate to please Miss Balcombe, he wants to gain the gratitude of all the negroes on the island."

To Las Cases, Napoleon observed: "Poor Toby here is a man stolen from his family, from his homeland, stolen from himself— could there be any greater agony for him? If this crime is the act

70

only of the English captain, then certainly that captain is one of the most evil of men; but if it was done by the whole crew, then the crime was committed by men who after all may not be as evil as one might think; for evil is always individual, almost never collective."

Frequently [Betsy wrote] when the nights were illumined by the splendid tropical moon, would he rise at three o'clock and saunter down to the garden long before old Toby, the slave, had slept off his first nap, and there he would regale himself with an early breakfast of delicious fruits with which our garden abounded. Our old Malay was so fond of the man Boney, as he designated the emperor, that he always placed the garden key where Napoleon's fingers could reach it under the wicket. No one else was ever favoured in the like manner, but he had completely fascinated and won the old man's heart. . . .

The old man retained ever afterwards the most grateful sense of Napoleon's kindness, and was never more highly gratified than when employed in gathering the choicest fruit, and arranging the most beautiful bouquets, to be sent to Longwood, to "that good man, Boney," as he called the Emperor. Napoleon made a point of inquiring, whenever I saw him, after the health of old Toby, and when he took his leave of him he presented him with twenty napoleons.

When she was a young woman in London, some years later, Betsy reflected on the character of the man known to the world as the remote, terrible warrior and statesman, the man she had once imagined as an "ogre with one large flaming red eye in the middle of his forehead," but who had turned out to be a fun-loving playmate:

I never met with any one who bore childish liberties so well as Napoleon. He seemed to enter into every sort of mirth

71

or fun with the glee of a child, and though I have often tried his patience severely, I never knew him lose his temper or fall back upon his rank or age, to shield himself from the consequences of his own familiarity, or of his indulgence to me. I looked upon him, indeed, when with him, almost as a brother or companion of my own age, and all the cautions I received, and my own resolutions to treat him with more respect and formality, were put to flight the moment I came within the influence of his arch smile and laugh. If I approached him more gravely than usual, and with a more sedate step and subdued tone, he would, perhaps, begin by saying, *"Eh bien, qu'as tu, Mademoiselle Betsee?* Has *le petit* Las Cases proved inconstant? If he have, bring him to me,"* or some other playful speech, which either pleased or teased me, and made me at once forget all my previous determinations to behave prettily.

Napoleon stayed at the Briars for two months. Then word came that Longwood, the residence five miles up the winding road into the interior, was ready for him to occupy; Napoleon was playing blind man's bluff with the Balcombe children when the news arrived. What was to prove the happiest time of the years in exile was over. In two days he would leave the Briars and his young friend:

On the appointed morning, which to me was a most melancholy one, Sir George Cockburn, accompanied by the emperor's suite, came to the Briars, to escort him to his new abode. I was crying bitterly, and he came up and said, "You must not cry, Mademoiselle Betsee; you must come and see me next week, and very often." I told him that depended on my father. He turned to him and said, "Balcombe, you must bring Missee Jane and Betsee to see me next week, eh? When will you ride up to Longwood?" . . . He gave me a beautiful little *bonbonnière,* which I had often admired, and said you can give it as a *gage d'amour* to *le petit* Las Cases. I burst into tears and ran out of the room. I stationed myself at a window from which I could see his departure, but my heart was too full to look on him as he left us, and throwing myself on the bed, I cried bitterly for a long time.

CHAPTER EIGHT

JULY 1960
GÖTEBORG

WHEN HE saw the British stamp and the return address—Department of Forensic Medicine, The University, Glasgow, W.2—Sten Forshufvud's first inclination was to tear the envelope open as fast as he could. This would be the answer from Hamilton Smith that he had been awaiting for nineteen days. Forshufvud knew just how long it had been: he had counted off each of those days.

Impatient as he was, Forshufvud stifled his first impulse and forced himself to walk slowly into the living room, holding the still unopened envelope, and sit down in his favorite armchair, the one under the etching of Napoleon's farewell to his Imperial Guard at Fontainebleau. He could feel his heartbeat quicken. He made himself breathe slowly. He filled his pipe. It was a moment to be savored.

It was almost three months since Forshufvud had returned from Paris with the precious strand of Napoleon's hair given him by Commandant Lachouque. He had tried to arrange for the toxicological laboratory in Stockholm, where he had friends, to test the hair with the new method devised by Hamilton Smith. Weeks had gone by and Forshufvud had finally decided that the laboratory was either unwilling or unable to go ahead with the test. And Forshufvud did not want to wait any longer. So he had telephoned Hamilton Smith in Glasgow. As he waited for the connection, Forshufvud hoped that Hamilton Smith would not ask—as he put it—"the name of the gentleman who once wore the hair": some instinct told Forshufvud to hold back that name, if he could, until the test had been made. In fact, Hamilton Smith did not ask, but promptly agreed to apply the test to the hair that Forshufvud would send.

Forshufvud had carefully wrapped the strand of hair and mailed it to Scotland in a registered envelope. He had briefly considered taking the precious specimen by hand to Glasgow, but the pressures of his work—he still had to earn a living—made it impossible for him to get away at the time, and he did not want to wait indefinitely for Hamilton Smith's test. In any case, Commandant Lachouque in Paris had more of Louis Marchand's lock of Napoleon's hair, so if his letter went astray the loss would not be irreparable. Rather than wait, he risked the mails.

Now Forshufvud opened the envelope, unfolded a single small sheet of stationery, and read in Hamilton Smith's handwriting:

The sample lettered H.S. which you sent to me gave a value of 10.38 micrograms of arsenic per gram of hair when analyzed by my activation method. This value shows that the subject has been exposed to relatively large amounts of arsenic.

Forshufvud knew that the amount of arsenic, 10.38 parts per million, was large indeed. The normal amount of arsenic in human hair is about 0.8 parts per million—that is, in modern times. In Napoleon's day, with fewer environmental sources of arsenic, the average if anything figured to be lower. So Napoleon's hair contained at the time of his death *thirteen* times the normal amount of arsenic!

Forshufvud leaned back in his armchair and indulged himself

75

in a rare moment of self-congratulation. Here at last was physical confirmation of his theory! His hunch four years ago, sitting in this same chair reading Louis Marchand's memoirs, had been right after all. He had unlocked the secret of St. Helena. Only now did Forshufvud let himself think about how he might have felt had Hamilton Smith's test proved negative; all those months of laborious research wasted. That danger at least was now safely in the past.

After his moment of exultation, Forshufvud began in his methodical fashion to ponder the future. He soon realized, as he thought about it, that a long road still lay ahead of him. Already he could hear the voices of the skeptics, those whose minds were chained to their pet theories: It was only a single test . . . the sample was too small . . . maybe the hair had been contaminated . . . maybe the arsenic came from the environment: the water, the drapes, anything, but not a deliberate act of poisoning . . . maybe the hair was not even Napoleon's.

Yes, there was still much work to be done: at this stage the case still hung, literally, on a single thread of hair. He needed more hair, more tests. He needed to know more about what could safely be concluded from the test, and what could not. Most of all, he needed to talk to Hamilton Smith face-to-face. He would go to Glasgow at the first opportunity.

CHAPTER NINE
JANUARY–JUNE 1816
LONGWOOD HOUSE, ST. HELENA

$\overline{}$ **A** DAY IN the life of Longwood
House:
It is dawn when Napoleon rings for the valet. His night has
been restless. The man who once could drop off at will, snatching
a couple of hours on the morning of battle after a night of
planning, can no longer command sleep. During the night he has
moved back and forth between the two campaign cots set up in
his two small adjoining rooms. The valet comes in with coffee
from the tiny room next to Napoleon's where he has spent the
night. "Let in God's good air," Napoleon says, and the valet opens
the shutters. Napoleon puts on a dressing gown and sits at a small
round table to drink his morning coffee.

The early morning light reveals Napoleon's spartan quarters.
His bedroom looks much like a campaign bivouac. The only
personal touch is the paintings Louis Marchand has hung on the
walls: Josephine, Marie-Louise, the child known as the King of
Rome. Napoleon's two rooms are at one corner of the sprawling,
pale-yellow stucco, twenty-three-room building called Longwood.
Most of his officers are lodged at the other end of the building;

the servants, who far outnumber the masters, are crowded into the attics above. All told, more than fifty people live in Longwood. It is a building that has been added to for various purposes over the seventy years of its existence. First built as a cowhouse and barn, it was later made into a summer residence for the lieutenant governor. Most recently, in order to house Napoleon and his entourage, the English have added a wing and converted the barn into living space.

Longwood is not a comfortable place to live. It rains much of the year on this upland plateau, even when the sun is shining in the valleys nearby. Because it has no cellar, the house is constantly damp, clothing soon mildews, there is green mold on the walls; in the hastily built addition the flimsy roof leaks. Worst of all, Longwood is infested with rats, as is all of St. Helena. The people who live there can hear the rats running in the walls, they get into the provisions, they frighten the children, and a chicken house has to be abandoned because the rats eat up the eggs. The servants try to patch the ratholes with tin, and sometimes they hunt the rats with dogs; the rats fight back and survive. The French consider poisoning the pests with arsenic, but give up the idea because if the rats died in the walls the stench would be unbearable.

After coffee comes the ceremony of shaving, at which Napoleon is assisted by two valets; one holds a mirror, the other hands him the instruments. Napoleon has made a habit of shaving himself ever since, as First Consul, he became a target for assassins. Stripped to the waist, he washes, scrubs, and has a valet rub his back and chest with eau de cologne—"a protection against many diseases," he advises his officers. To Las Cases he observes cheerfully that his hairless chest and prominent breasts—Napoleon is getting fat now—are "not of our sex."

Assisted by Louis Marchand, Napoleon dresses to go out. He usually wears knee breeches and a green hunting coat with velvet cuffs and collar; always he wears the famous cocked hat and the silver plaque of the Legion of Honor. In his pockets he puts a spyglass, a snuffbox, and a supply of the licorice he is constantly chewing. He goes out a door that leads from his bedroom to a garden that Marchand has created in his spare time. From this garden, Napoleon can contemplate the small world to which he is confined. Longwood lies on a barren upland plateau five miles by winding hillside road from the port at Jamestown. Despite the frequent rains, the land resists vegetation. The grass is coarse and sparse, and the few gumwood trees are bent by the constant southeast trade winds. For Europeans, the climate of the South Atlantic, where the seasons are reversed, is either too wet or too hot. Around the bleak, windy plain rise dark, jagged volcanic peaks. On one of these is Alarm House, where the English fire a cannon to announce dawn and sunset and the arrival of ships.

Around him, wherever he looks, Napoleon sees the concentric rings of his captivity. Directly in front of him, in full view, is the camp at Deadwood where the five hundred soldiers of the 53rd Regiment are stationed. Its red-coated sentries are posted within sight of each other all along the four-mile stone wall that encloses Longwood and the area immediately around it. Lookouts on the surrounding heights use semaphore flags to relay the news from Longwood about the captive: "General Buonaparte is out, but within the cordon of sentries"; "General Buonaparte is out, properly attended, beyond the cordon of sentries." If the lookout were to signal "General Buonaparte is missing," a blue flag would be raised at the command post ordering each army unit on the island to search the territory assigned to it. All of St. Helena is similarly prepared; the English have sent almost three thousand armed men there. All roads on the island are guarded; anyone out after nine at night will be arrested; the four possible landing places are heavily fortified with shore batteries against assault from the sea. Between the armed peaks Napoleon can see the English navy guarding the island's waters: five warships off Jamestown harbor, one always cruising to windward, another to leeward; six brigs circle the island day and night. Beyond the sentries, beyond the forts, beyond the circling ships, Napoleon sees the surest, most

79

implacable of his jailers: the empty, gray ocean stretching beyond the horizon in all directions.

Does Napoleon ever dream, as he gazes out to sea, of escaping from this lonely rock? Does the supreme military genius ever apply himself to the problem of getting past the sentries, the forts, the ships, the ocean itself? An impossible problem, it seems, but accomplishing the impossible was once a habit with Napoleon. Whatever he may be thinking on those solitary morning walks in the garden, none of the exiles reports any discussions of escape during these early days at Longwood. Napoleon's thoughts seem more turned toward the chance that some shift in the tide of European politics will sweep him back to Paris. He places some hope in Princess Charlotte, heiress to the English crown and an admirer of his; once she sits on the throne she will surely end his exile. He says to Las Cases that, barring events that cannot be foreseen, he sees only two circumstances that would result in his being called back to power: "The need the kings might have of me against the upheaval of the peoples, or the need the peoples might have of me against the kings; for, in the immense battle of the present against the past, I am the natural arbiter and mediator; I had aspired to be the supreme judge . . . but destiny ruled otherwise." When a rumor reaches the exiles that one of Napoleon's marshals, Bertrand Clausel, is leading a revolt against the Bourbons, Las Cases foresees the Emperor's return to power, but Napoleon only says: "Do you think he would be stupid enough to step aside for me? I have many followers, but he will too if he is successful . . . and besides, the last one on the scene is always right. People forget the past for the present."

Napoleon's immediate goal is to keep his name from being forgotten in the world he once dominated. For that, the exiles have to penetrate the censorship that governs all correspondence in and out of Longwood. In practice this is not difficult, though the exiles will be reluctant, even years later, to disclose their methods. Napoleon seldom leaves Longwood and never goes to Jamestown, but the others can frequently ride the five miles down to the tiny port, where on the street and in the waterfront shops they pick up the news and mingle with sailors from passing ships. Cipriani in particular—Cipriani, the dark, fearless Corsican who has been around the Bonapartes since childhood—goes into Jamestown on Longwood business and undertakes unnamed missions for Napoleon. Cipriani is Napoleon's eyes and ears; the two men are frequently together, and usually alone; no one knows what they discuss. In Europe, letters are regularly received that have evaded the English censors at St. Helena, and just as regularly the exiles receive uncensored correspondence from abroad. At Longwood the valet Saint-Denis, who has an especially fine handwriting, is charged with copying messages that will be smuggled out through a local merchant or with a sailor who can be persuaded by a few coins or the promise of reward at the other end. (The messages do not always get through. Forty years later, a visitor to a country house in Ireland will pry up the bottom of a snuffbox given to a departing English officer at Longwood and find a letter from Napoleon giving instructions for his son's upbringing.) With this correspondence, and with the accounts carried home by the visitors he has seen, Napoleon tries to keep alive his candidacy for a return to Europe.

Sometimes Napoleon goes horseback riding in the early morning. He is permitted to ride freely over the Longwood plain, beyond the red line of sentries, and in some of the nearby valleys, fertile after the barren plain; but beyond this specified area he must be accompanied by an English officer and this Napoleon refuses to accept. Occasionally on these rides he drops in on impulse at an islander's home. At one of these stops he meets Mary Alice Robinson, the attractive seventeen-year-old daughter of a tenant farmer. Napoleon nicknames her the Nymph and will visit her home a dozen times or more; the resulting rumors travel all the way to Europe. But tame rides around a limited circuit soon bore the man whose headlong horseback journeys were legendary; he rides less and less. If he does not ride, he strolls the garden humming an opera off-key or talking with one of his officers, and when it rains, as it so often does here, he retreats to his quarters to read from the library Marchand packed for him in Paris, augmented by books sent from Europe or borrowed from the English, or he reads three-month-old English newspapers he sometimes gets from the governor or a visitor. He is a fast and voracious reader; the floor around his sofa is littered with books he has tossed aside, many of them annotated in the margins with his scrawled observations.

Napoleon's bath, in midmorning if he has been riding, is a major undertaking. He may loll reading or talking for hours in the makeshift tub, a wooden box lined with tin; Marchand is busy hauling water from the kitchen to keep the tub as scorching hot as Napoleon wants it. Napoleon's doctor, Barry O'Meara, often is summoned at this time. Napoleon feels no need for O'Meara's professional skills in these early days. Other than an occasional day's illness, his health is generally good, and besides he has no faith in what doctors give their patients. He respects surgeons and when in power he promoted vaccination, but he consistently refuses doctors' medications, which he believes do more harm than good. "How many patients have you killed in your practice?" is his standard opening when he meets a doctor. O'Meara is valued as a source of local gossip. The thirty-three-year-old doctor in the English navy, who lives at Longwood, is uniquely able to move between the two worlds of St. Helena; sitting by the tub, he tells Napoleon in his fluent Italian what is going on beyond the ring of English sentries. O'Meara is an all-purpose source: while he is keeping Napoleon informed, he is reporting to the English governor, and, unknown to either of these, he is also reporting by letter to his naval superiors in London.

Lunch, usually around eleven, is either in Napoleon's room or, if the weather is good, in the garden. The meal, which he wolfs down in his usual quarter-hour, consists of boiling-hot soup— Napoleon considers chicken soup to be particularly therapeutic— two meat dishes, and a dish of vegetables. The food is prepared in the Longwood kitchen by the cooks Napoleon brought with him. But they do not serve it: that job is always reserved to Marchand and two trusted assistant valets, Saint-Denis and Abram Noverraz. Napoleon drinks a glass or two of watered wine, never more, always from his personal supply of Vin de Constance, the highly regarded South African wine from the Constantia vineyard near Capetown; the others at the table make do with whatever *vin ordinaire* is available. Most of the food is supplied by William Balcombe, Betsy's father, who has been named purveyor to Longwood by Admiral Cockburn. Within the house, the management of food is entrusted to Cipriani, the majordomo, and to the Count de Montholon.

Balcombe's appointment as food supplier reassures Napoleon. He is certain the English would prefer him dead and suspects they might take measures to make that wish a reality. He considers the possibility of poison—he says doctors and chemists have warned him to be particularly wary of wine and coffee—but dismisses it under present circumstances: "There's no danger of poison, Balcombe supplies the food and O'Meara and Poppleton [the resident English officer] are honest people who wouldn't lend themselves to such a thing." Having risked his life so often on the battlefield, Napoleon does not worry particularly about his safety, though when in power, he says, he survived "more than thirty authenticated plots" on his life, most of them mounted by the Count d'Artois, brother of Louis XVIII. His main precaution, he says, was to never tell anyone until the last moment where he was going and what route he was taking. Here he feels himself relatively safe. He says to Montholon: "I would not be in America six months without being assassinated by an agent of the Comte d'Artois. . . . I see nothing in America but assassination or oblivion. I prefer St. Helena."

Napoleon tries lunching with his officers, but their incessant quarreling wears on his nerves. He tells them: "You are only a handful of people at the end of the world. At least you could love each other." It does no good. The officers' problem is unemployment. Napoleon has carefully parceled out assignments to each of them, but there is too little work to go around, leaving them plenty of time to contend for favor in the exile court. Only Las Cases, the oldest among them, the historian who bears the brunt of Napoleon's dictating, is kept fairly busy. Bertrand, the quiet engineer, is unhappy because he is being superseded by Montholon; morose, he says little and stays with his family when he can. Bertrand has been with Napoleon ever since Egypt, and in Paris was grand marshal of the palace; by rights he should be in charge of the household. But at the insistence of his tall blonde wife, Fanny, who wants to keep her distance from Napoleon, Bertrand has chosen to live apart from Longwood. Napoleon, piqued, has put the household management in the hands of the Count de Montholon, the elegant, curly-haired courtier who only joined him in the last weeks in France. Besides, while Fanny Bertrand avoids Longwood, Albine de Montholon is always cheerful and accommodating. The rumor begins to circulate that the dark-haired, coquettish Albine has found her way to Napoleon's bed, with her husband's consent. "Isn't she pretty?" Napoleon asks Betsy Balcombe about Albine.

The worst off among the officers is Gaspard Gourgaud. Las Cases has his work and his son; Bertrand and Montholon have their wives and children; Gourgaud has no one. This big, swarthy man, just thirty-two, is full of energy and emotion that he cannot expend. His proudest boast, often repeated, is that he saved Napoleon's life in Russia. There is no opportunity for such heroics at St. Helena, though at the Briars—Betsy Balcombe mockingly reports—when a cow surprised them in a field while taking a walk, Gourgaud jumped in front of Napoleon, drew his sword, and proclaimed: "This is the second time I have saved the Emperor's life." At Longwood, Napoleon puts Gourgaud in charge of the stable of ten horses, but grooms do the work anyway, so his duties take little of his time and less of his energy. He rides furiously around Longwood plain. He thinks he is in love with Laura Wilks, the blonde, teenaged daughter of the former governor, but he can rarely glimpse, much less court her. He quarrels, mostly with

84

Montholon, complains to Napoleon, and sulks. Most of all, Gaspard Gourgaud is desperately bored, as he records in a week of his journal:

Tuesday, 25th: *Ennui. Ennui!*
Wednesday, 26th. The same.
Thursday, 27th. The same.
Friday, 28th. The same.
Saturday, 29th. The same.
Sunday, 30th. *Grand ennui.*

After lunch, Napoleon goes to the billiard room to dictate to one of his officers, usually Las Cases, sometimes to Marchand or Saint-Denis. He is trying to indulge what was always his greatest passion—work; but the once superhuman working day of sixteen or twenty hours is now down to little more than a quarter of that time. Usually in his dictation he is explaining and justifying his own career, but he ranges back in time to comment on the campaigns of Julius Caesar and he exercises his mind on topics as diverse as educational reform and a plan for irrigating the Nile valley. Dictating at top speed, he paces the room, pausing at times to handle the big globe on which his campaigns are traced, half the planet away from the tiny speck in the South Atlantic; or he peers with his spyglass out the hole he has had made in the shutter so he can see the English soldiers without being seen by them. "Write!" he barks at the officer, who is sitting at a desk, uncomfortable, in full uniform with high collar and sword at his side.

In midafternoon, Napoleon puts on a uniform to receive visitors, who are frequent in these early days. Napoleon wants to use his visitors to keep himself before the eyes of Europe; as for the visitors, usually English colonial notables whose ships are calling at St. Helena on the way home, they are delighted to attach themselves even for a moment to the most famous person of their time. Many of them will publish their impressions as soon as they get to England, a fact not lost on Napoleon. He imposes the intricate protocol of les Tuileries on these visits so that no one will forget that he is still the Emperor. The visitor must apply for an audience to Bertrand, who will issue him a written pass. The visitor is received in the billiard room by a couple of officers in gold-braided uniform, usually Montholon and Gourgaud. A servant dressed in livery of green tailcoat with gold trim opens the door of the adjoining drawing room and announces the visitor. Napoleon receives him standing in front of the fireplace, hat under his arm, Las Cases at his side to interpret. He will remain standing throughout the interview, even if it lasts an hour and more, even if he is sagging with illness or fatigue: he is forcing the visitor to stand in the presence of the Emperor. As always, Napoleon begins the interview by questioning the visitor about his or her background and interests. Whatever course the conversation takes, Napoleon displays the extraordinary range of his powerful mind. Most of all, he displays a man who knows he is more than a mere man, a man who is a natural-born ruler: an Emperor. That is the message Napoleon sends to Europe through his visitors.

One of the visitors—it is on January 14—is Commander John Theed, master of the H.M.S. *Leveret,* who brings newspapers to Longwood. When Theed is leaving, Fanny Bertrand gives him a souvenir of his visit: a locket enclosing some of Napoleon's hair.

Protocol is relaxed for visitors of lesser importance or for those, like the Balcombes, who are considered friends of Longwood; and for Betsy herself none of the rules apply. Once a week or so the Balcombes ride up to Longwood and Betsy visits with the man that she, and only she, can call "my old playmate." She remembers him as "more subject to depression of spirits than when at the Briars, but still gleams of his former playfulness shone out at times." There is billiards to play: "He took me into the billiard room, a table having just been set up at Longwood. I remember thinking it too childish for men, and very like marbles on a larger scale. The Emperor condescended to teach me how to play, but I made very little progress, and amused myself with trying to hit his imperial fingers with the ball instead of making cannons and hazards . . . and I was never more pleased than when I succeeded in making him cry out."

When Betsy finds Napoleon suffering from the aftereffects of having a tooth pulled, she says she is ashamed of him for complaining of pain after the battles he has been through, and asks for the tooth so she can have it made into an earring: "The idea made him laugh heartily, in spite of his suffering, and caused him to remark that he thought I should *never* cut my wisdom teeth;—he was always in extra good humor with himself whenever he was guilty of anything approaching to the nature of a witticism."

Sometimes, to her amusement, Napoleon practices his English on Betsy. He has been taking lessons from Las Cases off and on since the voyage on the *Northumberland,* and can read the London papers, but his spoken English, to her ear, is "the oddest in the world." In "one of his early attempts at expressing himself in English," he makes her father the butt of his mockery of English drinking habits: "If Balcombe been here, he would want drink one, two, three, ah! *cinq bouteilles,* eh? Balcombe go to Briars to get droonk?" Napoleon questions her about her studies: "Napoleon was very fond of extracting from me my little store of knowledge, acquired from, I fear, rather desultory reading. However, being fond of books and having a retentive memory, I could apparently chain his interest for some hours. 'Now, Mademoiselle Betsee,' he would say, 'I hope you have been goot child and learnt all your lesson'; which he said purposely to annoy me, as I was anxious to be thought full grown."

It is not always fun. On one visit: "I remember bounding up to Saint-Denis and asking for Napoleon; my joyousness was somewhat damped by the gravity with which he replied that the Emperor was watching the approach of the *Conqueror,* then coming in, bearing the flag of Admiral Pamplin. 'You will find him,' he said, 'near Madame Bertrand's, but he is in no mood for badinage today, Mademoiselle.' Notwithstanding this check, I proceeded towards the cottage, and in a moment, the whole tone of my mind was changed from joy to sadness. Young as I was, I could not help being strongly impressed by the intense melancholy of his expression . . . he was standing with General Bertrand, his eyes bent sadly on the 74, which was yet but a speck in the line of the horizon."

Looking back, the adult Betsy observed that "the thoughtlessness of youth, or the consciousness of being a privileged person, prompted me more than once, whilst conversing with Napoleon, to touch upon tender, if not actually forbidden ground, and to question him about some of the many cruel acts assigned to him; *entr' autres,* the butchery of the Turkish prisoners at Jaffa, and the poisoning the sick in hospital at the same place, came one day on the tapis." Napoleon takes the time to give her his side of the story, and the adult Betsy concluded that these events were among "the numerous and sad results of boundless ambition, united to unlimited power." On another visit Betsy sings a song about the execution of the Duke d'Enghien. When Napoleon learns the topic of the song, he asks the girl what she knows about it: "I told him he was considered the murderer of that illustrious prince. He said, in reply, it was true, he had ordered his execution, for he was a conspirator, and had landed troops in the pay of the Bourbons to assassinate him; and he thought from such a conspiracy, he could not act in a more politic manner than by causing one of their own princes to be put to death, in order the more effectually to deter them from attempting his life again."

At about four o'clock, Gourgaud orders the six-horse carriage harnessed for the afternoon ride. Napoleon sits with one of the wives, Fanny Bertrand or Albine de Montholon; they are accompanied sometimes by other officers or visitors. Napoleon instructs the drivers, two brothers named Archambault, to go at top speed around the most dangerous hillside curves. Betsy recalls: "These were drives which seemed to inspire Bonaparte with mischievous pleasure. He added to my fright by repeatedly assuring me the horses were running away, and that we should all be dashed to pieces." But Napoleon wants his young friend to be fearless: "The Emperor frequently urged my father to correct me whilst young, and said I ought never to be encouraged in my foolish fears, or even permitted to indulge therein."

If the Bertrands are not in the carriage this afternoon, Napoleon may tell the driver to stop at Hutt's Gate, their cottage. He goes in and plays for a while with the Bertrands' three children. One day he walks down a green valley behind their home and finds a spring shaded by three weeping willows. Its name is Geranium Valley; servants will be sent daily to get Napoleon's drinking water from the spring. He says to Bertrand: "If my body is left in the hands of my enemies when I die, you must bury me there."

The cannon of Alarm House announces sunset. As darkness falls, the noose of English sentries is drawn tight around Longwood House, and the exiles retreat to the interior. They gather in the candlelit drawing room, men in uniform, ladies in low-cut evening gowns, for chess or the card games of piquet and reversi. Napoleon proposes that their winnings be put in a fund to buy a slave's freedom, but, as with his effort to buy freedom for the Balcombe's slave Toby, nothing comes of this idea.

Dinner, usually at eight, is another occasion for imperial ceremony at the shadow court. Protocol is just as it was in the Tuileries. Cipriani, incongruous in embroidered green coat and black silk breeches, opens the dining-room door, bows deeply, and announces: *"Le dîner de sa Majesté est servi."* Napoleon offers his arm to the ranking lady, usually Albine de Montholon now that the Bertrands are living away from Longwood. The officers follow and are seated in order of precedence, and this provides them with a fruitful occasion to quarrel. There is no longer any power at this court, the power stayed in Paris at the Tuileries, but the officers do battle all the more fiercely over the shadow of what once was theirs. Gourgaud in particular finds the issue of precedence an outlet for his ever-ready temper. He tells his diary that he will kick Las Cases if the little man tries once more to go in ahead of him, and of Montholon he records: "I have had a discussion with my colleague regarding the places we should occupy at table. I have told him that I would yield to him in nothing. Sooner I'll fight him."

The dinner is served amidst the abundance of silver plate and Sèvres china, illustrated with scenes from Napoleon's campaigns, that Louis Marchand packed up when they were leaving Paris; for a moment, perhaps, the exiles can forget the sentries outside the window, the ocean that surrounds them, and imagine themselves back at the Tuileries palace. The illusion is shattered when a rat runs across the room. The many candles make the room stifling hot. Saint-Denis and Noverraz wait only on Napoleon; the drove of other servants includes English sailors gotten up in imperial livery. The menu is lavish: soup, two entrées, a roast, two vegetables, dessert. The food at Longwood is the cause of interminable bickering between the exiles and the English authorities. The French complain about the poor quality of the food, especially the meat and the wine; the English complain that the high style of living at Longwood is straining both their budget for the exile household and the resources of the island, which is subject to chronic food shortages. Both are right. Livestock and wine, imported from South Africa, are scarce and expensive, and after the long ocean journey they reach the table in poor condition: a fact no doubt less noticed by English colonials and soldiers than by people who only yesterday were dining on the best that Paris could offer. Dinner may last as long as forty minutes before Napoleon brusquely gets to his feet and leaves.

After dinner the shadow court returns to the drawing room to while away the hours until bedtime. Evening pastimes at Longwood are limited. They play cards again. Or they listen to Albine de Montholon play the piano and sing the Italian songs that Napoleon likes, or to Napoleon's monologues from the storehouse of his memory of the great events of his career. He refights the battles, and most of all the last one, the battle he almost won, should have won, the battle to which his thoughts obsessively return: Waterloo. "What a story my life has been," he says. Or

Napoleon sends a servant for a book and reads aloud: fiction, plays, poetry. He is particularly fond of the Gaelic poet Ossian and of the novel *Paul et Virginie*, which takes place on an island in the Indian Ocean. "We are going to the theater," he says if he is going to read a play, and he will interrupt himself to offer his criticism of the work he is reading. Of Racine's *Britannicus*, he observes that the conclusion is too abrupt, that the reader does not foresee as he should the poisoning of the main character. Napoleon reads badly, in a monotone, and he mangles the meter of poetry. Anyone caught dozing is likely to find himself forced to replace Napoleon as reader. Gourgaud writes of one evening: "The Emperor asked for *Zaïre* [the play by Voltaire] and read until midnight. We were all dropping with sleep and boredom."

No one, no matter how sleepy or bored, can leave the drawing room before Napoleon. At last he looks at the clock, and says: "What time is it? Bah, it doesn't matter. Let's go to bed." He goes to his rooms. He may keep one of his officers to read aloud to him. When at last he finds sleep, Louis Marchand puts out the three-candled reading lamp, lights the night light, and retires to his attic. An assistant valet remains in the tiny room next door waiting for Napoleon's ring at dawn that will announce another day in the life of Longwood House.

CHAPTER TEN

AUGUST 1960
GLASGOW

========================= $\mathbf{T}$ HE TWO men sitting in the Glasgow laboratory over the inevitable cups of tea had taken an immediate liking to each other. They were both specialists in the arcane field of toxicology, and so, as they discussed the properties of poison, they slipped easily into their common professional vocabulary. Their conversation was in English. Few people not born to it learn Swedish, and Hamilton Smith was no exception. Sten Forshufvud, like so many Swedes, had been forced early in life to learn the major European languages, and his English was fluent, especially when the subject was poison.

Hamilton Smith had taken his tall, erect visitor, whose distinguished manner did not conceal his almost boyish eagerness, on a tour of his laboratory, and now they were discussing Smith's research in arsenic poisoning and its analysis. Forshufvud was relieved that the encounter was going well. This day was as important to Forshufvud's quest as the day in Paris, the previous spring, when Commandant Lachouque had given him a single strand of Napoleon's hair. Hamilton Smith's analysis of the strand had found an unusual amount of arsenic, and now Forshufvud wanted to learn all he could about Smith's analysis and its significance. That was what had brought him to Glasgow.

The short, sandy-haired Glasgow scientist was explaining the nuclear-bombardment technique he used to analyze hair for the presence of arsenic. The hair was weighed and sealed in a polythene container. Then, at the Harwell Atomic Energy Establishment near London, the hair sample and a standard arsenic solution were both irradiated by thermal neutrons for twenty-four hours. The comparison between the two samples then showed the arsenic content of the hair, and from that figure the amount of arsenic in the body could be calculated. This new technique, which had been tested at length, gave as accurate results with a single strand of hair as did the old method, which required large quantities of hair. Unfortunately, Hamilton Smith observed, the test destroyed the hair itself, so no further testing was possible.

Forshufvud had a list of questions. Could the arsenic have come from an external source? He had in mind the possibility that Napoleon used some sort of hair lotion, or that the hair might have been contaminated during the many years between Napoleon's death and its analysis at Harwell. No, Hamilton Smith said decisively, that was impossible. External arsenic would show up quite differently. They could be sure the arsenic had been within the hair itself and had entered it through the root, from the body.

And, Forshufvud went on, choosing his words carefully, could one identify hair as that of a given person? With two or more strands, yes, said Hamilton Smith, in the sense that it is possible to tell if the strands all came from the same person. This was because the arsenic pattern in a person's hair is as distinctive as the patterns in that person's fingerprint. So, if Forshufvud supplied him with more hair, he could tell if the hairs came from the same person.

Now Hamilton Smith had a question for Forshufvud. It was the question Forshufvud had been avoiding since he had first telephoned Smith from Göteborg two months earlier. "Can you tell me who was the victim of this crime?" Smith asked.

Forshufvud said slowly: "The hair was that of the Emperor Napoleon the First."

Later Forshufvud recalled that Hamilton Smith's face went white: "pale like a corpse," as he put it. For an awful moment Forshufvud thought he had alienated the man whose help was so essential to his quest. It occurred to Forshufvud that Smith must be thinking the English had poisoned Napoleon, and that a Briton might well be dismayed at the idea that his Swedish visitor was about to lay this monstrous crime on his nation's doorstep. In fact, Forshufvud at that time had no idea who poisoned Napoleon; he had carefully put aside that question pending sufficient proof that a murder had indeed been committed. However, given the physical circumstances of Napoleon's life at St. Helena, it seemed highly unlikely that the English could have poisoned him without also poisoning his whole household. And so now he said reassuringly: "But I am quite sure it was not the English who poisoned him."

At that, Hamilton Smith drew himself up in frank indignation. "What do I care about that?" he exclaimed. "I'm a Scot!"

As they later recalled it, both men burst out laughing at the absurdity of the exchange. The incident broke the barriers of formality between the two rather reserved scientists; they were to become fast friends, and Hamilton Smith would over the coming years provide Forshufvud the indispensable support of his laboratory. Far from being put off, Smith's interest was kindled by the illustrious identity of the victim. It turned out he had assumed Forshufvud was a consultant on some current Swedish criminal case of the kind that Smith himself was occasionally called in on for his specialized expertise. Smith's offer to analyze the hair Forshufvud sent him had just been an act of professional courtesy. But to use his skill in helping determine how Napoleon died was an altogether different matter: some of the excitement that drove Forshufvud to devote much of his life to his quest had communicated itself to the Glasgow scientist.

Now Hamilton Smith, with as much eagerness as this reclusive Scot would ever display, told Forshufvud about the improvement he had designed for his method of analysis. He could now analyze the hair in sections. Forshufvud immediately saw that this was an extraordinarily important advance. The present method only tested the arsenic content of the entire hair; at best it could reveal that the person had arsenic in his system sometime during the time the hair was growing, but nothing could be learned from it about *when* during that period the arsenic entered the system. If small sections of that hair could be tested separately, the results would be much richer in information. The section-by-section pattern would show how much arsenic the victim had absorbed at what intervals over the time the hair had grown. If the arsenic was absorbed in a steady amount from the environment—something in the victim's room, say, or from the water he drank daily —the analysis would show a roughly constant amount from a section to section: a more or less straight line on a graph. If, on the other hand, the arsenic entered the body at intervals in large amounts, a graph of the sections would show jagged peaks and valleys. Since hair grows at a fairly constant rate of about 1.4 hundredths of an inch (.35 millimeter) a day, almost half an inch a month, it would then become possible to calculate the time between the peaks on the graph that represented doses of arsenic. If the hair had been cut with a scissors at an unknown distance from its root, one could not date such dosage accurately, though the amount of time during which all the dosages shown in that hair occurred would be known from the length of the hair. But, Hamilton Smith went on, if the hair were shaved at the root, on a known date, his new sectional analysis could date a dosage of arsenic with great accuracy, indeed almost to the day.

The implications for Forshufvud's quest were enormous. He knew now only that Napoleon at the end of his life showed the clinical symptoms of arsenic poisoning, and that his hair at death —and therefore his body—contained an "unusually large" amount of the poison. That was all. How much more could he learn from Hamilton Smith's new method! Forshufvud's thoughts turned to the lock of hair now resting in Louis Marchand's *reliquaire* in Paris, the lock from which his wife had extracted a single strand, the hair analyzed by Hamilton Smith—and destroyed in the process of the analysis. The Marchand hair was perfect for his purpose. It had been shaved, not cut, from Napoleon's head on the day following his death. Now, with Hamilton Smith's new sectional analysis, it was possible to determine whether Napoleon had gotten the arsenic in his system in a steady stream or in periodic large doses. And more: those dosages, if such they proved to be, could be calculated backwards along the length of the hair, and then compared to the existing written records of the dying man's symptoms day by day over the last months of his life. The evidence, one way or the other, could be conclusive: Forshufvud could prove, to himself and to the world, just how Napoleon had died. But, of course, he needed more hair. Forshufvud remembered with sudden regret Commandant Lachouque's offer to give him more hair—why had he not accepted? He could be handing that hair over to Hamilton Smith, right now, here in Glasgow.

Well, it could not be helped. The oversight in any event was not fatal. Lachouque had offered the hair before; surely he would offer it again. All it meant was a delay—a very frustrating one, now that the goal was in sight—and another trip to Paris.

Forshufvud's parting from Hamilton Smith was warm. He assured him he would be calling Glasgow as soon as he had obtained more hair. And—the surest evidence of scientific good-fellowship—the two men had already discussed publishing their findings. They agreed that when they did so they would give the name of the person Forshufvud referred to as "the gentleman who once wore the hairs."

CHAPTER ELEVEN

JULY 11, 1816
LONGWOOD HOUSE, ST. HELENA

THAT AFTERNOON, at four o'clock, Napoleon and Gourgaud called on Albine de Montholon in her room at Longwood. She had given birth to her second child, a daughter, a few days earlier. They found Montholon's attractive wife reading (Gourgaud noted in his diary) "the fables of La Fontaine and the story of Madame de Brinvilliers."

The story of Madame de Brinvilliers was no fable but one of the most celebrated murder cases in the history of France. Marie-Madeleine d'Aubray, Marquise de Brinvilliers, lived in Paris in the middle of the seventeenth century, during the reign of Louis XIV. In the year 1676, she was convicted and executed —she was beheaded and her body was burned—on the charge of having poisoned with arsenic a large number of people, including her father and both her brothers. Before she died, the Marquise made a detailed confession.

That confession, plus those of two of her accomplices, were the raw material on which was based the book Albine de Montholon was reading that afternoon. In effect the book was a detailed, step-by-step description of how to kill people with arsenic in the way least likely to be discovered. This was her story:

In 1663, Madeleine de Brinvilliers was thirty-three; she was petite, with blue eyes and abundant chestnut hair. She was quick to take offense, and she was extravagant and dissolute. For four years she had been having an affair with one Godin, a cavalry officer known as Sainte-Croix. Her father, a high Paris official, who disapproved of the way she flaunted her lover, had Sainte-Croix hauled out of her carriage and put in the Bastille. During his two months in prison, Sainte-Croix was befriended by an Italian expert on poison known as Exili—his real name was Eggidi —who earlier had served Queen Christina of Sweden as her protector against possible poisoners. When he got out, Sainte-Croix and the Marquise began visiting a well-known Swiss chemist named Christophe Glaser, who was apothecary to the King, at his quarters in the Faubourg Saint-Germain. They called the poisons they concocted "Glaser's recipe." Madeleine then appeared in Paris hospitals with gifts for the sick of jam and wine and biscuits. Many of those who ate her gifts died in agony; the attending physicians certified that they had died of natural causes.

The Marquise had not forgiven her father for jailing her lover. Three years later, in February 1666, she began administering small doses of arsenic to him. He complained of headache, loss of appetite and vomiting, itching, pains in the chest; he was very pale. His doctor could not diagnose or treat his illness, so the father went to his country house in the hope that a change of air would do him good. He did in fact get better, and he invited his daughter, who was still in Paris, to join him and keep him company. After she arrived, her father's symptoms broke out again, and he decided to return with his daughter to Paris and consult another physician. In Paris his illness grew much worse; he was having almost continuous bouts of vomiting. Believing he was close to death, he called a notary and made a new will in favor of the daughter who was caring so faithfully for him. As soon as the notary had left, the Marquise brought him a bowl of emetic wine—wine containing tartar emetic—that had been prescribed by his attending physician. He died on September 10, eight months after she had given him the first dose of arsenic.

There was a postmortem, but nothing was found to suggest anything other than death by natural causes. The Marquise would say in her confession that she had given her father twenty-eight to thirty doses of arsenic, and that a servant of hers named Gascon had administered about the same number more.

Four years later, in 1670, the Marquise killed her two brothers with arsenic. Her motive, she said, was to inherit their possessions. The older brother was poisoned by a servant, La Chaussée, whom he had employed at his sister's suggestion. His death took three months and, like his father, he suffered frequent fits of vomiting in the last stage. As with his father, physicians found no reason to think his death was other than natural. Madeleine's younger brother, attended by the same servant, La Chaussée, died in September of that year under similar circumstances. This time, however, a physician who performed an autopsy said the death was due to poisoning by arsenic. But no charge was made against the Marquise.

Madeleine de Brinvilliers also set out to poison her husband, the Marquis. In her confession she said the first symptom he showed was weakness of the legs: he found it difficult to stand and painful to walk. In this instance the Marquise changed her mind, stopped the poison, and her husband quickly recovered. The Marquis evidently was suspicious of his wife and her lover. When Sainte-Croix joined them at dinner, the Marquis instructed his servant: "Don't change my glass, and rinse it out every time you give me something to drink." After dinner, Madeleine retired to her bedroom with Sainte-Croix.

At various times, according to her confession, the Marquise administered arsenic to her servants and her friends and her several lovers, though not in lethal doses. A servant ate some ham given her by the Marquise and later suffered pain she described as like "being stabbed in the heart." One of her lovers, named Briancourt, also her sons' tutor, to whom she had described killing her father and brothers, threatened to expose her when she told him she was planning to poison her sister. Madeleine enticed Briancourt to her bedroom, where Sainte-Croix was waiting with a dagger to kill him. Briancourt managed to escape, but did not expose her.

Despite the death and illness she strewed around her, despite the suspicions of some of those close to her, and despite the doctor's finding of arsenic in her younger brother's death, Madeleine was not accused until after the sudden—but natural—death of Sainte-Croix. Her lover left behind a strongbox containing poisons and thirty-four letters from Madeleine in which she described the crimes she had committed with both Sainte-Croix and the servant La Chaussée. The Marquise went to Sainte-Croix's widow and demanded the letters, but they had been seized by a police officer named Picard. Picard later opened the letters. The widow of the Marquise's younger brother then filed suit against her, and she fled to London.

Four years later, in 1676, Madeleine returned to France and was arrested in a convent in Liège. La Chaussée was also arrested and was subjected to preliminary torture. He resisted that successfully, but, at the insistence of the Marquise's sister-in-law, he was then put to the torture of the boot, a wooden instrument in which the leg is gradually crushed. That made him talk; and he was broken on the wheel the day he confessed. Now the Marquise herself was put on trial. The trial lasted four months; Briancourt was brought forward to testify against her. Madeleine calmly and steadfastly denied the evidence of her letters and the testimony against her. She was convicted and sentenced to death.

The priest assigned to minister to her, a well-known theologian named Pirot, urged her to confess to save her soul, though, he conceded, she would undoubtedly have to spend some time in purgatory. "How shall I know if I am in purgatory or in hell?" she asked. At last she confessed her own guilt, but though she was put through the water torture—a funnel was placed between her teeth and her body was filled to bursting with water—she refused to name any accomplices. Accompanied by Pirot, Madeleine de Brinvilliers rode in the tumbrel to her execution through one of the biggest crowds in the history of Paris. She showed no fear and was cooperative with the executioner during the half-hour it took him to cut her hair and tie her to the block. He cut off her head with a single clean stroke.

At Longwood House, after Napoleon and Gourgaud had left Albine de Montholon, they discussed the case of the Marquise de Brinvilliers. Napoleon said he could understand a woman poisoning her husband, but not her father. Asked his opinion, Gourgaud said: "Neither the one nor the other; poison is the coward's weapon."

CHAPTER TWELVE

MAY 1961
GÖTEBORG

S TEN FORSHUFVUD was stunned by the news from Paris. He had just telephoned Henri Griffon, the head of the police toxicological laboratory, to ask if he had analyzed the strands of Napoleon's hair he had been given when Forshufvud was in Paris four weeks earlier.

Griffon told him he had not examined the hair and worse: he no longer even had it. He explained, to Forshufvud's dismay, that the hair had been taken away by the man who gave it to him: Commandant Henry Lachouque. It was Lachouque who a year earlier had given Forshufvud the strand of hair that, analyzed at the University of Glasgow, had shown an unusually high arsenic content. That strand of hair had started Forshufvud on the present stage of his quest, which until today had seemed to be going so well.

According to Griffon, Lachouque had claimed he needed the hair for an "exhibition." A few strands of hair for an exhibition, when Lachouque had many more strands of the same hair in his private museum where Forshufvud had seen them the year before? Forshufvud did not believe it: the story made no sense.

Something else was going on here: something Forshufvud did not yet understand. He had the uneasy feeling that he would get no more of Napoleon's hair, and no more help, from Lachouque—perhaps not from Griffon either. The gates of Paris were closing against him. It meant all the work of the last few months was going to waste, all the progress he thought he had made was an illusion. His case on the poisoning of Napoleon seemed to lie in ruins: the proof he had expected from those hairs in Griffon's laboratory had been snatched away from him. It would be difficult indeed—someone less determined than Forshufvud would have said impossible—to repair the damage. The road ahead was longer and harder than it had seemed before he telephoned Henri Griffon.

It was time to take stock. Forshufvud settled himself in his favorite armchair in the living room, the various portraits and busts of Napoleon gazing down on him. He was disappointed and resentful, but he would not let himself be defeated. He filled his pipe and, in his methodical fashion, reviewed the events that had occurred in Paris a month earlier as the first step toward planning his next move.

His trip had been well prepared. In the fall of the previous year, after his visit to Glasgow, he had written Lachouque in Paris to tell him about the new technique Hamilton Smith had devised to analyze hair in sections and thereby to calculate the dosages of arsenic that the victim had received. He had asked the Frenchman if he could spare him a few more strands from that same lock, the one shaved from Napoleon's head at death that Louis Marchand had brought back from St. Helena. Forshufvud had suggested that this time perhaps the hair could be analyzed in a French laboratory, using Smith's new method. Lachouque's replies had been cordial: he had agreed to set up meetings when Forshufvud came to Paris. Forshufvud had decided to go in April, the first time he could take a few days away from his dental practice: his consuming interest in the Napoleon case did not, after all, exempt him from the need to earn a living.

The meeting was scheduled for 10:30 on the morning of April 10 at the French army's historical office in the Ministère de la Défense on the Left Bank. It was altogether fitting, Forshufvud thought, that they were meeting only four blocks from Napoleon's tomb at Les Invalides and that the nearby Rue Las Cases bore the name of one of Napoleon's companions in exile at St. Helena. The building itself, the Hotel de Brienne, was full of memories of Napoleon's time. Built in the eighteenth century by the Conti family, it was later the home of Etienne Charles de Brienne, Archbishop of Toulouse—and a confirmed athiest— who was Louis XVI's finance minister just before the Revolution. When Napoleon was in power, his mother, Madame Mère, used the Hôtel de Brienne as her Paris residence. His brother, Lucien Bonaparte, used to meet his mistress there.

The room in which the meeting took place was darkish and chilly, like most French government offices. As Forshufvud later recalled it, eight men were seated around the table. The only one known personally to the Swedish visitor was Commandant Lachouque, whom he had met the year before. Among the others present Forshufvud remembered a doctor from the military hospital of Val de Grace, another military doctor, and the army's chief pharmacist, one Colonel Kiger. They asked Forshufvud to describe his case. As he looked around the table, he realized this was a formidable audience for an outsider—one who moreover was not even French—to address with the argument that France's national hero had been poisoned. Forshufvud was undaunted. He was not in any event easily daunted, and after his years of study at the University of Bordeaux he was comfortable with both the language and the ways of the French. He spoke confidently for about an hour. The group listened silently, and when they spoke, they seemed to him to be both interested in his thesis and sympathetic to it. No one greeted what he said with that eloquent scorn that Forshufvud knew from experience to be the special talent of the French expert. They agreed that the investigation should be pursued along the lines Forshufvud had proposed. There was even inconclusive talk about examining the body that lay beneath that gigantic slab a few blocks away. The meeting had gone better than Forshufvud had dared to hope.

Two days later, Lachouque had accompanied Forshufvud to see Henri Griffon. Griffon was head of the Paris police toxicological laboratory, and was known as France's leading expert on arsenic poisoning. They found him in his laboratory on the Right Bank, next to the Gare de Lyon. This meeting had seemed to Forshufvud to go even better than the one at the Ministère de la Défense. He and Griffon were at home with each other in the specialized language of toxicology, and the place itself, the familiar equipment and smells, reminded Forshufvud of all the laboratories in which he had conducted experiments over the years. Griffon quickly showed a personal interest in the case: the death of Napoleon was big game even for the chief toxicologist of France. The Frenchman had invented a hair-analysis technique of his own and, yes, he would arrange to use it in his laboratory. He said that "clearly" Napoleon had been poisoned. While Forshufvud watched, Lachouque handed Griffon a few strands from his precious Louis Marchand lock of hair.

After leaving Griffon's laboratory, Forshufvud walked by himself along the nearby bank of the Seine. As he looked across the river at the Quai d'Austerlitz, named for one of Napoleon's great victories, and back to the Place de la Bastille, where the Revolution from which Napoleon emerged had begun, Forshufvud reflected that it was right that the mystery of Napoleon's death should be solved here in the city where he was still such a constant presence. At that moment Forshufvud had no doubt that the case would indeed be solved in Paris, in Henri Griffon's laboratory. Getting Griffon himself to analyze the hair was a coup Forshufvud had not anticipated a few months ago. Forshufvud knew the French well enough to be certain that the results, whatever they might be, would always be suspect in French eyes if the tests were conducted in a foreign laboratory, and worst of all, a British one. Griffon, on the other hand, could speak on the question of whether Napoleon was poisoned with more authority than anyone else in France and, therefore, the world.

Forshufvud had felt, as he stood that day on the bank of the Seine, that he was close to the end of the quest that had occupied much of his time and most of his thoughts for the past two years. His elation had continued after he was home in Göteborg. He exchanged letters with Lachouque and Griffon; the Frenchmen were as cordial as they had been in Paris. Lachouque's letters indicated that he agreed with Forshufvud's thesis; he even advised him on how the case might best be presented. A Paris newspaper headline quoted Griffon as saying that "Napoleon must be exhumed." All was going very well, as far as Forshufvud could tell, until today, and the telephone call to Griffon. What had happened? What had caused Lachouque to in effect pull the rug out from under Forshufvud by withdrawing his strands of hair from Griffon's laboratory?

Forshufvud thought he knew the explanation for Lachouque's strange behavior. The French, not just Lachouque but others in the little closed circle of Napoleon experts, must have started thinking about the next question. If Napoleon was indeed poisoned, then who was the assassin? Forshufvud had avoided the question in his conversations in Paris, but of one thing both he and the French could be sure: the assassin, whoever he was, most probably had to be a trusted member of Napoleon's entourage. It would be tempting to try to blame the hated English, who had put Napoleon on St. Helena. But the circumstances of life at St. Helena—and the French experts knew those circumstances better than anyone—made it next to impossible for any outsider to the household to be the killer. The conclusion was inescapable: if Forshufvud was right, France's great hero was struck down by a traitor among those closest to him. It was not an appetizing prospect for a Frenchman to contemplate.

And there was more: if Forshufvud was right, the French experts had for six years failed to see the evidence staring at them out of the pages of Louis Marchand's memoirs, the evidence that

106

had first interested Forshufvud in the case. If this unknown Swedish outsider were proved right, many scholarly faces in France would be red: if anything new was to be discovered about Napoleon, *they* were the ones who were supposed to do it. Far better all around, for the self-esteem of not only the experts but France itself, if the Forshufvud thesis could be disproved or at least discounted. And that could be done—so it must have seemed to the French, Forshufvud reasoned—if he were denied access to the indispensable evidence of the hairs in Lachouque's possession. That was why Lachouque had taken his hairs back from Henri Griffon's laboratory. That was why the gates of Paris had closed against him. Forshufvud felt certain he could no more open those gates than he could remove the great slab of Napoleon's tomb— and to think that only a month ago he had reason to hope that the body itself would provide the final proof of his theory!

Forshufvud reflected unhappily that he would either have to abandon his quest or pursue it without the help—indeed against the opposition—of the French Napoleonists. To give up without a struggle was out of the question. Forshufvud was not a man who easily admits defeat, and his research work over the years had led him into more than one scientific battle. He knew he had gotten a pleasure out of those combats that was not at all scientific. "I won't let them stop me without a fight," he murmured, and—he later remembered—he glanced up at the portrait on the wall and thought: yes, that's what Napoleon would have said.

He would go ahead—but how? To move his case forward, he needed physical evidence, and that could be found in only one place: Napoleon's hair. Hamilton Smith was waiting in Glasgow to apply his new sectional analysis to the hair. In its absence, the case remained stalled where it had been the previous summer.

The hair was out there somewhere, Forshufvud was sure of that. Dozens of locks had been collected during Napoleon's life and at his death, and even at the time they were known to be precious relics. Many of those locks must have survived the intervening years, handed down the generations just as Louis Marchand's lock was handed down to his daughter and after her to her son. Among the present owners of those locks some must be willing to give up a few strands in the interest of science—and history. But who were the owners and how could Forshufvud reach them? Trying to trace even a single lock from its original owner to its present whereabouts struck Forshufvud as a formidable and tedious undertaking, particularly since those who could help him the most, the French Napoleonists, now seemed committed to his failure.

There was another way: publicity. Tell the world his theory, through whatever channels he could reach, and then pray that the news would reach a person or persons unknown who would come forward with the indispensable piece of evidence. It was a chancy way to proceed, and it was not to Forshufvud's liking. He had little experience of the popular press and, like most scientists, little respect for it: they always got things wrong. The researcher in him was offended at the idea of going public before his case was ready. Eventually, of course, he had always intended to publish his findings. Upstairs, in the desk in his third-floor study, were the handwritten pages of the manuscript he had started the year before. He had planned to wait until all the evidence he could muster was in and then lay his case before the court of history. That was the right way to do it, but now Forshufvud could not afford to wait. He would have to put his work out in its present incomplete form, make it known as widely as possible—and wait.

It was a gamble, he realized, but a well-calculated one, and it was always better to gamble than to lose by doing nothing. Napoleon would understand that.

CHAPTER THIRTEEN

OCTOBER 1816
JAMESTOWN, ST. HELENA

Cipriani waited with his basket until there were a dozen or so people in the office of Balcombe, Cole and Co. by the quay in the port of Jamestown. He needed witnesses for what he was about to do, and the group that was now in the office included the ideal spectators: English officers from a frigate at anchor in the harbor that was due to sail for England that afternoon. Satisfied, Napoleon's majordomo and agent opened the basket, brought out its contents, and asked the clerk to weigh them. The spectators saw a pile of battered silver platters and dishes from which the imperial eagles had been hacked off. Removing the insignia and damaging the silverware had of course greatly diminished its value. That did not matter. What mattered was that witnesses saw the transaction and would carry the tale to London.

"How is the Emperor?" one of the English officers asked Cipriani.

"Well enough," Cipriani told him. "Well enough for someone who must sell his silverware in order to live."

The silver weighed 952 troy ounces and was valued at 240

pounds; the amount was credited to the account of Longwood House. His transaction finished, Cipriani mounted his horse and set out on the five-mile ride up the winding road to Longwood. He had carried out his delicate mission. Once more the dark Corsican had justified Napoleon's confidence in him. He reported that the people who saw what happened seemed ashamed and indignant, and Napoleon said: "Anytime you're asked for money, sell as much silver as is needed till it's all gone."

The deliberately public sale of the silver was one of Napoleon's maneuvers in his running dispute with the new English governor, Hudson Lowe, over the budget of Longwood House. Acting on orders from Lord Bathurst, the Colonial Secretary in London, Hudson Lowe had told the French exiles that the amount spent annually on Longwood must be reduced from twelve thousand to eight thousand pounds. It was a strangely petty move: the cost of Longwood was trifling compared to the quarter-million pounds per year it cost the English to maintain the troops and ships stationed at St. Helena; and the amount now considered excessive for the fifty-odd residents of Longwood invited comparison with the Governor's personal salary, which was also twelve thousand pounds.

Napoleon had seized the opportunity to embarrass the English authorities. In fact he had plenty of money deposited in Europe on which he could draw, but what interested him now was the issue. "Have all my silver smashed with an axe by Noverraz," he told Montholon. Cipriani had the silver pieces broken up by the powerful Swiss valet in a courtyard in full view of the English garrison. The imperial eagles were removed, to deny them as souvenirs to the English, and were saved by Louis Marchand. Napoleon cared little about the silverware or, in fact, about the budget itself. So little did he care about Longwood's finances that he had entrusted their management to the Count de Montholon instead of to Grand Marshal Bertrand, who had administered the imperial palace at les Tuileries. Montholon's record made him a dubious choice for any position involving money. A good-looking and frivolous member of the old aristocracy, Montholon in his twenties had run through his legacy from his father; serving in the army under the Bourbons, while Napoleon was at Elba in his first exile, Montholon had been charged with embezzling the funds intended to pay his troops. Now, when the English complained about wine consumption at Longwood, Montholon replied that he was doing the best he could. He was even, he said, doing at "the Emperor's table" what he never did at his home in France: corking up partly drunk bottles of wine to be used the next day.

Whatever he may have thought of Montholon's ability as a manager, Napoleon was not about to blame him for Longwood's finances—especially not when he could use the budget issue as a tool to gain the sympathy of the English public. Napoleon's goal at this time was to persuade the English government—somehow, by whatever means he could find—to let him return to Europe, or England, away from this dismal, distant island where he had now been cooped up a full year and where he was above all bored: less had happened in that year than in any other twelve months of his adult life. Napoleon had just turned forty-seven, and he was not ready to be forgotten by the world. The difficult, petty-minded new Governor provided Napoleon with an opportunity to attract sympathetic attention to himself.

The two men had gotten on badly almost from the start. Lieutenant General Sir Hudson Lowe, who was the same age as Napoleon, had come to St. Helena five months earlier after a career in which he had served, without distinguishing himself, in a variety of military and diplomatic posts. For a number of years he commanded a regiment of Corsicans who joined the English during the French Revolution: Napoleon considered that the English had insulted him by sending as his jailer a man who had led "deserters" from his native island. Napoleon also professed to be repelled by the new Governor's physical appearance. An egg-shaped head over a high forehead, a long nose over a tight mouth, small furtive eyes—"hyena's eyes," Napoleon said—a face disfigured by red blotches of eczema. "He has a most villainous face," Napoleon observed after their first meeting.

Hudson Lowe's contemporaries were not impressed with his

111

talents. The Duke of Wellington, under whom he had served, said Hudson Lowe was a man who "knew nothing of the world, and like all men who know nothing of the world, he was suspicious and jealous"; on another occasion Wellington called him "a damned fool." Wellington thought Hudson Lowe "a very bad choice" for the job of Napoleon's guardian. Count Alexander Antonovich de Balmain, the Russian commissioner on St. Helena, reported to his government that "the responsibility with which he [Lowe] has been entrusted makes him tremble. He becomes alarmed at the slightest incident, puzzles his brain for hours about nothing, and does with an immense expenditure of energy what another would accomplish in a minute."

Although he did not know it, Hudson Lowe years earlier had had a humiliating encounter with a man who was now in Napoleon's household at St. Helena. It happened in 1808 on another, far more pleasant island: Capri in the Bay of Naples. Hudson Lowe was commander of the English garrison on Capri. To find out what the French forces on the mainland were doing, Hudson Lowe employed a couple of agents known to him as Suzzarelli and Franceschi. The second man was in fact an agent of Napoleon. He bribed Suzzarelli into serving as a double agent, and together they fed Hudson Lowe a steady diet of misinformation. The result was that a small French force was able to capture the heavily fortified, easily defended island. The man known to Hudson Lowe on Capri as Franceschi was, on St. Helena, the Cipriani who in that October was selling Napoleon's silverware on the dock in Jamestown. Hudson Lowe never did find out that the man who was now embarrassing him had earlier humiliated him, and both times in the service of Napoleon.

This anxiety-ridden man was terrified that he would bungle his awesome responsibility and that somehow Napoleon would escape to set Europe on fire again—and destroy the career of Hudson Lowe. There was always the specter of Elba: Napoleon had escaped his first exile because the British officer assigned to watch him had sailed over to Genoa to visit his mistress. It must not happen a second time: that much had been made clear to Hudson Lowe by his superiors in London. Having heard of two earlier mutinies at St. Helena, the new Governor had decided the likeliest way Napoleon would escape was by raising a revolt among the inhabitants and the garrison. This improbable fear, magnified by his irrational mind, informed much of Hudson Lowe's behavior toward the exiles at Longwood.

In his first months in the governor's residence at Plantation House, halfway across the island from Longwood, Hudson Lowe began enforcing petty rules that had been ignored by his more confident predecessor, Admiral Cockburn, and issuing new rules of his own. He rode up to Bertrand's residence on Longwood plain and announced to the Grand Marshal that all the exiles, officers and servants alike, must sign a declaration that they would stay on St. Helena for the duration of Napoleon's captivity—or be deported immediately. The demand caused turmoil among those of the French who nursed the hope of getting away from the rock before too long, without necessarily waiting out their master's fate. Fanny Bertrand, who had tried to throw herself overboard rather than go to St. Helena, was desperate to get to England and educate her children there. Now in her early thirties, the attractive blonde did not want to spend her remaining youth and beauty in exile. She spent days weeping and, in angry scenes with her morose husband, she threw dishes around their little home. Bertrand told the Governor that "family pressures" would require him to leave within a year, though he knew that duty required him to stay to the end. Eventually the officers all signed ambiguous declarations they had written. Bertrand wrote: "I declare it to be my wish to remain at St. Helena." The servants all signed a statement written by Napoleon promising to "remain here." It was not what London had demanded, but the Governor, as irresolute as he was vindictive, let the matter drop.

Most of the regulations Hudson Lowe sent up to Longwood, usually in a letter that an aide delivered to Bertrand, were designed to restrict Napoleon's ability to talk with the islanders and write to the world outside. Aware that the exiles were regularly smuggling letters past his censorship, the Governor proclaimed it a crime for any islander to have any dealing with anyone at Longwood without his specific permission—which did not keep the mail from getting through. (In fact, when Hudson Lowe deported a servant named Santini, Napoleon took the opportunity to have a bill of particulars against the English written on a piece of white satin cut from a dress, and sewn into the lining of Santini's coat: it was published in England under the title of "The Remonstrance from St. Helena.") Hudson Lowe reduced the area in which Napoleon could ride without an escort, knowing that Napoleon would never accept an escort imposed by the Governor, and he revived a rule, laid down in London but never enforced by Cockburn, that an English officer must see Napoleon at least twice a day.

Napoleon's response was to frustrate Hudson Lowe when he could and, failing that, to use the regulations as a grievance against the English in general. When his riding area was reduced, Napoleon stopped going out on horseback—and told his doctor, Barry O'Meara, who he knew would tell the Governor, that the English would bear the blame for killing him by depriving him of exercise. He frustrated the rule that he must be seen twice a day simply by staying in his two little rooms at Longwood for days at a time. In June, during the austral winter, when Longwood plain was enveloped in fog and rain, no Englishman saw Napoleon for eight straight days.

Hudson Lowe was wild with anxiety. Only a month earlier London had warned him to watch out for escape attempts: there were rumors of an expedition being organized in Brazil, of a Bonapartist agent on St. Helena, of an American named Carpenter fitting out a ship in the Hudson River. And now this. Was Bonaparte even at Longwood? Could he somehow have escaped under cover of the fog and now be on his way to Europe, laughing at the man he had so easily duped—and Lowe's own career be in ruins? The Governor sent emissaries up to Longwood to tell

Bertrand that Napoleon must let himself be seen or he would order his men to break down the door.

An English officer knocked on the door leading from the garden to Napoleon's rooms and shouted: "Come out, Bonaparte!" No response.

Eventually Napoleon called O'Meara to his room, where he now kept a pair of loaded pistols. "Any person who endeavors to force his way into my apartment," he told O'Meara, "shall be a corpse the moment he enters it. If he ever eats bread or meat again, I am not Napoleon. This I am determined on: I know that that I shall be killed afterwards, as what can one do against a camp? I have faced death too many times to fear it." The prospect that the captive would be killed by an English soldier was, as Napoleon knew, almost as frightening to Hudson Lowe as the thought of his escape: the twice-a-day rule remained on paper only.

Though he could frustrate some of the Governor's rules, the feud with Hudson Lowe was in fact costing Napoleon dearly. The narrow circle of his captivity was shrinking. Visitors became rare because of a dispute over who should sign their passes; yet visits by travelers on ships calling at St. Helena were a way for Napoleon to send messages to the outside world and were one of the few distractions of life at Longwood. And there were the commissioners. In June, representatives from three of the Allied powers— France, Austria, and Russia—had arrived at St. Helena. The French and Austrian commissioners had been instructed to make sure with their own eyes that Bonaparte was in fact in captivity; the Russian, Count Balmain, was told only to observe and report what was going on. Napoleon at first thought Balmain and the Austrian, Baron Sturmer, might be useful. Tsar Alexander had once been his friend; maybe he could be convinced to intervene and end Napoleon's dismal exile. As for the Austrian, Emperor Francis was after all Napoleon's father-in-law; at the very least he might bring news of Marie-Louise and the child known as the King of Rome. But neither commissioner brought any message from his master. (The only message about Napoleon's family came indirectly. A young botanist with Sturmer gave Louis Marchand a note from his mother, employed by Marie-Louise, with a lock of Napoleon's son's hair.) Instead, the commissioners asked only to see Napoleon, presumably to make sure he was really there. Napoleon refused to receive them in their official capacity because, he said, that would mean recognizing the right of the Allies to keep him a prisoner. He would see them privately, as individuals, he said, but that in turn was refused by the commissioners. They were never to meet: a possible channel of communication remained closed.

The French commissioner was another matter. The Marquis de Montchenu, at fifty-nine, was a vain aristocrat who had little to boast about in his parasitic career besides his lineage. His young secretary did the work and reported separately to Paris. Montchenu arrived with letters for some of the residents of Longwood, including Fanny Bertrand, Las Cases, and Montholon, but Napoleon himself expected no help from him or his master. "Louis owes me nothing," he observed. The most self-made of men despised Montchenu's aristocratic pretensions: "In that booby's eyes, belonging to an old family is the only source of merit. It was such as Montchenu who were the chief cause of the Revolution. God help the nation that is governed by such." When he heard that Montchenu had written to Europe about Betsy Balcombe's escapades with him, he sent Barry O'Meara to the Briars "with [Betsy wrote] a message to me, which was how I might revenge myself. It so happened that the Marquis prided himself on the peculiar fashion of his wig, to which was attached a long queue. This embellishment to his head Napoleon desired me to burn off with caustic. I was always ready for mischief, and in this instance had a double inducement, on the Emperor's promise to reward me, on receipt of the pigtail, with the prettiest fan Mr. Solomon's shop contained. Fortunately I was prevented indulging in this most hoydenish trick by the remonstrances of my mother."

Napoleon knew the idleness he was imposing on himself

116

could not be good for his health, but he had never permitted the needs of his body to stand in the way of his ambition. In the time of power, Napoleon had made superhuman demands on his body: the days in the saddle, wearing out one horse after another, and the sleepless nights during campaigns; the twenty-hour workdays at the Tuileries. Now the logic of his position demanded just the opposite of his body: days and nights lying around, listless in front of a smoky fire, in his damp, cramped quarters, seeing no visitors. In fact, Napoleon's health was suffering during that first year of exile. In May he fell so ill he sent Louis Marchand to get Doctor O'Meara. Normally he saw O'Meara only when he was well, for conversation and gossip; if he was ill, he preferred to stay alone and doctor himself with barley water and long baths. He complained of gout to O'Meara, and he told Las Cases that "my legs refuse to work for me." He said that he was constantly cold and that the sunlight gave him a headache. His gums began to bother him, and O'Meara found that they were "spongy, pale, and bled on the slightest touch." The recurring symptoms suffered by Napoleon, and also at times by Gourgaud, were attributed by O'Meara to "diseases of the climate": a catch-all diagnosis for whatever could not otherwise be explained. As usual, Napoleon waved off the medicines O'Meara proposed with remarks like "Medicine is fit for old people." He agreed that lack of exercise was damaging to his health, but told O'Meara that was better than conceding the Governor's right to treat him as a prisoner when he went out riding.

Napoleon's stormy relations with Hudson Lowe reached a climax on August 18, two months before he ordered Cipriani to sell his silver. A few days earlier the Governor had quarreled with Bertrand and had ordered the Grand Marshal's home surrounded by sentries who let no one go in or out; a soldier who let Doctor O'Meara through to care for a sick servant was himself arrested. Now Hudson Lowe had ridden up to Longwood, accompanied by Admiral Pulteney Malcolm, the naval commander, to complain about Bertrand. Hudson Lowe made his complaint and Napoleon,

117

angry, addressed himself to the Admiral: "Bertrand is a man who has commanded armies, and *he* treats him like a corporal. *He* treats us as if we were Corsican deserters. Governments have jobs for two kinds of people, those they respect and those they despise: *he* is one of the latter. The job they have given him is that of an executioner."

"I have to obey my orders," Hudson Lowe said.

"So, if you were ordered to assassinate me, you would obey?"

"No, the English are not assassins."

By now Napoleon was waving his arms and shouting: "I can't write a letter without his seeing it. . . . I can't receive a woman without his permission. . . . He kept a book sent to me by a Member of Parliament, and he boasted about it. . . ."

Admiral Malcolm tried to intervene: "Sir Hudson Lowe kept those volumes because they were dedicated with the title of Emperor. He was forbidden to give them to you."

Napoleon plunged on: "And who gave you the right to dispute that title? In a few years your Lord Castlereagh, Lord Bathurst and you, you will be buried in oblivion, or if you are known, it will be only for the indignities you have committed against me."

The Governor left abruptly. Later Napoleon bitterly reproached himself for losing the iron self-control he had so prized in the days of power when, if he displayed anger, it was always for a well-calculated purpose. He said to Las Cases: "I must not receive that officer again. He makes me lose my temper. It's beneath my dignity. Words escape me that would have been unpardonable at the Tuileries. If there is an excuse here, it is that I find myself in his hands and in his power."

Napoleon was never to see Hudson Lowe after that day. They conducted their guerrilla war through intermediaries. Sitting in his office at Plantation House, across the island, Hudson Lowe labored for long hours, finger in the corner of his mouth, over the wording of letters he then sent by courier to Longwood House. Napoleon's formal replies, when he answered at all, were in the form of letters dictated by him but signed by Bertrand or Montholon. When he wanted to make an accusation that might not look good on paper, or simply to vent his anger, Napoleon used Barry O'Meara as a conduit. Sitting in his garden or lolling in his bath, Napoleon would summon the doctor and launch into a tirade about the man he referred to by a collection of epithets, one of his favorites being *sbirro Siciliano*—Sicilian spy. O'Meara recalled that Napoleon said on one occasion: "While surrounding the house with his staff, he [Lowe] reminded me of the savages of the South Sea Islands, dancing round the prisoners whom they were going to devour. Tell him," continued Napoleon, "what I said about his conduct." O'Meara continued: "For fear that I should forget, he repeated his expressions about the savages a second time, and made me say it after him." And O'Meara would relay the Governor's response to his patient.

Napoleon's tactic of sending Cipriani to Jamestown to sell his silver succeeded in its immediate purpose. On Christmas Day, 1816, Cipriani rode down to the port with four baskets containing 290 more pounds of battered silverware. When he heard about this transaction, Hudson Lowe summoned Cipriani to his office. "Why do you need so much money?" he demanded.

"To buy food, Excellency," Cipriani replied.

"Why do you buy so much butter, so many fowls?"

"Because the allowance granted by your Excellency does not give us enough to eat."

The Governor had not recognized the man he knew as Franceschi eight years earlier on Capri. The English authorities in London, embarrassed by the publicity the affair of the silver was getting, called off their effort to cut the Longwood budget. It was a victory of sorts, in a battle of sorts. Not much for the man who fought from Austerlitz to Waterloo. But, on St. Helena, it was the only battle Napoleon could find to fight.

CHAPTER FOURTEEN

OCTOBER 1961
HAMBURG

 STEN FORSHUFVUD settled himself uncomfortably into his seat, as usual unable to find room for his long legs, and waited for the last flight to Göteborg to take off. He was exhausted, but he was far too excited to sleep on the short flight home to Sweden. It had been a long day, and a very successful one. In the black leather briefcase he held carefully on his lap was the biggest prize he had bagged to date in the Napoleon case.

The telephone call that brought him to Hamburg had come that same morning at eight o'clock. The caller identified himself in French as Clifford Frey, a textile manufacturer from Munchwilen, Switzerland. Was he speaking to the Sten Forshufvud who wrote the article about the poisoning of Napoleon? He was indeed. Frey went on to say that he had in his possession a lock of Napoleon's hair that came originally from the valet Abram Noverraz. He would be happy to provide Forshufvud with some of those hairs for further testing. As it happened, Frey would be in Hamburg, Germany, that afternoon. Could Forshufvud by any chance meet him at the airport restaurant at, say, six-thirty that evening?

Forshufvud agreed immediately. A hair from Abram Nover-raz was exactly what Forshufvud wanted. According to Louis Marchand's memoirs, Noverraz was the servant who shaved the hair from Napoleon's head on the day after his death. He sailed on the *Camel* with Marchand and the others returning from exile, and then went back to his native Switzerland. Of all the hair that Forshufvud might obtain, this one from Noverraz was the best suited for the next step in his campaign: the analysis of the hair section by section. After agreeing to meet Frey, Forshufvud hung up and promptly booked his flight. Then he cancelled all his plans for the day: meeting this stranger in Hamburg was the most important thing he could do with this day of his life. Only then did he remember that he and Frey had not agreed on how they would recognize each other. As he left, he told his wife he hoped to catch the last flight home that night, but added: "Don't wait up for me."

By late that afternoon, Forshufvud was at the Hamburg airport restaurant. He glanced around, but all he saw was a wealthy German woman with her beery husband, and, as he put it, a band of uproarious Danish Vikings on their way home, no doubt, from berserking on the Reeperbahn, Hamburg's street of pleasures. Forshurfud took a table from which he could see the entrance and settled himself down to wait for the man he was to meet. As he waited, he thought about the man who was responsible for the occasion: Abram Noverraz, the powerful, six-foot valet who, in 1814, had single-handedly held off a raging Royalist mob beseiging Napoleon's carriage when he was on his way to his first exile in Elba. Napoleon called him "my Swiss bear."

The man who entered the restaurant and looked around was also powerfully built, erect and close-cropped, with the sunburnt face of an Alpine skier. It was Clifford Frey. After their greeting, Forshufvud suggested they share a meal. Frey declined; he wanted to get home that night, and it was a six-hour drive. They got right down to business.

Frey took an envelope from his briefcase and handed it to

Forshufvud. The envelope bore the name of the sender—*Abram Noverraz, La Violette près Lausanne, 1e 8e, 7bre, 1838*—and was addressed to *Monsieur Mons-Riss, St. Gall, Suisse.* It was postmarked Lausanne, September 9, 1838. In it Forshufvud found a letter and a smaller envelope. The letter, in the same hand as the writing on the envelope, was signed J. Abram Noverraz and said in part: "It is a pleasure to send you, Monsieur Mons, some hairs of the Emperor Napoleon which I have taken from his head after his death, it was the sixth May 1821." The smaller envelope was marked, in the same handwriting: *Cheveux de l'immortel Empereur Napoléon.* The hairs themselves were attached to a small piece of pasteboard with an intricately knotted twine, and the knot was sealed with a small clot of wax. "It is just what I need," Forshufvud said to Frey. "You will play an essential role in proving my case."

Frey explained, at Forshufvud's request, how the lock had come into his possession. A Madame Mons-in-Hoff, widow of the grandson of the "Monsieur Mons" to whom Noverraz had addressed his letter, had sold the lock and envelope many years ago to Frey's father, Clifford Sr., an officer in the Swiss army, who had left the relic to his son.

Frey asked: "Would you like to buy the hairs for one thousand dollars?"

Forshufvud was taken aback. He had been finding his quest increasingly costly in money as well as time. After a moment's reflection, he pointed out that the market value of Frey's relic would be greatly increased if he and Hamilton Smith could use some of the hairs to prove that Napoleon had been poisoned.

Frey had agreed, and then carefully set forth the conditions on which he would let Forshufvud use the hairs. No more than twenty of the fifty-odd hairs in the lock would be used for the analysis. The knot must on no account be undone; the hairs must be slipped free or cut on either side of the knot. Clifford Frey would receive a report of the test results, and the remaining hairs would be returned with the envelopes and the letter from

Noverraz. A paper describing the results would be submitted for publication in a suitable scientific journal. Forshufvud smiled to himself as he listened: these shrewd stipulations were just what he might have expected from a Swiss businessman. No matter: that was no concern of Forshufvud's one way or the other. As long as he got those indispensable hairs, he did not care whether Frey was motivated by love of truth or love of money.

Forshufvud had readily agreed to all of the Swiss businessman's stipulations. Now, on the flight back to Göteborg, he could relax and enjoy the thought of what he had accomplished. He was delighted to be holding the Noverraz hair in his briefcase. He was, if anything, even more delighted at his success in, as he later put it, "running the French blockade." Last spring he had found out to his great disappointment that the French circle of Napoleon experts was not going to help in his quest, because, Forshufvud guessed, his theory, if proved, would upset too many of their own cherished and published theories and raise too many unwelcome questions about treason in Napoleon's household.

The French blockade had left Forshufvud with no alternative but to look elsewhere for the hair that alone could prove his theory. Not knowing where to look, he had decided all he could do was to publicize his case, in its admittedly incomplete form, and hope the news would reach someone who could come forward with more hair. He and Hamilton Smith, with Anders Wassen, a Swedish toxicologist, wrote an article detailing the results of the test Smith had performed on the single strand of hair Forshufvud had obtained in Paris; the article named Napoleon as the victim. The article had appeared in the October 14 issue of the British scientific journal *Nature.*

The first reactions came from the Napoleon experts, notably the French circle, who predictably enough denounced the Swedish interloper who was trespassing on their territory. One hair was not enough, maybe it was contaminated, maybe it was not Napoleon's. . . . Forshufvud shrugged off their attacks on him; he had expected no less. He was waiting for another kind of response. It had come earlier than he had dared to hope: Clifford Frey's call from Switzerland that same day had come only two weeks after the *Nature* article appeared.

Napoleon had certainly changed his life, Forshufvud reflected while the airplane began its descent to Göteborg and home. Here he was plotting press campaigns and meeting strangers in foreign airports—it was all a far cry from the laboratories in which he had spent so many of his working days. He had good reason to be pleased with himself. He might be an amateur at this game, but so far, it seemed, he was playing it pretty well. He had not let the French blockade stop him, anyway. He realized, too, that he was beginning to enjoy the game. Napoleon was taking up every moment he could spare these days. But Forshufvud did not begrudge the time. Days like this one made it all worthwhile.

The next step was to get the Noverraz hair in his briefcase over to Hamilton Smith in Glasgow. The Scots scientist would then apply his new method of analyzing the hair in sections. The result would be a chronological graph of Napoleon's exposure to arsenic over the crucial last months of his life. Forshufvud's theory would stand or fall on what that graph revealed.

CHAPTER FIFTEEN

NOVEMBER 1816
LONGWOOD HOUSE, ST. HELENA

====================== $\mathbf{N}$APOLEON WAS sitting on a tree trunk in the garden of Longwood House. Three of his officers—Las Cases, Montholon, and Gourgaud—were with him. It was midafternoon, the weather was better, and Napoleon was in a good mood. The valet Saint-Denis brought him a plate with five South African oranges, a gift from Admiral Malcolm, and a knife and some sugar. Napoleon gave one orange to Las Cases for his son. He cut the other oranges into slices, sugared them, and handed the slices to the officers. "I've been working all day with Bertrand on fortifications," he said. "It made the day seem short."

A cold wind came up—it was spring below the equator—and Napoleon went into the house with Las Cases. Through the billiard room window, they saw appear a group of uniformed Englishmen on horseback: Hudson Lowe, accompanied by aides and soldiers. A valet came to the billiard room to say that the Governor's assistant, Thomas Reade, was asking for Las Cases. "Go see what that animal wants with you," Napoleon said. A quarter-hour later Louis Marchand, visibly upset, reported to

Napoleon that the English had arrested Las Cases and his son in their room and had seized all his papers.

Late that evening, when Napoleon was sitting in his bathrobe in his room, Barry O'Meara appeared with more news. The Doctor had met Hudson Lowe on the road to Jamestown, and the Governor had said: "You will meet your friend Las Cases in custody." In town, O'Meara had found out that the charge against Las Cases was clandestine correspondence—"clandestine" being any communication, written or oral, that did not go through Hudson Lowe. A young mulatto named James Scott, a freed slave until recently assigned to Longwood as Las Cases' servant, had confessed to taking letters from Las Cases for delivery in England, where he was due to go with a new master on the next ship. The letters were written in white satin and sewn into Scott's clothing. One was addressed to Lucien Bonaparte in Rome; the other, to a Lady Clavering in London, a friend of Las Cases, asked her to place an item in a London paper that would, discreetly, let Longwood know the letter had arrived. Scott's father learned of the plan and denounced his son to the Governor. Las Cases and his fifteen-year-old son, Emmanuel, were now being held at a cottage on the edge of Longwood plain, and his papers—the hundreds of pages dictated by Napoleon, and more written by Las Cases—were in the Governor's possession.

Napoleon had good reason to be upset. One of Longwood's secrets had been revealed, and his major work at St. Helena, his justification to history of his career, was in enemy hands. His remaining officers, who agreed only in detesting Las Cases, thought that the little man they called the Jesuit had set himself up for arrest as a way of getting away from St. Helena. The circumstances surrounding his arrest were in fact peculiar. Only a few days earlier, Las Cases had proposed sending the letters via Scott; Napoleon told him the idea was "crazy" and assumed he had given it up. And, two weeks ago, Las Cases had been caught sending another unauthorized message through the same Scott. Hudson Lowe had let Las Cases off with a warning but had ordered Scott out of Longwood. That message had been addressed to the young French wife of Baron Sturmer, the Austrian commissioner.

Las Cases had been anxious to get in touch with the Baroness ever since her arrival earlier in the year. He had known her in Paris, two years ago, when she had been plain Mademoiselle Boutet, the plump, pretty daughter of a minor official who did tutoring to supplement his salary. He had tutored Las Cases' son; Las Cases' wife had befriended the daughter and had tried to help her find work as a governess. Now, Las Cases thought, the former Mademoiselle Boutet would surely remember his family's kindness and would use her new station in life to help the exiles. Napoleon had derided Las Cases' hopes: "How little you know the human heart! So her father was your son's tutor! So your wife befriended her when she needed it! My dear Las Cases, she is now a baroness, and you are the person she most dreads meeting, the person whose presence here is most embarrassing to her." Napoleon was right: the Baroness sent back word to Longwood that she knew no one by the name of Las Cases, and her husband reported the incident to the Governor.

Strangely, Hudson Lowe did not punish Scott, beyond firing him from Longwood, for carrying the message: slaves at St. Helena were routinely flogged for far less. Even more strange, Scott had returned to Longwood at some risk, slipping through the sentries at night, to pick up the second message, had then left part of one letter under a rock, and had told the whole story to his father. Las Cases himself, in a letter written from his prison, said he had fallen into a trap, presumably set by Hudson Lowe, who was known to want to reduce Napoleon's entourage and who had a particular aversion to Las Cases.

Once arrested, Las Cases seemed content enough to be deported. He managed to avoid accepting an offer from Hudson Lowe that would have permitted him to stay, and when Bertrand visited him in his cell, he told the Grand Marshal rather mysteriously that his destiny now lay elsewhere. His great historical work,

127

Napoleon's account of his career, was essentially completed. Life at Longwood was hard for the frail, birdlike aristocrat. He was poorly equipped to withstand the constant hostility of his much younger colleagues. His quarters were miserable; the roof leaked constantly. Both he and his son were having trouble with their health. Las Cases' eyes were failing, so much so he could no longer take Napoleon's dictation. Both of them had suffered recurring bouts of unexplained illness with symptoms similar to those displayed by Napoleon. Just before their arrest, Emmanuel had fallen very ill. All in all, there was reason enough for Las Cases to want to leave the island of exile.

One month after their arrest, Las Cases and his son were sent to the Cape of Good Hope, where they had to wait eight more months before they were allowed to board a ship for Europe. While he was at the Cape, Las Cases shipped a supply of Napoleon's favorite wine, the South African Vin de Constance, to St. Helena; and he noted with pride that people at this distant edge of Africa named their best fighting cocks, fastest racehorses, and favorite bulls—Napoleon. Hudson Lowe had kept Las Cases' manuscript under seal, and later sent it to London; the author would not get it back until 1821, after Napoleon's death. But when he left St. Helena, Las Cases was able to take another souvenir of his stay: a lock of hair that he had picked up from the floor two months earlier, when the footman Santini was giving his master a haircut.

Las Cases' fellow officers, jealous of his favored position with Napoleon, were as happy to see him go as he evidently was to leave. When it briefly seemed the little man might be staying after all, Montholon flew into a rage unusual for this polished courtier. Napoleon, on the contrary, was disappointed to lose him. Las Cases had been valuable as his English interpreter as well as the recorder of his history, and he found the old aristocrat's conversation more interesting than that of the others, whose knowledge and interests were far more limited. Napoleon was especially concerned about the manuscript now in Hudson

Lowe's possession, and no doubt being read by him. He summoned Saint-Denis, who had transcribed the manuscript into 925 pages of his small, precise hand, and questioned him about those parts of it—Las Cases' own account of St. Helena—that had not been dictated by Napoleon. He asked how his opinions of such figures as Admirals Cockburn and Malcolm were reported, and finally he got around to Hudson Lowe:

"Does he say anything about the Governor?"

Saint-Denis smiled and said: "Quite a bit, sire."

"Does he report that I said, 'He's a vile man,' and that his face is the meanest I've ever seen?"

"Yes, but often the terms are more moderate."

"Does he say I called him *sbirro Siciliano* (Sicilian spy)?"

"Yes, sire."

"That's his name."

When it was clear that Las Cases was leaving, Napoleon drafted a letter of farewell. After dinner, now with only Gourgaud and the Montholons, he asked Gourgaud to read the letter aloud and invited comments. Gourgaud, jealous, complained that the letter was too full of praise for a man who had only served the Emperor for eighteen months. He added: "I can see that in this world one must never tell the truth to sovereigns and that intriguers and flatterers are those who are most successful."

"My wish is that one day Las Cases will be your best friend," Napoleon said.

"Never, I detest him. . . . He is a hypocrite; one day your Majesty will realize that."

Napoleon shrugged and answered from his long experience of human behavior in the fires of war and politics: "Well, what do you expect? That he'll betray me? Speak ill of me? My God! Berthier, Marmont, that I loaded with honors and favor—how did they behave? I defy anyone to take me in. Men would have to be villainous indeed to be as much so as I believe they are."

129

CHAPTER SIXTEEN

JULY 1817
LONGWOOD HOUSE, ST. HELENA

=============================== Barry O'Meara was invited to dine alone with Napoleon that evening, not in the dining room but in the small room next to his bedroom where Napoleon now spent much of his days. Dinner was served on a small round table, without imperial ceremony; Napoleon sat on his sofa and O'Meara on a small chair.

Napoleon rarely dined with his remaining officers now. When he did, usually only three people were present: Gourgaud and the two Montholons, the Count and his wife Albine. Some evenings Napoleon dined alone with Albine. The Bertrands seldom came to Longwood House in the evenings. Their relations with Napoleon were rather cool now. Bertrand, the skilled engineer who had no talent for intrigue, had been eclipsed by the courtier Montholon, and his very proper wife resented the attractive Albine's favored position with Napoleon. Gourgaud and the Montholon couple quarreled incessantly, and besides, Napoleon complained, their conversation at dinner put him to sleep. He missed talking with the historian Las Cases, deported six months earlier.

By contrast, he enjoyed O'Meara's company. He could not trust the young doctor, who after all was an English officer, but he trusted no one anyway; and O'Meara, because he could circulate freely on St. Helena, could bring news of the world outside the narrow circle of Longwood. As for O'Meara, who was aware of his historic opportunity, he liked to draw Napoleon out in conversation, and then go to his room and record his words in the journal he was keeping. The two men often debated about the English national character. Napoleon said English policy was guided by economic interest, and quoted the Corsican nationalist Paoli on the English: *"sono mercanti"* (they are merchants). In these conversations, Napoleon at times took a more detached view of himself than he did in the self-justifications he dictated to Las Cases, as in this comment on his fall:

None but myself ever did me any harm; I was, I may say, the only enemy to myself; my own projects, that expedition to Moscow, and the accidents which happened there, were the causes of my fall. I may, however, say that those who made no opposition to me, who readily agreed with me, entered into all my views, and submitted with facility, were those who did me the most injury, and were my greatest enemies; because, by the facility of conquest they afforded, they encouraged me to go too far. . . . I was then too powerful for any man, except myself, to injure me.

Napoleon felt little need of O'Meara's professional services, for, despite occasional days of illness, his health was relatively good in the first half of 1817. On various occasions he complained of the persistent swelling in his legs, of headache, and of his sore gums, and a couple of times he was laid up with a diarrhea that O'Meara diagnosed as dysentery. Still, he felt better on most days than he had the year before. He made a point, as usual, of telling O'Meara what he thought of his profession: "You medical people will have more lives to answer for in the other world than even

131

we generals. . . . When [physicians] dispatch a number of souls to the other world, either through ignorance, mistake, or not having properly examined their complaints, they are just as cool and as little concerned as a general with whom I am acquainted, who lost three thousand men in storming a hill. Having succeeded, after several desperate attempts, he observed, with great sangfroid, 'Oh, it was not this hill I wanted to take, it was another; this is of no utility'; and returned back again to his former position."

That evening Napoleon was in particularly good spirits. After dinner, he told O'Meara he wanted to see him drunk: Napoleon, who never drank more than a glass or two of wine, was fond of telling the English that they were a nation of drunkards. He mocked the English custom of separating the sexes after dinner, and said to O'Meara: "If I were an Englishwoman, I should be very discontented at being turned out by the men to wait for two or three hours while they were guzzling their wine." Now he sent Louis Marchand for a bottle of champagne, drank one glass himself, and made O'Meara drink the rest. "Doctor, drink, drink," he said in English.

Napoleon talked about Admiral and Lady Malcolm, who were due to leave for England after a year at St. Helena, where he had been the naval commander. Napoleon liked the Admiral as much as he detested Hudson Lowe. Malcolm was an attractive, gray-haired man in his mid-forties who, Napoleon said, had a good heart and said what he thought. Though he could not criticize the Governor, Malcolm disapproved of his harsh treatment of Napoleon. Lady Malcolm, a gaunt, heavily made-up woman who suffered from curvature of the spine, was openly sympathetic to the fallen Emperor. Her brother owed his life to Napoleon: he was the Captain Elphinstone, seriously wounded the day before Waterloo, whom Napoleon had ordered his surgeons to treat. Two weeks earlier the Malcolms had come up to Longwood for a farewell visit. Napoleon proudly showed Lady Malcolm a supposed bust of his son (in reality it was a fake), which had arrived a week before and was now on the mantelpiece. Napoleon took the opportunity to recite his grievances, to be transmitted to London, and added that his mistreatment would only add to his renown: "I have worn the imperial crown of France, the iron crown of Italy; England has now given me a greater and more glorious crown, such as was worn by the savior of the world—a crown of thorns. It is to the persecutions of England that I shall owe the brightest part of my fame."

Lady Malcolm's family was responsible for an odd incident in the running war between Napoleon and Hudson Lowe. An English traveler had recently arrived from China with a chest of gifts for Napoleon, sent by Lady Malcolm's other brother, John Elphinstone, who was the East India Company's representative in China. Among them was a beautifully carved ivory chess set. The chest was sent up to Plantation House for the Governor's inspection. It contained no hidden messages, but Hudson Lowe discovered, to his distress, that the chessmen were embossed with an imperial crown and the letter *N*. For days, Hudson Lowe puzzled over whether he should let the chessmen with their imperial crests go up to Longwood: would that action perhaps mean that he, and through him the English government, was recognizing Napoleon as Emperor?

A difficult issue: the Governor consulted Admiral Robert Plampin, Malcolm's successor. "If the crowned *N* bothers you, all you have to do is not to look at it," Plampin advised. Finally, though not before the story had made the rounds of St. Helena, Hudson Lowe sent the problematic chess set to Longwood with a letter to Bertrand explaining that he was doing so even though a strict interpretation of his rules would forbid the gift. Napoleon replied, in a letter signed by Bertrand, that playing cards, linen, and "the little silverware that is left" all bore crowns, and were they forbidden too? This caused the Governor to send a 1,200-word letter in which he carefully explained that a crown made after Napoleon had abdicated, and by an Englishman at that, was altogether different from a crown made by the French when he was still on the throne. The story provided St. Helena with a rare occasion for laughter, and Count Balmain wrote to St. Petersburg that Hudson Lowe's "conduct toward them is a little crazy, even the English are beginning to say so."

Napoleon had asked O'Meara to invite the person who brought the chest of gifts to call on him at Longwood. The traveler, a black-bearded Englishman named Manning, was reputed to have seen the Grand Lama of Tibet. "I am very curious to get some information about this Grand Lama," Napoleon said to O'Meara. "I have never read any accounts about him that I could rely on, and have sometimes doubted of his existence." At their interview, Manning thanked Napoleon for setting him free some years earlier when he was arrested while traveling in France. Napoleon took out his atlas, written by Las Cases, and asked Manning to trace his route to Tibet. Manning then answered Napoleon's barrage of questions about the Grand Lama, whom he described as an "intelligent boy of seven years old." Napoleon asked some questions about the Chinese language and wanted to know if the Russians had penetrated Tibet.

Hudson Lowe, when he was not dealing with such immediate issues as the imperial chessmen, was worrying as always about the possibility that Napoleon would escape. He had come to Longwood one day in March to announce that he was going to put up a fence around the building, have its gates locked at night, and hold the keys himself until dawn. But Napoleon himself seems never to have taken the idea of escape seriously. At least twice, the second time only a few days before his dinner with O'Meara, Napoleon had refused to act on an offer by an English captain to smuggle him off the island.

That second time, Napoleon had joined for a few minutes in a discussion with Gourgaud and Montholon over a map of the island spread out on a table: "Through the town in broad daylight would be best. Going along the coast, with our hunting rifles, we could easily overcome an outpost of ten men. I'll pretend to stay in my bedroom. Only Marchand will know I'm not there . . ."

But then abruptly he said: "It is a very seductive picture, but alas it is madness. I must either die here or France must come and get me." Napoleon placed equally little hope in the rumor, which had reached St. Helena in various forms, that the Spanish colonies in America were going to revolt and ask Joseph Bonaparte, then living in Philadelphia, to be their king. Joseph would of course negotiate his brother's release; some of those at Longwood began to imagine themselves in Buenos Aires. Napoleon was skeptical. He had twice made his brother a king, first of Naples then of Spain, and had been disappointed in the results. He thought Joseph lacked the strength to be a ruler. "He is too good a man to be great," he told O'Meara.

Whatever his thoughts may have been, Napoleon spoke less and less about a return to power. When he talked about France after his fall, it was usually to comment on the problems of his successors. The Bourbons, he told Gourgaud, "can only stay in power by the use of terror; if they show weakness, they are lost." To O'Meara he said: "Ere twenty years have elapsed, when I am dead and buried, you will witness another revolution in France." When O'Meara said the English thought he still wanted to regain his throne, Napoleon answered: "Bah! If I were in England now, and a deputation from France were to come and offer me the throne, I would not accept it, unless I knew such to be the unanimous wish of the nation. Otherwise I should be obliged to turn executioner and cut off the heads of thousands to keep myself upon it. Oceans of blood must flow to keep me there. I have made noise enough in the world already, perhaps too much, and am now getting old, and want retirement."

After almost two years in exile, Napoleon was putting most of his hopes for getting away from St. Helena on a change in the English government. He knew from the papers that reached Longwood, or were reported on by O'Meara, that the story of the selling of the silverware, and the message carried by the servant Santini in his lining, had caused enough of a stir in England to force a debate in Parliament. The Whig opposition, led by Lord

Holland, whose wife was an admirer of Napoleon, attacked the treatment of the exile as overly harsh. But the government had not fallen and Lord Bathurst, the Colonial Secretary, had been able to prevent any change in policy toward Napoleon. In June, Napoleon summed up his situation to Gourgaud: "There could be great events at the death of Louis XVIII. If Lord Holland were in the government, perhaps I would be brought back to England, but what would give us the most hope is the death of the Prince Regent, which would put the little Princess Charlotte on the throne. She will bring me back."

On July 4, the day after Napoleon's dinner and champagne with O'Meara, the Malcolms sailed for England. Each carried a souvenir of their last visit to Longwood. Lady Malcolm had a cup and saucer of Sèvres porcelain depicting Cleopatra's Needle. The Admiral had a lock of Napoleon's hair.

Louis Marchand, twenty-four at the beginning of the exile, was Napoleon's chief valet and was known for his devotion to his master. He was at Napoleon's bedside more than anyone else during the last days of the Emperor's life. His account of those last days, in memoirs that were not published until the 1950s, provided the first clues to the real cause of Napoleon's death.

Henri-Gratien Bertrand had been grand marshal of Napoleon's palace at les Tuileries. A military engineer who served with Napoleon in Egypt, he had been with the Emperor the longest of the four officers who went to St. Helena. His memoirs, unpublished until the middle of this century, also provided important new evidence about Napoleon's death.

Fanny Bertrand, whose father was English, had been at Elba during Napoleon's first exile. She tried in vain to prevent her husband from taking his family to St. Helena. Once there she insisted, to Napoleon's displeasure, on their living apart from the other exiles.

Count Charles-Tristan de Montholon was a member of the pre-Revolutionary aristocracy. More of a courtier than a soldier, he served Napoleon in various minor positions until he was dismissed in 1812. Though he had never seen combat, he was a major general under the first Bourbon restoration. He rejoined Napoleon after Waterloo and went with him to St. Helena.

Albine de Montholon had been married twice
when she met Montholon. Napoleon, who
thought the match unsuitable, dismissed
Montholon for marrying her against his express wishes. At St. Helena it was widely believed that she was Napoleon's mistress.

Gaspard Gourgaud was an artillery officer who served with Napoleon in Russia where, he said, he saved the Emperor's life. At St. Helena he proved to be moody and hot-tempered — "a real Corsican," Napoleon said. Gourgaud's repeated quarrels with the Montholons caused Napoleon to send him home in 1818.

Count Emmanuel de las Cases, a member of the old aristocracy, lived in England during much of Napoleon's time in power. At St. Helena he recorded, and he later published, Napoleon's own accounts of his career. He left St. Helena in 1816.

Napoleon is seen (above) on board the English warship *Bellerophon* in a painting by Q. W. Orchardson. He had surrendered to the English in the hope he would be allowed to spend his exile in England, but he was sent from the *Bellerophon* on another ship to St. Helena. In this scene he is looking for the last time at the receding shore of France.

Jamestown, the tiny settlement that is the only port at St. Helena, is seen (right) in an 1806 engraving by J. Clark and J. Hamble. Napoleon landed here in October, 1815. The road winding up the hillside leads to Longwood Plain in the interior.

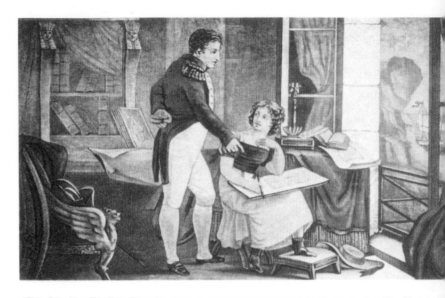

Napoleon spent the first two months of his exile at the Briars, the home of the Balcombe family. At left, he is seen helping fourteen-year-old Betsy Balcombe with her French lesson. His playful relationship with the high-spirited English teenager provided juicy gossip back in Europe. After his brief stay at the Briars, Napoleon moved to Longwood House (below), where he was to live, surrounded by English soldiers, for the five remaining years of his life. This picture of Longwood House was made from a sketch by Louis Marchand.

Lieutenant General Sir Hudson Lowe was governor of St. Helena from early 1815 until after Napoleon's death. Petty-minded and suspicious, and fearful that Napoleon would escape as he had from Elba, Hudson Lowe rigidly enforced restrictions on Napoleon's movements. Napoleon blamed his declining health on the confinement and lack of exercise that resulted from the governor's restrictions.

Count d'Artois was the younger brother of both
Louis XVI, guillotined during the Revolution,
and Louis XVIII, the first king of the Bourbon
Restoration. During his quarter-century in
exile, he mounted plots on the life of Napoleon, for whom his hatred was fanatical. He
succeeded to the throne as Charles X on his
brother's death in 1824, was ousted by the July
Revolution in 1830, and died in exile.

Sten Forshufvud (above) is seen in his study at Göteborg, Sweden, where he pieced together the evidence that solved the mystery of Napoleon's death. He first suspected arsenic poisoning when he found new information about Napoleon's last days in the memoirs of Louis Marchand. He then began to search for authentic specimens of Napoleon's hair that could be tested for arsenic content by a new method devised by Hamilton Smith (left), senior lecturer in the department of forensic medicine at the University of Glasgow, Scotland.

Barry O'Meara (below, right), seen holding his memoirs, A *Voice from St. Helena*, was an Irish-born doctor serving in the English navy aboard the *Bellerophon* when he accepted Napoleon's invitation to accompany him into exile as his personal physician. At Longwood House, he provided Napoleon with news of the island, and also reported about the exiles to the governor, Hudson Lowe, and to his naval superiors in London. The governor, who distrusted O'Meara, succeeded in getting him recalled in 1818.

Francesco Antommarchi (below), a Corsican doctor and pathologist, was Napoleon's resident physician from September 1819 to Napoleon's death. He performed the autopsy. His medical account of Napoleon's last days, often discounted by hostile historians, was given new credibility by the memoirs of Marchand and Bertrand.

1797

1802

1815

1817

his series of portraits shows Napo-
on's changing appearance over al-
ost a quarter-century. 1797 — at
venty-eight, he is the leading general
f the Revolution. 1802 — he is First
onsul and master of France. 1813 —
fter the disaster of Russia, the Emperor
in his last days of power. 1815 — on
oard the ship that took him to St.
lelena, Napoleon leans against the
un the English called "the Emperor's
annon" and gazes out to sea. In the last
iree representations, all at St. Helena,
Japoleon is seen getting steadily
eavier as the end approaches. Napo-
on's obesity in his last years was an
nportant piece of evidence in Sten
orshufvud's case.

1813

1819

1820

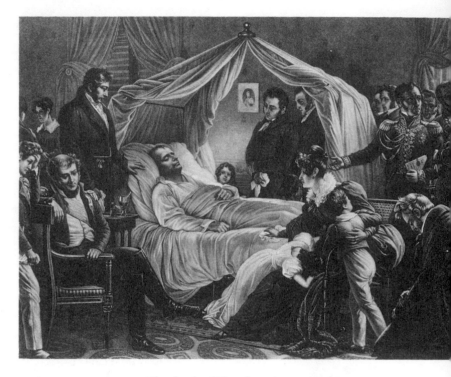

The death of Napoleon is recreated in a painting by Steuben. Dr. Antommarchi stands at the head of the bed, his hand on the pillow. Louis Marchand, the chief valet, stands clasping a napkin or towel on the far side of the bed. Bertrand is seated in the foreground; his wife Fanny is seated at the foot of the bed; the three children are the Bertrands'. Montholon is standing, arm outstretched toward the dying man, at the foot of the bed.

CHAPTER SEVENTEEN

DECEMBER 1961
GÖTEBORG

========================= Two months went by before Sten Forshufvud got the results of Hamilton Smith's second analysis of Napoleon's hair. Forshufvud had run into difficulty getting his precious lock of hair over to the University of Glasgow. After he had obtained the lock from Clifford Frey at the Hamburg airport, along with the conditions the Swiss businessman placed on its use, Forshufvud had asked a Swedish company to insure the hair for the equivalent of $25,000. He recalled later that the company representative had laughed at the idea of insuring a few strands of hair for that amount; even Lloyd's of London had refused to do it. Eventually, Clifford Frey had come to Göteborg to pick up the lock and take it in person to Hamilton Smith in Glasgow.

Forshufvud spent those two months getting ready for the information he expected from Hamilton Smith. He spent all the time he could spare up in his third-floor study working through his books and journals and the rapidly growing accumulation of his handwritten notes. Some of his books were so worn by now that he had to fasten them together with used pipe cleaners. He was confident that Smith's tests would bring him useful results, and he enjoyed what he was doing: this methodical research was the kind of work he knew from his years in the laboratory.

Once more, Forshufvud had plunged himself for days on end into that distant world centered on the fetid sickroom of Longwood. Once more, he was watching the dying Emperor and his companions coming and going at his bedside. The devoted Louis Marchand was there almost all the time. The doctor, Francesco Antommarchi, was there briefly on most days, despite Napoleon's aversion to him. The Count de Montholon was there more and more often, Forshufvud noticed. No visitors came from the outside world anymore.

Forshufvud was tracing Napoleon's symptoms, as described in the witnesses' memoirs, over the final seven months from September 1820, when he fell seriously ill, to the end on May 5, 1821. He was matching the descriptions of Napoleon's condition against what he knew of arsenic poisoning to see just when Napoleon might have been dosed with arsenic. Forshufvud had long ago established that the sick man in those last months displayed the great majority of the many recognized symptoms of both chronic and acute arsenic poisoning: the testimony of the memoirs on that point was overwhelming. The next step, which Forshufvud was now performing, was to plot the occurrence in time of those symptoms to see if they coincided with the evidence of the hair that Hamilton Smith was now analyzing.

Napoleon's last illness, as the witnesses described it, had not been a gradual descent into death. Bouts of acute illness alternated with periods when Napoleon felt well enough to get out of bed and take a few steps. Not many steps, for, as he complained to Marchand, "My legs won't hold me"; weakness in the lower legs is a symptom of arsenic poisoning. To put his notes in order, Forshufvud taped several sheets of paper together and traced on them a time-line for the last seven months. On it he listed every symptom Napoleon suffered on the date on which it was reported by Antommarchi, Marchand, or one of the other witnesses. Once he had filled in the time-line—it was several feet long, and to see it as a whole Forshufvud had to lay it on the floor of the study—the picture of Napoleon's last illness fell into perspective. The paper stretched out on the floor looked like a textbook illustration of arsenic poisoning. The symptoms did not appear spread out evenly along the line, but were clustered in groups between periods of partial recovery. The evidence was that, in those seven months, Napoleon suffered six episodes of acute poisoning: from the eighteenth to the twenty-first of September; the tenth to the eighteenth of October; the twenty-fifth of October to the first of November; the twenty-eighth to the thirtieth of December; the twenty-sixth to the twenty-ninth of January; and the twenty-sixth and twenty-seventh of February. In the intervals between those acute attacks he continued to show the symptoms of chronic poisoning. After February the nature of his symptoms seemed to change. He recovered somewhat in mid-April, when he wrote his will; the final illness then started and lasted about two weeks.

The evidence of the witnesses was ready: now Forshufvud needed only the physical evidence from Hamilton Smith in Glasgow. During those weeks of waiting, Forshufvud was well aware that all his work, the time-line into which he had put so much effort, might well prove to have been wasted. Hamilton Smith's analysis might show a constant amount of arsenic in the sections of a single hair: this would be evidence, not of deliberate poisoning, but rather that Napoleon had absorbed arsenic each day from some source in his environment—drinking water, perhaps, or drapes in the sickroom. Or the hair might show *no* abnormal amount of arsenic. This would indicate that one of the two tests, this one or the earlier one that showed high arsenic content, had been a fluke. Either result would wreck the case for a deliberate administration of poison. Forshufvud did not let these possibilities stop him. He knew from his many years in the laboratory that a scientist usually has to go up many blind alleys before he finds the road to the truth. There was something more in Forshufvud's determination: he had come, in the long hours of studying those last months in the sickroom at Longwood, to have quite a different view of Napoleon. The man he had previously known was the all-powerful Bonaparte: the conqueror on the field of battle, the ruler of Europe. That Napoleon needed no one's sympathy; he was, as few men have ever been, the master of his destiny. The man who lay suffering helplessly on his campaign cot at Longwood, betrayed by one of those closest to him, desperately needed help. Napoleon had wanted the cause of his approaching death to be understood, and now, almost a century and a half later, he needed Forshufvud to prove the truth about those last months. Forshufvud would let nothing stop him from carrying out the mission that fate had entrusted to him. He would not fail Napoleon.

Hamilton Smith's report arrived early in December, as usual by mail, and as usual in a handwriting that Forshufvud found almost as hard to read as Napoleon's impatient scrawl. Forshufvud saw at a glance that Smith's work had been worth waiting for. This was a treasure of scientific information far larger, far more conclusive, than the single test Smith had been able to perform on the Louis Marchand hair eighteen months earlier.

In his letter, Hamilton Smith carefully described how he had gone about the tests. Following the instructions of Clifford Frey, the Swiss owner of the hair, Smith had extracted twenty hairs from the lock without undoing the twine knot sealed with wax. He could see that one end of each hair had been shaved, not cut with scissors, just as Louis Marchand had reported in his memoirs. Dead hair becomes brittle over the years, and some of the hairs had broken while being removed from the knot. To these scraps, Hamilton Smith had applied his old test which showed only the total content of arsenic. Two sets of these scraps, tested separately, showed an arsenic content of 3.27 and 3.75 parts per million. This was less than the content in the earlier hair, but it was still between four and five times the normal amount of arsenic in human hair, which is 0.8.

One hair measured thirteen centimeters, long enough to be

analyzed in sections by Smith's new method. This hair, and one measuring nine centimeters, were put in fine silicone tubes and sent by Smith to the Harwell Atomic Energy Research Establishment, where they were irradiated with thermal neutrons for twenty-four hours in a nuclear reactor. This made the arsenic in them radioactive. The hairs were then returned to Smith's laboratory in Glasgow. He fixed them on paper and cut them into five-millimeter pieces which he then could measure separately with a Geiger counter for their arsenic content. Smith had laid out the results for the longer hair on a graph. The graph was a jagged line ranging from a low of 2.8 to a high of 51.2. The arsenic in the shorter hair ranged from 1.06, not much above normal, to a high of 11. All told, Smith had performed 140 tests on this batch of hair.

That jagged line on Hamilton Smith's graph was the physical evidence that Napoleon was not accidently killed by some source of arsenic in his environment. With the graph in his hand, Forshufvud could now be certain that someone had administered periodic large, but not immediately fatal, doses to the victim. It was just what an assassin would have done had he wanted to cover his tracks. He would administer those repeated doses, no one sufficient to kill, in the hopes that the victim's symptoms would be diagnosed as those of some other disease. It was the classic method. And it had worked—for 140 years. *Until now,* Forshufvud thought jubilantly.

Now Forshufvud took out his time-line of taped-together sheets and laid it out on the floor of his study. He took Hamilton Smith's graph and calculated back along the line of growth of the hair from the day it was cut, May 6, the day after Napoleon died. Each five-millimeter section represented about fifteen days' growth: fifteen days of Napoleon's life. Forshufvud compared the peaks and valleys of Smith's graphs with the clusters of symptoms and periods of recovery on his time-line. They matched, and matched perfectly. All along those last months of life, the peaks of arsenic in the hair coincided in time with the clusters

141

of symptoms of acute poisoning reported by the witnesses. Forshufvud got up from the floor and stood for a long time gazing down at the papers spread out before him. So much work had gone into what those papers represented: his own work, Hamilton Smith's, the memoirs of the long-dead witnesses. Forshufvud had proved his case to his own satisfaction. He felt the profound but quiet pleasure of the scientist who had designed an experiment to test a theory when, after months of work in the laboratory, the result of the experiment confirms the theory. In Forshufvud's case it was not months but years—six years since the night he read Louis Marchand's memoirs and first suspected arsenic.

Forshufvud could, and did, take pride in the methodical way he had gone about his self-appointed mission, yet he knew fate had a hand in it too. Fate that two servants, Louis Marchand and Abram Noverraz, had saved the hair that provided the crucial evidence. Fate that Marchand's memoirs were read by a man with the rare combination of interest in Napoleon and knowledge of toxicology. Fate that Hamilton Smith in Glasgow had invented the methods of testing that alone made it possible to extract the evidence of the hair. Fate again that Clifford Frey in Switzerland had picked up a newspaper two months ago and read about Forshufvud's theory—and decided for whatever reason to provide him with the Noverraz hair which had just given such spectacular results. Fate, or luck, played a bigger role in human events than many were willing to admit. Napoleon knew that, he was a fatalist. The general who prepared his campaigns with such exceptional care once said: "I've been in sixty battles and at the beginning of each one I never knew how it was going to turn out." That man would have appreciated the chain of events, some due to Forshufvud, some to fate, that had led to this moment.

And, Forshufvud realized, he would need a lot more help from fate. His mission was far from over. He had proved that Napoleon was poisoned during the last months of his life. But that fact immediately raised other questions. Had the poisoning begun

142

then, or had Napoleon been poisoned earlier during the six years of his exile on St. Helena? And the greatest question of all—the one Forshufvud had been putting off since the beginning of his quest—who was the assassin? Forshufvud knew he would not stop now: he would follow the case to its end. And that meant a lot more work, and, with a hand from fate, a lot more evidence.

But that was all right. Forshufvud was sure, having come this far, that more evidence would turn up somehow, through the attention his theory was getting in the scientific press, or in some other way he could not foresee. And he had a date to meet Dame Mabel Brookes, granddaughter of Betsy Balcombe's younger brother, in London in the spring. That should prove interesting.

CHAPTER EIGHTEEN

SEPTEMBER 1817
PARIS

MONSIEUR WAS worried. The news his agents brought him at the late-night meetings in the Pavillon de Marsan was bad and it was getting worse. Two years had passed, and the shadow of the Usurper was growing longer every day. In the southwest of France, a "vast conspiracy" had just been uncovered. From America came rumors of plots. What was happening at St. Helena?

The Count d'Artois, known as Monsieur, was the younger brother of King Louis XVIII. Since Louis was ailing and childless, Monsieur could expect to be the next King of France—if the Bourbons stayed in power. At sixty, Monsieur's long face, with its prominent nose and distinctive, pendulous lower lip, was crowned with white hair. His manner was misleading. Monsieur was unfailingly courteous in an aristocratic way; he was warm and generous with his inner circle of faithful followers. He was also a fanatic. He was fanatical in his hatred of the Revolution and all its works, and what he hated above all was that most monstrous child of the Revolution: Bonaparte the Usurper.

In 1789, when he was thirty-two, the Revolution had sent

Monsieur into an exile that was to last a quarter of a century. In Holyrood Castle in Edinburgh, where he lived on a subsidy from the English government, he planned one expedition after another to overthrow the Revolution that had ousted him and executed his oldest brother. Monsieur never accompanied the Royalist soldiers who landed in France; all of the expeditions failed. When General Bonaparte became First Consul, Monsieur sent him a message, through Josephine, offering to erect a statue to him in Paris if he would put his second brother on the throne. Napoleon said to Josephine: "Did you answer that this statue would have as its pedestal the corpse of the First Consul?" After that, getting rid of Bonaparte became Monsieur's obsession. From his headquarters in England, Monsieur mounted a series of plots to assassinate Bonaparte, plots of which his brother was not aware. He maintained a network of agents of France, but it was infiltrated by Napoleon's agents and the plots all failed. One that almost succeeded was known as the plot of the "infernal machine." This was a bomb that was supposed to go off when Napoleon's carriage went by on the way to the opera one evening. Napoleon escaped only because the driver, named César, was drunk and drove faster than usual; the carriage had passed when the infernal machine exploded. More recently, Monsieur was believed responsible for an attempt to assassinate Napoleon when he was on Elba.

Now at last Monsieur's long exile was over. The Bourbons were back in France: Louis was in the Tuileries in place of the Usurper, and Monsieur had installed himself in the Pavillon de Marsan, a wing of the Louvre. But the Bourbons' hold on power was shaky. The dynasty that for centuries had ruled France by divine right now held the throne only by right of the foreign armies that had defeated Napoleon at Waterloo. How little support the Bourbons had among the French people had been made all too obvious two years earlier when Napoleon came back from Elba and swept them out without firing a shot.

In the interest of holding on to the throne, King Louis was willing to accept at least some of the huge changes wrought in

France by the Revolution and Napoleon. Not Monsieur. He and his followers, known as the Ultras, wanted to set the clock all the way back and restore the ancien régime in its entirety ("including the abuses," one of them said). Monsieur and the Ultras had set up what amounted to an alternate government of France known as the *petit bureau*. Monsieur and the men called his nocturnal advisers conducted their nightly meetings at the Pavillon de Marsan in a permanent air of conspiracy. The *petit bureau* was the command post of a network of spies, informers, provocateurs, and thugs that covered the nation, infiltrated all parts of the government, and secretly competed with Louis' men for control of France. Monsieur had agents in the police and abroad; in the army, suspect above all institutions of sympathy for the Usurper, he kept three spies in every regiment, one each for the officers, the noncommissioned officers, and the men. At the night meetings it was said the monarchy would not be safe until no officer was left in the army who had served the Usurper. In the cafés, Monsieur's agents tried to provoke the soldiers into showing Bonapartist leanings; they could then be punished. A wave of desertions resulted; one officer then advocated the deterrent of taking the soldiers' pants away from them at night.

Monsieur's agents combed the nation in search of conspiracies to restore the Revolution and the Usurper. In the Bourbons' first months back in power the Verdets, a private army of thugs wearing Monsieur's green livery, staged a reign of terror in the provinces bloodier than the Terror of the Revolution. But still more conspiracies, usually among old soldiers vegetating on half pay, were reported to the man in the Marsan. Behind them all was the shadow of the Usurper. Rumors circulated that *he* had been seen in the countryside. A hen laid an egg bearing *his* effigy; both the hen and her owner were sent to jail, where the hen died.

The year before, Marsan had been shaken by the Didier affair. Jean-Paul Didier was an odd character. He had been dean of the law school at Grenoble, had gone bankrupt in a scheme to reclaim some marshes, and had been active at one time or another

146

on all sides of France's turbulent politics as royalist, revolutionary, and Bonapartist. In 1816, according to an agent's account, Didier began recruiting Napoleon's unemployed veterans in and around Grenoble for a plot to overthrow the Bourbons; it was said he told them they would be joined by the Emperor leading an army of 600,000 blacks. On May 4, about sixty men, led by a sergeant from the army of Egypt beating a drum, set out on the road taken by Napoleon on his return from Elba, picking up some two hundred peasant followers. It was a place of particularly humiliating memory for the Bourbons: here the returning exile had won over their army without firing a shot. Napoleon had stepped toward the troops sent to stop him, alone and unarmed, opened his coat to bare his breast, and said: "If there is one soldier among you who wants to kill his Emperor, here I am!" But without Napoleon the little band organized by Didier was easily defeated; the sergeant from the army of Egypt died crying *"Vive l'Empereur!"*

By the time the plot was reported to Paris, the number of rebels had been inflated to five or seven thousand. Its leaders, including Didier, died on the guillotine. At almost the same time the police uncovered another plot in Paris. Three of its leaders were sentenced to the death prescribed for parricide. Each man was led to the guillotine barefooted with a black veil over his head. The executioner cut off his hand at the wrist. Then he cut off his head. Most recently, in May of that year, the government press announced the uncovering of a "vast conspiracy" aimed at "putting supreme power in the hands of the Usurper or his son." This plot was organized by a police spy named Randon who nonetheless was rounded up and executed with the rest of the conspirators.

If the news from France was alarming, the reports reaching Monsieur from America were just as bad. There was fertile ground for conspiracies among the 25,000 French people living in the new United States. Joseph Bonaparte was living in Bordentown, New Jersey, and was known to have enough money to finance a plot in favor of his brother. With him, and in other parts of America, were quite a number of Napoleon's veterans, including that General Grouchy whose inaction had cost France the Battle of Waterloo. The Bourbons' chargé d'affaires in the United States, Hyde de Neuville, watched what was being done and said in the French colony and reported regularly to Paris. Once it was a report that sixteen or seventeen ships had sailed from Baltimore for an undisclosed destination: could it be St. Helena? Another time American pirate ships were said to be heading toward a rendezvous off Africa and then were going to St. Helena. Joseph and Grouchy were going to Mexico, where Joseph would become king. In May, at the time of the "vast conspiracy" in France, two of Napoleon's servants, expelled from Longwood by Hudson Lowe, arrived in America where, wrote Hyde de Neuville, they would find "in all the ports of the Union brave auxiliaries, arms, and money," and "it would not be in the power of the American government to put obstacles in their way." And more: an old Bonapartist officer named Charles Lallemand planned to seize an island off the coast of Brazil and use it as a base from which to free the captive of St. Helena.

Now, in the fall of 1817, Monsieur was hearing reports of a strange undertaking called the Champ d'Asile. Two of Bonaparte's officers were said to be founding a settlement of some kind in Texas, near Galveston Bay. As settlers they were recruiting only veterans of the French army, and among them were some from what had been the most fearsome force on earth: Bonaparte's Imperial Guard. Theoretically the Champ d'Asile was to be a peaceful agricultural community, a utopian haven for soldiers of the Emperor who had been repudiated by their nation. But they could easily move down into Mexico to help Joseph establish his rule there, or, from New Orleans, where there were many Bonapartists, take ship for St. Helena and free the captive from his rock —and the Usurper would march back into Europe at the head of his invincible Guard!

The reports from America, compounded of fact and rumor,

worried not just Monsieur but also his brother's prime minister, the Duke de Richelieu. The danger of escape was much on Richelieu's mind that year. He warned his colleagues to keep a close watch on "this rock in the middle of the Atlantic. One can say that *he* has lost all credit in France, I want to believe it, but I would not feel comfortable about putting that belief to the test." Richelieu did not trust the English to be vigilant enough: *he* might have escaped while the English thought he was still at Longwood; a new government in London might even set him free. Richelieu wrote his ambassador in London: "For God's sake, do not lose sight of St. Helena. The guard and garrison must be frequently changed, because this devil of a man has an astonishingly seductive effect on any who come near him, witness the crew of the *Northumberland.* . . . If the same troops stay assigned to his guard for a long time, he will find supporters among them."

Yes, the news in the fall of 1817 was more alarming than ever. Even chained to his distant rock, Bonaparte was casting his gigantic shadow over both sides of the Atlantic. One thing was clear to the worried white-haired aristocrat and his nocturnal advisers meeting secretly in the Pavillon de Marsan: as long as the Usurper lived, the rule of the Bourbons was in danger.

CHAPTER NINETEEN

MARCH 1818
LONGWOOD HOUSE, ST. HELENA

BETSY BALCOMBE was walking with Napoleon in the garden at Longwood. It was late afternoon. Napoleon pointed at the gray ocean they could see between the somber peaks bristling with English cannon and with a "sickly smile" said: "Soon you will be sailing away towards England, leaving me to die on this miserable rock. Look at those dreadful mountains—they are my prison walls. You will soon hear that the Emperor Napoleon is dead." Betsy burst into tears. She reached for her handkerchief, but she had left it in the pocket of her saddle. Napoleon took his handkerchief, wiped away her tears, and told her to keep it as a token of their parting. Later, after dinner, the Balcombes prepared to say farewell:

> He asked me what I should like to have in remembrance of him. I replied, I should value a lock of his hair more than any other gift he could present. He then sent for Monsieur Marchand, and desired him to bring in a pair of scissors and cut off four locks of hair for my father and mother, my sister,

and myself, which he did. I still possess that lock of hair; it is all left me of the many tokens of remembrance of the Great Emperor.

The Balcombes were leaving St. Helena ostensibly because Mrs. Balcombe was in poor health, but in fact because the Governor thought they were entirely too friendly with Napoleon. William Balcombe's position as food purveyor to Longwood gave him easy access to the exiles; Hudson Lowe suspected that Balcombe was smuggling out those letters that kept turning up, embarrassingly, in Europe. No incident involving Longwood and the Balcombes was too small or seemingly harmless to arouse the Governor's fury. On New Year's Day, Napoleon sent a servant to the Briars with pastries for Betsy and her sister Jane; a sentry intercepted him, and Hudson Lowe ordered the gift returned to Longwood. In September, Napoleon had sent Barry O'Meara with a Longwood horse named Mameluke for Betsy to ride in a race to be held at the Deadwood military camp. Betsy rode Mameluke to victory in the race. When this news reached the Governor, he summoned Balcombe and O'Meara to his office and rebuked them both savagely. Betsy went to the Governor's office alone to take the blame for the incident. Hudson Lowe listened, then walked away from the girl without a word. After these and other incidents, William Balcombe, sensing himself in some peril from the Governor, found it expedient to take leave in England for his wife's health.

In William Balcombe, Napoleon was losing a valuable link to the outside world, and in the family he was losing his only friends among the English colony on St. Helena. By now Betsy was no longer the adolescent whose pranks he had shared at the Briars. She had grown into a very pretty young woman of seventeen, much courted by the officers of the garrison: her relationship with Napoleon could no longer be that of child and affectionate uncle. Yet they remained friends, and there were moments she would remember with pleasure. The time that Napoleon showed her a machine, operated by an air pump, that produced the first ice ever seen on the island: "He explained the process to us, and he tried to enlighten me as to the principle upon which air-pumps were formed; he advised me, moreover, to get a book upon elementary chemistry, for my amusement and improvement; and finished, as usual, by turning to my father, recommending to him to enforce a lesson a day." The evening they sat on the steps of Longwood with a six-string guitar sent by Napoleon's sister Pauline; Betsy played and Napoleon sang *"Vive Henri Quatre"* in his "most unmusical voice." It was duly reported to the Governor's office that "General Bonaparte sang and whistled this evening to accompaniment of a guitar. A lady sang also."

The departure of the Balcombe family was the latest in a series of blows Napoleon suffered in the first months of 1818. On New Year's Day the exiles had gathered in the billiard room at Longwood. Napoleon was giving out candy to the Bertrand and Montholon children when a servant reported that a ship had arrived from England with important news. O'Meara hurried down to the port; Napoleon was excited. Perhaps a new governor had been appointed, perhaps a new cabinet: "If only it could be the death of the Prince Regent." Told that O'Meara was returning, Napoleon watched him approach through his spyglass: "He's galloping hard! It must be good news. Surely the Governor is being recalled. That certainly concerns O'Meara. That settles it. If it were something else, he would have stayed in town. Self-interest comes first."

But there was no news about either Hudson Lowe or the English government. The news of a death in the royal family did not come until a month later, and it was not that of the Prince Regent. Princess Charlotte, the young woman in whose expected reign Napoleon had placed so much hope, was dead in childbirth.

In February, Gourgaud left Napoleon, the second of his four officers to go. He left after a year of increasing bitterness in the exile household. Gourgaud, young, hot-tempered, and unable to keep his mouth shut, had been quarreling ever more violently with the Montholons; soon he was threatening Montholon with a duel. In the confined environment of Longwood no one could escape their quarrel; it poisoned the air. Napoleon was exasperated. Once he could silence anyone with a word; now he could only lose his temper with Gourgaud. He blamed the young general for his troubles with the Montholons. Where Gourgaud was moody—"a real Corsican," Napoleon said—the curly-haired, handsome Montholon was always even-tempered and attentive to his master's wishes. Napoleon knew Montholon was acting out of self-interest, but he told Gourgaud, "After all, I only like people who are useful to me and as long as they are useful. What do I care what they think! I only pay attention to what they say to me: if they betray me, they will only be doing what many others have done."

When Gourgaud complained that he had no woman, while Montholon and Bertrand had wives, Napoleon said: "Bah! Women! When you don't think about them, you don't need them. Be like me." But Gourgaud did not think his master did without women. He thought Albine de Montholon was Napoleon's mistress, and he let Napoleon know what he thought. In his diary he recorded his evidence for that belief. On one occasion he surprised Albine going to visit Napoleon, who was not dressed, in his bedroom; when Gourgaud told this to her husband, Montholon stammered: "I don't know. I'm not saying no." Another time, when Montholon was sent out while Albine visited Napoleon in his bath, Gourgaud said to him: "That's nice, you're chased out when she comes in." Napoleon's relationship with the attractive, accommodating Albine infuriated the jealous Gourgaud: "Let the Emperor have mistresses if he likes, but I am not going to humiliate myself before them." As for Albine's husband, Gourgaud wrote: "Poor Montholon! What role are you playing?"

The end came at a stormy scene in early February. Napoleon sent for Gourgaud, who found him in the billiard room playing chess with Bertrand. "What after all do you want?" Napoleon asked. Gourgaud said once more that he felt mistreated and wanted to leave. Gourgaud appealed to Bertrand for support: but the engineer stood leaning against the wall and as usual said nothing. The issue as always was the Montholons. Napoleon said he would treat the Montholons as he pleased, and added: "If I were to go to bed with her, what would be wrong with that?" Gourgaud said he had supposed "his majesty's taste was not that depraved." Napoleon then told him to leave. Giving bad health as the reason, Gourgaud left St. Helena the following month, but not before telling the foreign commissioners in Jamestown that Napoleon could escape anytime he wanted to, but preferred captivity to freedom in America.

In late February, Napoleon suffered another and much more serious loss. One evening during dinner Cipriani suddenly fell to the floor writhing in pain. Four days later he was dead of, O'Meara said, "inflammation of the bowels." Cipriani was listed as a servant: there was no autopsy, no questions were asked about his abrupt death. In Cipriani, Napoleon lost his most trusted confidential agent, a loss that on St. Helena could not be replaced. Their ties went back to their early days on Corsica. During Napoleon's first exile on Elba, Cipriani had been his agent on the mainland, the one who warned him the Allies were talking of sending him to St. Helena. On St. Helena, Cipriani gathered intelligence from the shopkeepers in Jamestown when he was buying supplies, and he arranged for letters to be smuggled out. Gourgaud called him Longwood's "minister of foreign affairs" and "minister of police," and once observed that Napoleon "would sacrifice us all for Cipriani." Napoleon never talked about what Cipriani did for him, and neither did the dark, fanatically loyal Corsican. His death was mourned by his close friends, Louis Marchand and O'Meara; the latter wrote of him that "Cipriani was a man possessed of strong, but uncultivated talents. Though artful, he had the appearance of openness and candor. He was regarded by his master in a very confidential light." Napoleon appeared profoundly depressed in the days following Cipriani's death.

Napoleon's own health had taken a turn for the worse the

previous fall. In August an English traveler named Basil Hall had found him in good health and spirits, though his face was pale as marble. (Hall told Napoleon about the inhabitants of an island in the Far East who had no weapons because they had no war. "No war!" Napoleon exclaimed.) But in September he fell ill, and in October he complained to O'Meara of "a dull pain in the right hypochondriac region, immediately under the cartilages of the ribs, which he said he experienced yesterday morning for the first time . . . said he felt something in the right side which never was there before." O'Meara thought this might be a symptom of hepatitis. Two weeks later O'Meara reported that Napoleon "was never free from dull pain, or an uneasy sensation in the right side; his appetite was diminished; his legs still swelled, especially toward night; occasional nausea; great want of sleep." When the Balcombes saw him about this same time, Betsy wrote, "the havoc and change it [his illness] had made in his appearance was sad to look upon. His face was literally the color of yellow wax, and his cheeks had fallen in pouches on either side of his face. His ankles were so swollen that the flesh literally hung over his shoes; he was so weak, that without resting one hand on a table near him, and the other on the shoulder of an attendant, he could not have stood. . . . My mother observed, when we had left, that death was stamped on every feature."

Napoleon thought his slow death was just what the English government wanted. The restrictions imposed on him, he told O'Meara, were designed "in the course of time to bring on disease, which in a frame impaired by confinement and the blood being decomposed, must prove mortal, and that I may thus expire in protracted agonies, which may have the appearance of a natural death. This is the plan, and a manner of assassinating just as certain, but more cruel and criminal than the sword or the pistol."

At other times Napoleon's repeated illnesses had revived his fear of poison. His fear usually centered on the wine. In June Gourgaud found a strange flavor in a bottle of Napoleon's wine; it was one of the rare times that Napoleon shared the wine reserved for his own use. Napoleon said: "That scoundrel Reade [the Governor's assistant] is capable of trying to poison me; he has the key to the wine cellar, he could change the corks." Gourgaud advised him not to be the only one to drink his wine because no one would dare poison them all—it would attract too much attention. Napoleon shook his head: "The fact is I'd be dead." But when Cipriani told him that a shipment of wine had been sent by Hudson Lowe, Napoleon refused to drink it. On an earlier occasion O'Meara was asked to test the Longwood wine for the presence of lead: no result was ever reported.

As for the Governor, his ever-present fear of escape had been raised to fever pitch by the reports of a plot being mounted in Pernambuco in Brazil. In January the French commissioner, the Marquis de Montchenu, had received an account of the plot from the French chargé d'affaires in Rio de Janeiro. The next month the Russian commissioner, Count Balmain, reported: "Bonapartist plots at Pernambuco have greatly excited the governor. He works incessantly on the fortifications, is placing new telegraph posts and batteries in various places, and has doubled the guard at Longwood. I see him always on horseback, surrounded by engineers, and galloping in all directions."

Princess Charlotte and Cipriani dead, Gourgaud and the Balcombes gone: one by one Napoleon's friends and allies were disappearing. And there was the threat of worse to come. Hudson Lowe was always eager to find pretexts to banish from St. Helena anyone who was close to Napoleon. A year earlier a rumor reached Longwood that he was thinking about deporting Montholon. "I should feel the loss of Montholon most sensibly; he is most useful, and endeavors to anticipate all my wants," Napoleon said to O'Meara, and added that the Count had "nothing to fear in France . . . being of a noble family, he might readily find favor with the Bourbons if he chose." The Governor did not move against Montholon, but now, in early 1818, he was maneuvering to get Barry O'Meara recalled to England.

CHAPTER TWENTY

MAY 1962
GROSVENOR HOUSE, LONDON

STEN FORSHUFVUD gazed across the tea table at the woman he had come to London to meet. They were sitting in the lounge of her suite at Grosvenor House in Park Lane, one of London's finer hotels. Dame Mabel Brookes was a handsome woman in her mid-seventies, with strong features and a direct, no-nonsense look in her blue eyes. Very aristocratic in a fin-de-siècle way, Forshufvud thought: she must have been quite beautiful in her youth.

In her native Australia, Dame Mabel was known as the author of several books, as a tireless promoter of civic causes, her latest being a new women's hospital, and as the wife of Sir Norman Brookes, the noted tennis player. She was also the great-granddaughter of William Balcombe, and that was why she had suddenly become important to Forshufvud's quest. Some months earlier in Melbourne, where she lived, she had read an article in the *Medical Journal of Australia* that quoted from the article in which Forshufvud and his colleagues had first made public their evidence that Napoleon was poisoned. It must have been about the same time that Clifford Frey had read a similar article in the

Swiss press and telephoned Forshufvud. Dame Mabel had immediately written Forshufvud, in care of the London scientific journal, *Nature*, where the original article appeared. She told him she owned not one but two locks of Napoleon's hair, both from St. Helena. One was the lock Napoleon gave to Betsy Balcombe during the family's farewell visit to Longwood; it had been handed down to her in the Balcombe family. The other lock was the one Fanny Bertrand gave to Commander John Theed in January 1816; Dame Mabel had acquired it from Theed's descendants. She wrote that she was willing to send samples from each lock to Hamilton Smith in Glasgow for testing.

Forshufvud was overjoyed: his effort to attract people with locks of Napoleon's hair had borne fruit for the second time in a few months; once more he had run the French blockade. Forshufvud knew of Betsy's lock from her memoirs, and had often wished for a strand of it; but until Dame Mabel's letter he had no idea where Betsy's descendants lived or even if the lock still existed. Dame Mabel had also written that she was coming to London in the spring and invited Forshufvud to meet her there. The samples of hair were duly sent and analyzed, and now Forshufvud had come to London to meet her and tell her the results.

Dame Mabel poured tea, and said in a straightforward manner: "Doctor Forshufvud, I am delighted that you are presenting the evidence that the Emperor was poisoned. You know, it is a tradition in our family that Great-Grandfather believed the very same thing. I heard it often as a child. So, as a descendant of William Balcombe, I owe you our thanks for the crime you are exposing. Now please tell me, do the samples of hair I sent your friend Doctor Smith add to the case?"

"Very much so, my dear Dame Mabel, very much so, and it is I who must thank you," Forshufvud said in his most courtly manner. He briefly explained the method of testing hair devised by Hamilton Smith and the results of the first two tests. But both those hairs were shaved from Napoleon's head the day after his death. Now for the first time he had available hair from earlier periods, and both samples showed the evidence of arsenic poisoning. Betsy's hair, two strands analyzed in three one-centimeter sections, showed arsenic content ranging from 6.7 to 26 parts per million, far above the normal content of 0.8. The Theed hair, three strands analyzed in four one-centimeter sections, registered from 3.5 to 76.6 parts, and some scraps tested together showed 37.6. The great difference in arsenic content from one section to another, and therefore from one period in Napoleon's life to another, was once again evidence for deliberate poisoning as opposed to some constant environmental source.

As Forshufvud spoke, Mabel Brookes nodded in quick comprehension. He realized he did not have to repeat anything: he was dealing with a very quick-witted lady. "Now," he went on, "the hairs from Mademoiselle Betsee"—Dame Mabel laughed at his use of Napoleon's way of addressing the girl—"these hairs are clearly most important to the case." He explained that Napoleon's exposure to arsenic could be dated fairly accurately because it was known, from Betsy's memoirs, that the hair was cut on the day of her last visit, March 16, 1818. It was safe to conclude that the hair cut that day by Louis Marchand grew in 1817 or the first months of 1818. "And we know from Barry O'Meara and Marchand that Napoleon was many times sick with the symptoms of arsenical poisoning during the last part of that time," he concluded.

"Yes," Dame Mabel said, "and Great-Aunt also described how ill the Emperor was at that time." Forshufvud had to think a moment before he realized that the person who lived in his mind's eye as a teenaged girl could also be the great-aunt of this lady in her seventies. He nodded, and Dame Mabel asked: "And how about the hair from Commander Theed?"

Forshufvud said the Theed hair was a problematic piece of evidence. It was known that Fanny Bertrand gave him the hair on January 14, 1816, but no one recorded when it was cut or how far grown it was when cut. So it could not be dated with any certainty. If it were cut just before Theed received it, and if it

159

were cut close to the skull, the hair would be evidence of poison during the first days at St. Helena. If not, if it were cut weeks or months earlier, or far from the skull, then it would suggest Napoleon was poisoned while still in France, during the Hundred Days. They talked about the extraordinary travels of these tiny, critical bits of evidence: from that remote island in the South Atlantic to England, then to Australia, and now to a laboratory in Scotland. "I believe Napoleon's hair was quite distinctive," Dame Mabel observed. "Great-Aunt wrote that it was so soft and silky that it could be mistaken for the hair of an infant. The locks I have certainly seem that way to me."

"Your great-aunt was quite correct," Forshufvud said. "Two years ago in Paris—it was before the French Napoleonists tried to push me out of the case—Commandant Lachouque recommended me to Princess Clotilde Mathilde Bonaparte, sister to Prince Napoleon, as a person who might possess some hairs. I should say that she was a very witty and charming lady. She indeed had hairs, but they were sealed in a medallion. The Princess said: 'I don't think they would be of any use to you, because I believe they were taken from Napoleon as a baby.' But now that I have seen his hair myself, I think perhaps the hair the Princess had was from Napoleon the adult. However, since she had no knowledge of when it was cut, it would have no value as evidence."

Dame Mabel asked: "Do the hairs I sent help you in finding out who was the poisoner?"

"Better to say they help tell us who did *not* do it. Now that we have evidence of poison in 1818 and earlier, we can rule out as suspects those who came later to St. Helena. I have in mind particularly Doctor Antommarchi, who did not arrive until 1819. We can also eliminate those who left before the last days." He paused for effect and added: "That means we can no longer consider as suspect William Balcombe."

Dame Mabel, surprised, exclaimed: "You don't mean you would suspect him! Why, William Balcombe was a great friend to the Emperor, and, if I may say so, he was an honorable man who would not consider such a thing."

Forshufvud laughed, pleased at the reaction he had provoked, and said: "No, in reality, I did not suspect your great-grandfather and I shall tell you why. At first one might consider him suspect because he provided the food for Longwood. But not if one thinks about it. Yes, William Balcombe could have poisoned the food that passed through his hands. But consider what would have happened. Balcombe could not know that a piece of food would be eaten by Napoleon alone. He would have to poison the whole household. If all of Longwood died or fell sick at once, there would be a scandal and people would quickly think of poison. Bodies of the dead would be examined and traces of arsenic would be found. The whole world would know that the English had poisoned the Emperor. That would never do! We must always remember that the first rule of this assassination was that it must go undetected, that the Emperor must be seen to have died a natural death. I believe this means we must seek the assassin within the walls of Longwood House. No one outside the household could poison Napoleon without poisoning others as well. So we can free the English of suspicion, not just your great-grandfather but also Sir Hudson Lowe."

"Dreadful man! Great-Grandfather considered him responsible for the Emperor's death."

"Perhaps a dreadful man," Forshufvud said. He felt that the evil nature of the Governor had been much exaggerated by French writers eager to heap blame on the English, but he had no desire to press the point with a member of the Balcombe family. "But in any event not an assassin. He did not have the opportunity."

Mabel Brookes then asked about Cipriani: "Great-Grandfather was always suspicious about Cipriani's sudden death, just weeks before the family left St. Helena. I learned a strange fact when I visited St. Helena. I was told that Cipriani's grave in the Protestant cemetery has completely disappeared, along with the

161

headstone Napoleon ordered for him and also the record of his death. What do you think, Doctor Forshufvud? Was Cipriani poisoned?"

Forshufvud nodded and said he thought it quite likely. He observed that the assassin would not have to take the same precautions with Cipriani that he did with Napoleon. He could kill him with a single large dose of arsenic. The victim would die just as Cipriani in fact had died. The assassin could be confident that the body of a servant would not be examined for traces of arsenic. The motive would be found in Cipriani's special relationship with Napoleon. He was the Emperor's confidential agent, his spy. If Napoleon asked anyone to watch over his household, to watch particularly for a possible assassin, the person he asked was surely Cipriani. If anyone at Longwood had begun to suspect there was a poisoner in the house, that person, also, would probably be Cipriani. For a poisoner, then, Cipriani was the most dangerous resident of Longwood. There was good reason for his murder.

"What about General Gourgaud?" Dame Mabel asked. "His behavior seems to me quite peculiar."

"A difficult person," Forshufvud said, "but that hot-tempered young man who could not keep his mouth closed had anything but the personality of a secret agent." In any event, he pointed out, Gourgaud could be eliminated as a suspect because he left the island the same month as the Balcombes. Forshufvud thought Gourgaud might have been a victim himself. He was ill several times, with symptoms similar to those of Napoleon, and he was known to be suspicious of the wine. In 1816 he asked O'Meara to test the wine for lead, and the following year he and Napoleon discussed the possibility that the wine was poisoned.

"Did the Emperor himself suspect poison?"

"The Emperor was the target of assassins many times in his career. Certainly he must have thought about poison. At St. Helena he spoke several times about poison, but always he accused the English, in my opinion the wrong people. Also, when he accused the English he may have been playing the political game. But if he suspected that there was a poisoner in his own household, to whom would he dare speak of it? Only perhaps to Cipriani. So we shall not know."

Forshufvud went on, in response to her questions, to summarize what was known about arsenic at St. Helena. Both O'Meara and Marchand wrote in their memoirs that the use of poison to get rid of the rats was considered at Longwood, and Marchand specified that the poison was arsenic. So evidently the poison was available. The book on the Marquise de Brinvilliers, known to be at Longwood, was a manual for poisoning someone without being detected; and the techniques were in any event well known in the Europe of that time. "The Marquise played an important part in my own understanding of the events at St. Helena," Forshufvud recalled. "In 1922, when I was nineteen years old, I was sick in a boardinghouse in Stockholm. The landlord offered me a book to read—it was about the Marquise de Brinvilliers. When I read the memoirs of Louis Marchand thirty-three years later, I saw the similarity between events he described and what happened in Paris at the time of the Marquise. So I thought of arsenic. And when I read Gourgaud, I immediately saw the importance of the presence of that book at Longwood. So the confession of the Marquise helped solve another crime!" Forshufvud then explained that the quantity of poison needed was quite small. The entire amount used to poison Napoleon over the six years at St. Helena could have been kept in a small envelope.

Mabel Brookes poured another cup of tea, and the conversation turned to the Balcombe family. Dame Mabel was the family historian, trustee of its oral tradition, handed down from her grandfather, Alexander, who sat on Napoleon's lap as a four-year-old. She had written a book, *Saint Helena Story*, about that time. "Our lives were greatly affected by Napoleon," she said. "Were it not for the Emperor I would no doubt be English rather than Australian." The opposition of Hudson Lowe, based on the family's friendship with Napoleon, prevented William Balcombe from returning from England to his position at St. Helena. In

163

1824 he was appointed Colonial Treasurer of Australia, and the family sailed for Sydney, except Betsy, who was by then married.

"What was the life of Mademoiselle Betsee after St. Helena?" Forshufvud asked.

"I don't think hers was a very happy life. It seems her marriage turned out badly, though we don't know much about it. I found a letter written to Betsy in 1826 by George Heathcote —he was a young ensign at St. Helena—in which he asks: 'Where is this husband who I heard treated you so cruelly?' Later Betsy taught music to support her daughter. You know, her life remained connected with the Bonapartes. Joseph Bonaparte called on her in London in 1830 and gave her a cameo ring which I now have. Years later, when Louis Napoleon became Emperor of France, he gave her an estate in Algeria. He kept a copy of her memoirs in his library. It is now in my library. But Betsy ended her life not in Algeria but in London, in 1873." She paused. "Poor Betsy. I should imagine that she looked back on her life at St. Helena, and especially the months the Emperor was at the Briars, as the happiest times of her life. She was born at the wrong time. The qualities that Napoleon admired in her—her courage, her intelligence, her strong will—were not thought to be ladylike in those days."

"I believe she shares those qualities as well as her beauty with her great-niece," Forshufvud said gallantly.

Dame Mabel smiled, apparently pleased by the comparison. "You know, Doctor Forshufvud, when I visited St. Helena there were times when I felt I was walking hand-in-hand with Betsy. So many of the paths and places were familiar to me from reading her descriptions of them. Longwood, the Briars, the place where three roads meet where old Huff was buried." She told Forshufvud she had bought the Briars and given it to France in memory of her family's association with the Emperor.

Forshufvud reflected that Mabel Brookes had visited the places that he was seeing in his own mind's eye these days. She had followed Betsy's footprints; he was following those of Napoleon—and his assassin. "I too hope to go to St. Helena," he said at last. "But only when my work is complete."

"When will that be?"

"When I can prove who killed Napoleon."

CHAPTER TWENTY-ONE

AUGUST 1819
LONGWOOD HOUSE, ST. HELENA

THE FIFTEENTH was Napoleon's birthday. He was fifty years old. "Just a few years ago, on this date the ambassadors of the kings of Europe were at his feet offering their masters' homage," Montholon observed. "Today they want to break into his home." "They" were the English. Fearful as always of an escape, Hudson Lowe was threatening again to break down Napoleon's door if he did not let himself be seen twice a day, and Napoleon was resisting in the only way he could, by hiding from sight inside Longwood House and letting it be known he would kill the first man through the door.

There was no celebration at Longwood House: this day passed like all the others. Napoleon at fifty was no longer the man he was in les Tuileries, the superhuman figure all Europe held in awe. It was as if his star were falling as quickly and as prematurely as it had risen: he had rocketed to supreme power when he was only thirty, and now at fifty he was old before his time. The iron constitution that had borne his flaming ambition was badly deteriorated. Three years of idleness and recurring illness had left his body fat and flabby and weak. His spirits were low. The aimless days dragged by; Longwood was an ever more depressing place to live. The sprawling building was half empty now, and silent since the Montholon children had gone; their play had dented the monotony of the days. Sometimes Napoleon wandered through the silent rooms, lashing out at the furniture with a billiard cue in bored fury. He told Bertrand and Louis Marchand that he expected to die soon.

Napoleon's hopes had faded. He never spoke of a return to power now, and the bad news from Europe had ended even his hope of living as a free private citizen. In March he had learned that the Allied sovereigns, meeting at Aix-la-Chapelle the previous November, had voted unanimously to keep him in exile, in English custody, for the rest of his life. A year earlier Napoleon had tried to send a message to Tsar Alexander, once his ally, through the Russan commissioner at St. Helena—but at Aix the Russian delegate made the motion to confirm his exile. It was the Russian also who referred to him as "the Revolution concentrated in one man." The logic was inescapable for the sovereigns of the Holy Alliance of reaction who lived in constant fear of the revolutionary contagion that had broken out in France in 1789. Keep that *one man* bottled up on his distant island and the disease of revolution could be contained; let him loose, on any terms, and soon the rabble would be storming the palaces of Europe. For good measure, the sovereigns approved England's treatment of him, rejected his complaints, and reminded the English above all not to let the *one man* out of the bottle.

In the days after he got the news from Aix, Napoleon shut himself up in his two tiny rooms, saw no one but Louis Marchand, and barely spoke to him. Yet he still had one hope: that the English could be persuaded to at least change his place of exile. Earlier a rumor had reached Longwood that he might be moved to Malta: if he could not live in England, that island would be closer to home and better than this one. Napoleon hated St. Helena. He blamed his recurring poor health on the island and its governor. He was so often sick because of the "disease of the climate" diagnosed by Barry O'Meara. And he was sick from the idleness and lack of exercise imposed on him by the petty tyranny of Hudson Lowe. In fact, the Governor, along with his pettifogging series of regulations, had sent out feelers offering to compromise their differences, for, as much as he detested his prisoner, he could not afford to be blamed for his death. If Napoleon would only let himself be seen twice daily, so the English would know he was in fact there and not escaping, then he could have a considerable degree of freedom.

But Napoleon could not accept the political price, as he saw it, of coming to terms with the Governor, for it would mean admitting his status as a prisoner. And that would mean abandoning his claim to be the Emperor, chosen by the will of the people of France, the *one man* who had healed the wounds of the Revolution and brought the nation its greatest glory and prosperity, its great modern institutions, and who had then voluntarily abdicated, in favor of his son, the throne he had earned. If he gave up that claim, what his enemies said about him would be true: that he was just General Bonaparte, the Corsican adventurer, the Usurper who had stolen the throne that belonged to the Bourbons. No, his career might well be over, but still ahead lay the judgment of history. Napoleon would give his life, a martyr here on St. Helena, to defend the legitimacy of what he had done, of what he had been, before that judgment. And there was more: if he came to terms with Hudson Lowe, he would no longer be able to complain about his treatment and would lose his chance of convincing the English to move him away from this hateful island. So the guerrilla war between Longwood House and Plantation House had to continue.

And so, on April 2, Napoleon had received his first visitor in almost two years, Charles Milner Ricketts, an English official on his way home from Calcutta. Napoleon wanted to see him because Ricketts was cousin to the Prime Minister, Lord Liverpool. Napoleon did not receive him in the imperial style, standing and in full uniform; now he was portraying not the Emperor but a sick man. Ricketts was accompanied by Bertrand, and "I was ushered into a very small room where Napoleon was lying on a camp bed with only his shirt on, with a colored handkerchief round his head, and with his beard of three or four days' growth. The room admitted so little light that at first I could not discern his features, though subsequent introduction of candles gave me a tolerable view of them. . . . I had very few remarks to make, and not many questions put to me, but he frequently said to me, *'Comprenez-vous?'* . . . He seemed to be a little deaf." In the interview, which lasted four hours, Napoleon argued his usual case that he was slowly being killed by St. Helena and Hudson Lowe. But Ricketts, despite the scene staged for him, did not have the impression Napoleon was seriously ill, and he so reported in London. The Colonial Secretary wrote to Hudson Lowe: "Nothing could have been more fortunate than Mr. Ricketts' visit to St. Helena." It was one more defeat for Napoleon.

In fact, Ricketts' observation was largely accurate. Napoleon was in relatively good health. He suffered those occasional days of unexplained illness that had afflicted him ever since he arrived at Longwood, he called for hot towels for his feet, which were always cold, and he sometimes told Louis Marchand he had a pain in his side that felt like being stabbed with a razor. Despite these symptoms, Napoleon was far better now—after a year without a physician at Longwood—than he had been eighteen months ago, when Mrs. Balcombe thought he was dying. But of course this fact had to be hidden, and Napoleon ordered his two remaining officers, Bertrand and Montholon, to take every opportunity to tell the world how sick a man he was.

Napoleon's entourage was diminishing along with his hopes of getting away from St. Helena. Albine had left a month ago, taking with her the three Montholon children, and leaving behind questions that would never be answered: she was, or was not, Napoleon's mistress; her daughter Napoléone, born on the island, was, or was not, the Emperor's child; Basil Jackson, the young English officer who had visited her so often at Longwood and later met her in Brussels, was her lover or a spy for Hudson Lowe, or both, or neither.

The belief that Albine was sharing Napoleon's bed was widespread enough at St. Helena to find its way into the foreign commissioners' reports to their governments. Baron Sturmer, the Austrian, reported that "Madame de Montholon was able to triumph over her rivals and climb into the imperial bed." Captain George Nicholls, the English officer resident at Longwood House, reported regularly on Albine's visits to Napoleon's room, and on one occasion noted that Napoleon had sent the valet Saint-Denis to get her at two o'clock in the morning. Fanny Bertrand, who disliked Albine, told the English doctor James Roche Verling that the little Napoléone did not resemble Montholon at all and hinted that the girl was her namesake's daughter. Fanny attributed Montholon's favored position in the exile court, at her own husband's expense, to his acceptance of what happened between his master and his wife.

Whether or not Albine was Napoleon's mistress, it was certain that her departure and that of her children made the slow days still more empty. Albine de Montholon was always cheerful and accommodating—in contrast to the stiff-necked, melancholy Fanny Bertrand—and if in her mid-thirties her dark-haired beauty was somewhat faded, she provided a feminine grace that was now sorely lacking in Longwood House. She was also a hard bargainer. Before she left, giving poor health as the reason, Albine extracted a large financial settlement from Napoleon; he also gave her the carved ivory chessmen whose imperial crests had cost Hudson Lowe so many hours of worry.

Napoleon watched her leave through a shutter, and, turning away, almost tripped on a rat. Later he said to Bertrand that Albine was an "intriguer" who "only gave her heart for good bills of exchange." When he had realized Albine was determined to leave, Napoleon told her husband he could go with her, but Montholon refused: the courtier-aristocrat would stay on alone. And Bertrand, the quiet, loyal engineer who had been with Napoleon for so many years, since the early days in Egypt—even

Bertrand was talking in his morose way about leaving. The servants were getting out too: in the past year half a dozen, including Lepage, the cook, had gone home on one pretext or another, and most of the rest would leave if they could.

Except Louis Marchand: his chief valet, always attentive, never complaining, served him with equal devotion on the good days and on the bad ones. The handsome, vigorous young man did not complain even when his master would not let him marry a local woman who had borne a child that was either Marchand's or the Emperor's—though Napoleon allowed other servants to marry. Marchand and Montholon, Montholon and Marchand, one a valet, the other an aristocrat: Napoleon was coming to rely more and more on these two faithful followers. He spent his days alone or with one of the two. In the mornings he might walk in the gardens with Montholon; in the afternoons he dictated to Marchand; in the evening, or in the middle of the many sleepless nights, one of them would be summoned to read aloud to him. There were no more imperial dinners in the half-deserted establishment; Napoleon took his meals alone or with Montholon. Bertrand came to Longwood House every day, but, because he lived outside the grounds and had his beautiful, bitter wife to worry about, he was not on hand when Napoleon wanted him; and the distance between Napoleon and his oldest follower grew.

When Napoleon fell ill, it was Louis Marchand who took care of him. By now, in August of 1819, he had been without a doctor since July of the previous year, when Hudson Lowe had at last succeeded in obtaining the recall to London of Barry O'Meara. The Governor suspected that O'Meara was more loyal to Napoleon than to himself, and his medical opinion that the prisoner was suffering from hepatitis was intolerable because it reflected on health conditions at St. Helena and therefore on the English government. He had heard Montholon contradict O'Meara's description of Napoleon's health; and he said someone, whom he did not name, had told him the doctor was poisoning Napoleon with mercury.

Napoleon was sorry to see the young Irish-born doctor go.

With Cipriani dead and Balcombe gone, O'Meara was one of his few remaining sources of information about the world outside the narrow circle of Longwood, and his conversation helped while away the long days. When they parted, Napoleon shook the doctor's hand—an extremely rare gesture from the Emperor—and said: *"Adieu,* O'Meara. We shall never see each other again. May you be happy." Once in London, O'Meara struck back at Hudson Lowe. The Governor, he said, "made to me observations upon the benefit which would result to Europe from the death of Napoleon Bonaparte, of which event he spoke in a manner which, considering his situation and mine, was peculiarly distressing to me." This statement, which was read as hinting that Hudson Lowe wanted him to poison Napoleon, resulted in O'Meara's dismissal from the navy on the grounds that he was "an improper person to continue in His Majesty's service." His hinted accusation was never investigated. After O'Meara had left Longwood, Marchand found a supply of ointments and medicines that he had prepared for his patient's use. Napoleon told Marchand that he would use the ointments, "but as for anything that is supposed to go in my stomach, you can throw it in the fire."

Efforts to get a doctor to replace O'Meara foundered on the mutual suspicions of Napoleon and Hudson Lowe. The exile's health was too important an issue, too politically sensitive, to be left to medical judgment; Napoleon and the governor each wanted a doctor loyal to himself alone. Hudson Lowe proposed two English doctors who were rejected by Napoleon because they were proposed by Hudson Lowe. Another English doctor, John Stokoe, a naval surgeon on the ship *Conqueror,* was caught in the crossfire between the two antagonists. He had met Napoleon once while visiting O'Meara at Longwood. When, in January, Napoleon collapsed while dictating to Montholon, Bertrand sent an urgent message to Stokoe asking him to come. The Doctor came, with the Governor's permission, then and on two more occasions, and Montholon transmitted to him an offer to come to Longwood as Napoleon's resident physician.

But now Hudson Lowe turned against Stokoe. Like O'Meara, he thought Napoleon was suffering from hepatitis; that would never do. And worse: the Governor's censors had intercepted a letter from O'Meara's business agent in London addressed to Stokoe but containing a letter for Bertrand. Stokoe, like William Balcombe before him, sensed that a cold wind was blowing from Hudson Lowe's headquarters; he asked for leave for his health and boarded a ship for England. But the same ship carried a recommendation that he be court-martialed, and now, in mid-August, Stokoe was on his way back to St. Helena and due to stand trial at the end of the month. The main charge was that he had "stated facts relative to the health of General Buonaparte which did not fall under his observation"—he had stated that Napoleon had been suffering from hepatitis for sixteen months—and a secondary accusation was that in his reports he referred to the patient as "the patient" instead of "General Buonaparte."

Being Napoleon's doctor was a dangerous undertaking for an Englishman subject to military discipline and Hudson Lowe. But Napoleon, skeptical as he was about the profession, did want a doctor on hand for those occasions when he was seized with sudden pain or weakness—and so, for his own reasons, did Hudson Lowe. A physician was on the way. More than a year earlier, Bertrand had written—with the permission of the English—to the Bonapartes clustered in Rome asking them to send out a majordomo to replace the dead Cipriani, a cook, and a Catholic priest, of which there were none on St. Helena. Napoleon, an agnostic, had no desire for the priest's professional services, but he enjoyed discussing theology, some of his servants were believers, and, as he had said to Las Cases one Sunday, if they had a Mass to attend it would at least help pass the time. Later Bertrand added a doctor to the list of people wanted at Longwood, and, in August, Montholon wrote Hudson Lowe stressing the urgency of getting a physician for Longwood. The group from Rome, identities unknown, were said now to be journeying toward St. Helena.

CHAPTER TWENTY-TWO
APRIL 1963
GÖTEBORG

         THE CASE was shaping up nicely, Forshufvud reflected. He was sitting in his third-floor study reading the latest report from Hamilton Smith in Glasgow. As always, Smith's style was utterly sober and scientific, betraying no hint of the dramatic events to which its content bore witness. Forshufvud wondered in passing what it would take to make his Scots colleague write an exclamation mark—the end of the world, perhaps.

  Hamilton Smith was reporting on his analysis of a new sample of Napoleon's hair. This sample had been sent directly to the Glasgow scientist by one Colonel Duncan Macauley. Colonel Macauley, who lived in Arundel, Sussex, was a descendant of Admiral Pulteney Malcolm. Like Clifford Frey and Dame Mabel Brookes, he had read about Forshufvud's theory and Hamilton Smith's finding of arsenic in Napoleon's hair. He had written to Smith volunteering a sample from a lock of hair handed down in his family from Admiral Malcolm, to whom it was given by Napoleon when the Admiral and Lady Malcolm paid a farewell call at Longwood House on July 3, 1817.

  The section-by-section analysis of the Malcolm hair showed

arsenic content ranging from 1.75 to 4.94 parts per million, from about twice to six times normal. The reading was lower than those for previous hairs. Most important to Forshufvud was the telltale jagged pattern of the reading—high in one section of the hair, low in another. This was the most convincing evidence of deliberate poisoning.

Forshufvud realized with regret that the episodes of poisoning to which the Malcolm hair bore witness could be dated only with probability, not with certainty, because none of those present that day at Longwood House had recorded when the hair was cut, nor how far from Napoleon's skull. If Napoleon had someone cut the lock on the spot for the Admiral—as he had told Louis Marchand to cut a lock for Betsy Balcombe—and if the lock was cut fairly close to the skull, then the hair was evidence of poisoning late in 1816 and in early 1817. But perhaps Marchand saved, for just this use, clippings from the last haircut he had given his master. How often did Napoleon have his hair cut? Not very often, judging from the longish-haired Napoleon portrayed in paintings from that period. Suppose the hair was cut, say, four months before it was given to Malcolm: that would point to poisoning in early 1816 or even late 1815. But either way the hair filled an important gap in Forshufvud's knowledge. Setting aside the problematical Theed hair of January 1816, the Malcolm hair was the earliest that could with certainty be dated from St. Helena. For the first time Forshufvud had sure evidence of poisoning during the first two years of the exile.

Forshufvud now reviewed his voluminous notes on Napoleon's health during the times to which the Malcolm hair might testify, notes taken from Dr. O'Meara's memoirs, with their almost daily record of his patient's condition, and from the memoirs of Louis Marchand and others then at Longwood House. The eyewitnesses' testimony was that during the year 1816, and early in 1817, Napoleon suffered a number of brief periods of illness in which he showed several of the symptoms of chronic arsenic poisoning. The attacks were moderate, not severe, and that was consistent with the relatively low—though still far above normal—arsenic content of the Malcolm hair. Because of the uncertainty in dating, Forshufvud knew he could not match any one peak of arsenic revealed by the Malcolm hair with any one of Napoleon's illnesses; but he could say that during the time that the Malcolm hair testified to arsenic, so did the record of Napoleon's health.

After he had absorbed and evaluated his new evidence, Forshufvud began to think about his next move. The case had advanced further in the past eighteen months than he could have dared to hope. When he and his colleagues first made the theory public, their case hung only on the single strand of hair from Louis Marchand's *reliquaire* that Forshufvud had obtained in Paris back in May of 1960. By now their original article had brought forth a total of four more hair samples, all analyzed, all consistent with the medical evidence and with the poison thesis. Each new hair was like a new cable strengthening the case; each supplied ammunition with which Forshufvud could return the fire of those critics, the inner circle of French Napoleonists, who had been deriding the poison theory.

But only a handful of people knew about the new evidence. Perhaps he should tell the world about it, as he had done before, and wait to see what would come back to him: more evidence or, who knows, help of some other kind that could not now be foreseen. Going to the public had worked before, it could work again, and, at the very least, he would have the satisfaction of answering his French critics. Yes, Forshufvud concluded, that was what he should do, he should take the offensive, just as Napoleon would have done. He settled down to write to Hamilton Smith in Glasgow.

CHAPTER TWENTY-THREE

FEBRUARY 1820
PARIS

MONSIEUR WAS shattered by the news that was brought to him that night at his office in the Pavillon de Marsan. His son, the Duke de Berry, had been stabbed in the side only minutes ago, while about to enter the Opera, and now lay dying.

The Duke de Berry, a forty-two-year old playboy who played at being a soldier, was more than the younger son of the Count d'Artois. He was the single hope of the Bourbon dynasty, for, without him, the family could provide no heir to the throne after Monsieur and his two sons. Old Louis XVIII would never have children; nor, in all probability, would d'Artois, now in his sixties, have another son; nor would the only other male Bourbon, Monsieur's other son, the Duke d'Angoulême. Only de Berry seemed capable of producing an heir. Monsieur would succeed to the throne upon the death of his brother Louis, then d'Angoulême, but after him, with the Duke de Berry gone—no one. The Bourbon line would be extinct.

The assassin was caught four blocks from the Opera and quickly confessed. He was a thirty-seven-year-old saddler in the royal stables named Louis-Pierre Louvel. It was rumored that he had received the Legion of Honor from Bonaparte during the Hundred Days. He had been planning the assassination for four years, he said, but until that night his courage had always failed him. Before he was guillotined, Louvel said: "I cannot avoid believing that if the Battle of Waterloo was so fatal to France, it was because there were Frenchmen at Ghent [headquarters of the Bourbons during the second exile] and Brussels who had sown treason in our army and aided the foreigner."

The Pavillon de Marsan was dark with sorrow for the lost son and with fear that the dynasty would be lost with him. Bonaparte again—always Bonaparte! Would Monsieur and his family, rulers of France by the will of God, would the Bourbons never be free of the shadow of the Usurper?

CHAPTER TWENTY-FOUR

MARCH 1820
LONGWOOD HOUSE, ST. HELENA

FIVE O'CLOCK in the morning. Napoleon is up and wearing a dressing gown, red morocco slippers, and a broad-brimmed planter's hat. He waits impatiently for sunrise, when the English sentries will be withdrawn from their nighttime positions immediately surrounding the building. Then it will be time to get to work on the gardening project. As soon as the sentries are gone, he waddles outside carrying a big bell. When the first ray of the sun appears between the mountains, he vigorously swings his bell, shattering the silence of Longwood House. He picks up a pebble, throws it at a garret window and roars:

"Ali, Ali, you're sleeping!"

The valet Saint-Denis, known as Ali, opens his window. When his servant's face appears, Napoleon bellows: "Come on, you loafer, can't you see the sun?"

It is Louis Marchand's turn next. Napoleon hurls a pebble at his window also and calls out: "Marchand, *Mam'zelle* Marchand, it's day, get up!" When Marchand joins him in the garden, Napoleon says: "All right, take that spade and make me a hole to plant this tree." While Marchand is digging, Napoleon lumbers around inspecting the work, finds a recently planted tree, and comes back: "Marchand, bring some water, water this tree." A moment later: "Go get me my measure." And: "Go tell Archambault to bring some fertilizer, and tell the Chinese to cut some sod, we don't have any left."

To Saint-Denis, shoveling earth into a wheelbarrow, Napoleon says: "What, you haven't finished with that earth?"

"No, sire, but I haven't been playing."

"For that matter, you rascal, have you finished the chapter I gave you yesterday?" Because he had the best handwriting at Longwood, Saint-Denis always made the final copy of Napoleon's manuscripts. He says: "But, sire, your Majesty didn't give it to me until last night."

"Try to finish it today, I have another one for you."

To Pierron, the chef, who is laying sod, he says: "You still haven't finished that wall? Do you have enough sod?"

And again to Saint-Denis: "What time was it when I woke you last night?"

"Sire, it was two o'clock."

"Ah!"

Napoleon sends for Montholon, and when the Count appears, he asks: "Do you have news for me? They say there is a ship in sight."

"I don't know, sire. I haven't seen anyone."

"Take my spyglass: go see if you can see it."

Now Napoleon sends for his doctor, Francesco Antommarchi, and says to him: "Well, Doctor, are you satisfied with your patient? Is he obedient enough?" He holds up his spade and laughs. "This is worth more than your pills, *dottoracio*. You won't drug me anymore." He digs with the spade for a while, then says: "This work is too hard, I can't go on with it." He puts down the spade: "But I've always done what I wanted with my body. I'll train it to do this work too."

For the first time in five years, Napoleon was doing what he did best. He was deploying his forces, keeping them moving, joking with the troops, setting the example by being first on the job. True, it was not the continent of Europe, it was only a couple of infertile acres at the edge of the world; and his forces were a handful of servants and four Chinese laborers, not the 600,000 men of the Grand Army or the prefects of France that he regularly summoned to les Tuileries to be interrogated on the projects he had assigned them. No matter. Napoleon was in his element. He was back at work. He was more cheerful, more alive, than he had been since he moved to Longwood more than four years ago.

Doctor Antommarchi had succeeded where his predecessor, Barry O'Meara, had failed. Since his arrival last September, he had been urging Napoleon to get out of the house and exercise. Napoleon as usual refused to subject himself to the indignity of the English sentries: "Among the redcoats? Never!" One day in November, without any explanation, he had changed his mind. When Antommarchi suggested he take a hand in the gardening project now underway, Napoleon said: "Dig the earth! Yes, doctor, you're right. I'll dig the earth." The next day he took personal command of the gardening work, which was followed by the construction of ponds using piped water recently installed by the English. One day that month he and Montholon strolled out in the garden stark naked and took a dip in a pond. He resumed his horseback rides, and he visited the site of the new house the English were building for him. He did make a gesture toward defying the English requirement that he let himself be seen twice a day. When he was going out to garden, he had two of his servants dress in similar fashion—the huge hat, slippers, and dressing gown—to confuse the officer in charge of making certain he was there.

Antommarchi had come to St. Helena as a member of the "little caravan"—the others were two priests and two servants—sent from Rome by Cardinal Fesch, Napoleon's uncle, in response

181

to a letter from Bertrand. Rome was the headquarters of the Bonapartes who had fled from France after Waterloo. Madame Mère shared a palace in the Strada Giulia with her brother, the Cardinal, and his huge collection of Flemish and Italian paintings. Napoleon's extravagant, oversexed sister Pauline also lived in Rome; she was married to a Prince Borghese but spent her time with a succession of lovers. Louis and Lucien were in Rome off and on, and Madame Mère corresponded regularly with the rest of her exiled son's brothers and sisters.

The choices Cardinal Fesch had made for St. Helena were strange ones. Napoleon's doctor at Elba and during the Hundred Days, Foreau de Beauregard, had been eager to join the exile, but Fesch rejected him because, he said, the Doctor wanted too much money—the Cardinal was famously stingy except when buying paintings—and intended to take his wife with him. Instead, Fesch chose Antommarchi, a thirty-year-old Corsican, working at a hospital in Florence, who had more training and experience in pathology than in practicing medicine and who had no previous connection with the Bonapartes. The selection of priests was especially strange. Fesch knew his nephew had little love for the Church, of which he himself was a high official. Napoleon often spoke contemptuously of priests and especially monks and, when Emperor, he had combatted Rome, had imprisoned the Pope, and had only allowed the Church to operate in France under a Concordat that severely limited its power in civil life. Bertrand's letter had asked for a "well-informed priest under the age of forty" who was not "anti-Gallican." Fesch's choice was none of these things. Instead of seeking out an urbane priest, one who accepted the special position of the church in France and who could sustain an intellectual conversation with Napoleon, the Cardinal had unearthed one Antonio Buonavita, sixty-seven and ailing, who had spent most of his career in Mexico and whose conversation, far from urbane, was barely intelligible thanks to a recent stroke. He sent a second priest, a semiliterate young Corsican named Angelo Vignali, on the grounds that Church rules required missionary priests to go in pairs so one could hear the other's confession. Nor were the two servants well suited to their assignment. The majordomo, Jacques Coursot, was willing enough but did not even know how to make coffee, and the cook, Jacques Chandellier, was competent but in poor health.

But then: the Cardinal and Madame Mère knew there was no purpose to the journey of the little caravan and so the qualifications of its members were irrelevant. They knew that Napoleon was *not at St. Helena*. They had known this fact for some time now. Napoleon's mother and her brother had fallen under the spell of a German clairvoyant who had it from the Virgin that, as Pauline wrote to a friend, "His Majesty has been taken away by angels and transported to another country where his health is very good." When the five men he had chosen finally left, Fesch wrote to Las Cases, now living near Frankfurt: "The little caravan left Rome at a time when we ourselves believe they will not arrive at St. Helena because there is someone who assures us that, three or four days before January 19th, the Emperor received permission to leave St. Helena and in fact the English are taking him elsewhere. What can I say to you? Everything in his life is miraculous and I am very inclined to believe in this miracle." Later he wrote Las Cases that "there is no doubt that the jailer of St. Helena makes Count Bertrand write you as if Napoleon were still in his chains." Pauline mocked her mother's and her uncle's credulity, but finally had to give up to keep peace in the family.

If Napoleon was not at St. Helena at all, but with the angels in that land where his health was very good, there clearly was no hurry in sending him the people he had requested. It took Fesch the better part of a year to make his five choices. They left Rome on February 19 and took two months to travel overland to the Channel and then to London. In London, the Colonial Office delayed them another three months on the pretext that the officials did not know when the next ship was sailing for St. Helena; the English said Napoleon was in excellent health and hinted that the five could abandon their mission in good conscience.

Antommarchi took advantage of his time in London to consult two colleagues who had treated his future patient, Barry O'Meara and John Stokoe—the latter in the city between his arrival from St. Helena and his return there to stand trial—and English specialists in tropical medicine. He also sought to arrange an English edition of the text of Paolo Mascagni, the famous anatomist, which he had completed after the author's death.

On their long journey to St. Helena the members of the little caravan had witnessed an extraordinary scene that testified to the worldwide fame of the fallen Emperor they were going to serve. It happened when their ship, the *Snipe,* made a last stop on the West African coast before heading out into the South Atlantic toward its destination. Antommarchi was on the deck watching as African men paddled dugout canoes toward the *Snipe* carrying provisions for sale. The canoes were light and fast; the men paddling them were strong and vigorous. The five travelers were happy to see the canoes and their provisions because the Captain was keeping the best of his food supply for sale in St. Helena. Antommarchi heard this conversation between a dugout and the deck:

"Where are you going?" one of the Africans asked.
"To St. Helena."
"To St. Helena! Is it true that he is there?"
"Who? the Captain asked."
The African looked at the Captain disdainfully, turned to us, and repeated the question; we answered that he was indeed there. He stared at us, shook his head, and finally said: "Impossible." We glanced at each other; we did not know who could be this savage who spoke English and French and had such a high opinion of Napoleon.
"Do you know him?"
"Since long ago."
"You saw him?"
"In all his glory."

"Often?"

"In the Well Guarded City [Cairo], in the desert, on the field of battle."

"Did you serve under him?"

"In the Twenty-first. I was at Bir-am-bar, at Samanhout, at Cossier, at Cophtos, everywhere that valiant demibrigade went."

"Do you remember General Desaix?"

"None of those who were on the campaign of Upper Egypt will ever forget him. He was brave, energetic, generous; I served him for a long time."

"As a soldier?"

"Not at first. I was a slave, I belonged to one of the sons of the King of Darfur. I was taken to Egypt, mistreated, sold. I came into the hands of an aide-de-camp of the Just One [Desaix]. They dressed me in the European manner and gave me some household tasks, which I did well; the Sultan was satisfied with my zeal and kept me by him. As soldier, as grenadier, I would shed all my blood for Napoleon. One word repaid us for all our effort. Our wishes were satisfied, we feared nothing once we saw him."

"Did you fight under him?"

"I was wounded at Cophtos, I was evacuated to Lower Egypt, I was in Cairo when Mustafa appeared. The army moved out, I followed, I was at Abukir. What precision, what vision, what charges! It is impossible that Napoleon could be vanquished, that he could be at St. Helena."

Now, at St. Helena, Antommarchi found himself unhappy with his life at Longwood House, and Napoleon, though he took his advice to exercise, was often angry with his new doctor. The young Corsican was by temperament poorly suited to the strange little world of the exiles. After four years, life at Longwood had settled into a dreary pattern of monotony and isolation; those who could not adapt to that life had left. The officers and servants seldom left the grounds, seldom spoke to anyone but each other. Their daily routine was dominated by the brooding presence of their master. They had to be on call at all hours of day and night, though in his periods of isolation Napoleon might go for weeks without speaking a word to them. Such a life was not for Antommarchi. At thirty, he was a handsome man with wavy black hair and fine features and, if he had come to devote himself to "the man of the century," he also wanted a life of his own. He was likely, after making himself available to the patient in the morning, to saddle a horse and ride down to Jamestown in search of whatever diversion the tiny port had to offer. All too often, he was absent when Napoleon sent for him. Antommarchi was also by nature resentful of authority and impatient with the strict protocol that governed everyone around the Emperor. It was noticed with disapproval that Antommarchi went so far as to address his patient as "you" rather than "His Majesty." Louis Marchand tried to advise the doctor on proper behavior: "Be more serious in the presence of the Emperor when you answer questions put to you, and when you speak of the Count de Montholon and the Grand Marshal, be careful not to refer to them as Bertrand and Montholon; the Emperor can speak of them that way, but you cannot permit yourself that."

Between outbursts of temper, Napoleon spent a good deal of time talking with Antommarchi, as he had with O'Meara, and the doctor, like his predecessor—whose room he occupied—kept a journal in which he recorded Napoleon's conversation as well as his own observations on his patient's condition. Napoleon interrogated him on his medical background and asked Antommarchi to show him the anatomical plates for the text he had edited. After studying the plates, Napoleon exclaimed: "Two hours of anatomy for a man who could never stand the sight of a cadaver!" On one of the doctor's first visits, he saw Antommarchi looking at his clock and said: "That was Frederick the Great's alarm clock. I took it in Potsdam; that's all Prussia was worth." He reminisced about the island on which he and Antommarchi were both born, and said he had considered going there instead of to Elba at the time of his first exile. He described his plans for Corsica had he gone to rule it: "The salt marshes near Ajaccio could be used for growing coffee and sugarcane; it has been tested; I intended to develop that. I wanted to encourage industry, commerce, agriculture, the sciences, and the arts . . . bring in foreign families, increase the population; in a word, make the island self-sufficient, independent of continental markets. I had a plan for fortifications which I had thought over for a long time; it would have been impregnable." And he told Antommarchi about his chronic constipation and his "heroic remedy, *soupe à la reine*, made up of milk, egg yolk, and sugar . . . it is the only medicine I use."

If he was sometimes dissatisfied with Antommarchi, Napoleon was disgusted with the two priests sent out by his uncle the Cardinal. He had hoped for someone with whom he could talk theology, but instead, he said, Cardinal Fesch had sent him "missionaries, propagandists, as if I were a penitent." He thought the older priest, Buonavita, had come to St. Helena only to be buried, and could not stand to listen to his impeded speech; Napoleon told him to go home, and he did. Young Vignali once gave it as his opinion that Alexander was the greatest man of ancient Rome. That was too much for Napoleon: the unfortunate priest was ordered to read two hundred pages a day of Rollins's ancient history and to take notes on it. Napoleon allowed the priests to convert the dining room into a chapel on Sundays, but specified that Mass could be held only on those occasions recognized in the Concordat he had negotiated with the Pope. He blamed Cardinal Fesch for the poor quality of the priests, and recounted to Antommarchi his childhood memory of a family gathering around a relative's deathbed. Fesch was "seized with holy zeal" and began reciting prayers until the dying man had to plead: "Leave me alone! I have only a few minutes to live, I want to spend them with my family."

When he was gardening, Napoleon would call a halt to work

at around eleven, when the heat of the day came on, and would sit down to a hearty lunch with his standard half bottle of his own wine. After a nap, he was likely to dictate to either Montholon or Marchand. He had finished his great work, the account and justification of his career, most of it with Las Cases in the first fifteen months of exile. Now he would dictate his thoughts on whatever topic was currently on his restless, far-ranging mind. Often it was a criticism of what he had been reading. The military expert had this to say about Virgil's *Aeneid:* "The second book of the *Aeneid* is considered the masterpiece of this epic poem; it deserves that reputation for its style, but is far from deserving it for its substance. The wooden horse may have been a popular tradition, but this tradition is ridiculous and utterly unworthy of an epic poem; we see nothing similar in the *Iliad* where everything conforms to the truth and to the practices of war." He went on to list in detail the improbabilities in the work, concluding: "That is not the way an epic should proceed, and that is not how Homer proceeds in the *Iliad.*" On another occasion he described Voltaire's play *Mohammed* as a flawed masterpiece and asked: "Would it be so hard to remove those flaws that do not affect the essence of the work?" Napoleon answered his own question by dictating to Marchand a lengthy, scene-by-scene proposal for revising the play. Among many other changes he proposed to remove the two episodes in which Mohammed poisons his foes as unworthy of the protagonist, whom he considered a great man. If revised as he suggested, Napoleon concluded, the work "could be read without indignation by enlightened men in Constantinople as well as in Paris."

Napoleon's guerrilla war with the English Governor continued in a diminished fashion, as if the exile had lost interest in the conflict. On days when he did not go out to work in the garden or ride horseback, he played hide-and-seek with the officer responsible for seeing him the required twice a day. The priest Vignali was short and heavy-set like Napoleon, so he was dressed in the Emperor's clothes and the famous cocked hat and told to sit with his back to the window; when the officer looked in the window, Vignali turned around abruptly to show him he had the wrong man.

Occasionally Napoleon repeated his often-expressed fear of English poison. Hudson Lowe held a meeting to discuss that fear with the foreign commissioners, at which Montchenu, the French commissioner, quoted Montholon as saying: "We don't believe anything of the kind ourselves, but it is always a good thing to be able to say." Montholon was emerging as the dominant figure among Napoleon's followers. The smooth-spoken, handsome courtier had supplanted his rival, the retiring, morose Bertrand, as Longwood's chief spokesman to the English, and he often went down to Jamestown to visit his fellow aristocrat, the French commissioner. When he had recovered from a long illness, during which Napoleon was in particularly good health, Napoleon told him that hereafter he would take all his meals with Montholon. With his family gone, Montholon could spend all his time with Napoleon, and he never complained. By contrast, Bertrand was visibly impatient to go. Napoleon's taciturn engineer asked for a nine-month leave to take his unhappy wife and their four children to England and return to St. Helena. If Bertrand left, Montholon, the one-time frivolous aristocrat who joined him in the last days, would be the one remaining among the four officers Napoleon had asked to join him in his exile.

CHAPTER TWENTY-FIVE

FEBRUARY 1970
NEW YORK CITY

GREGORY TROUBETZKOY was a Napoleon buff. More precisely, an 1812 buff. Because of his family background, and by personal inclination, Troubetzkoy was a student of that disastrous conflict which set Napoleon on the downward path that led three years later to St. Helena.

The Troubetzkoy family was deeply involved in the tragic events of that epoch. In *War and Peace,* Tolstoy's classic account of the Napoleonic wars as seen from the Russian side, the family appears under the name Drubetskoy; Tolstoy's mother was a Troubetzkoy. Another Troubetzkoy, Prince Alexander, was an aide to Tsar Alexander I at Tilsit in 1807, when the Tsar and Napoleon met on a raft to seal an alliance that ended five years later in war and disaster. Still another member of the family, Serge Troubetzkoy, was exiled to Siberia in 1825 for his participation in the Decembrist revolt against Alexander's successor, Tsar Nicholas I.

Gregory Troubetzkoy's parents were among the many Russians who fled their homeland during the upheavals of Russia's Revolution and civil war. Born in Morocco in 1930, he lived there and in France before coming to the United States after the Second World War. He grew up in a household steeped in Troubetzkoy family traditions that were all the more important to people living in exile from their native land. As an adult, Gregory Troubetzkoy maintained an interest in the events centered on the year 1812 in which his family had played so prominent a part. Like many Russians, Troubetzkoy had powerfully contradictory feelings about the central figure in the drama. Napoleon was Russia's enemy, his Grand Army brought death and destruction to the land, but Napoleon also brought the winds of change blowing from revolutionary France, and his defeat was a defeat for those revolutionary ideas in Russia just as it was in France.

Given his avocation, Troubetzkoy would notice an item in a New York newspaper—a Reuters dispatch datelined Glasgow—that referred to a person who believed, after an analysis of Napoleon's hair, that the Emperor had been poisoned. Troubetzkoy read the brief story with interest, but without immediate personal concern. He clipped the item and filed it away with his Napoleonic memorabilia.

Some years later, Troubetzkoy acquired an original page of Napoleon's handwriting. Written at St. Helena, it was Napoleon's scrawled outline for the second chapter of his account of the campaign of Italy. The dealer from whom he bought it, Charles Hamilton of New York, who was also Troubetzkoy's friend, had attached to the paper about twenty strands of Napoleon's hair. The dealer told Troubetzkoy that he had bought both the manuscript page and a lock of hair, from which these strands were taken, at an auction sale in London.

At first Troubetzkoy was puzzled by the reddish-brown color of the hair; he had expected Napoleon's hair to be "Italian black." He went back to a favorite Russian author, the partisan leader and poet Denis Davidov (who appears in *War and Peace* as Denisoff, the officer with a lisp), and read his account of the Tilsit meeting, where he saw Napoleon face-to-face. "The hair on his head was not black, but dark blond," Davidov had written.

Troubetzkoy vaguely remembered that he had read years earlier about the finding of arsenic in Napoleon's hair from St. Helena. He dug out the clipping and, after some time spent in the library and on the telephone, he located the author of the poison theory, Sten Forshufvud, in Göteborg, Sweden. Troubetzkoy wrote to Forshufvud to offer some of his lock of hair for analysis. In his letter, he told what he knew about the origin of the hair. In 1825 the Count de Las Cases was living in Passy, near Paris. By then he was the world-famous author of the *Mémorial de Sainte-Hélène*. On July 22 of that year he sent the page of Napoleon's writing and the lock to "W. Fraser in Delhy." Las Cases noted that the hair was "gathered by me in Longwood circumstance indicated in the *Mémorial.*" In his own letter, Troubetzkoy quoted the *Mémorial* for October 16, 1816:

At the usual hour of his dressing, the Emperor had his hair cut by Santini; I was by his side, a little bit to the rear, a large lock of hair fell to my feet. The Emperor seeing me bending down asked what it was. I answered that I had let something fall which I was picking up. He pinched my ear, smiling. He had just guessed. . . .

Troubetzkoy did not know—nor did Charles Hamilton, the dealer—who "W. Fraser" was, why Las Cases sent him the lock and manuscript, or where the lock had been from the time it was sent to "Delhy" until it turned up in London more than a century later. At Forshufvud's suggestion, Troubetzkoy sent six hairs— one long strand and five short ones—directly to Hamilton Smith in Glasgow.

Now Troubetzkoy was reading a letter from Forshufvud reporting on the analysis of the Las Cases hair. The one long strand, analyzed in sections, showed arsenic content from 11.1 to 18.1 parts per million, and the content of the short pieces ranged from 9.2 to 30.4. In his letter Forshufvud explained the significance to his case of the Las Cases hair:

Of course we are not sure how far from Napoleon's scalp Santini cut those hairs. It is most probable that they were taken from the nape of the neck and cut off close to the skin. If so, they prove that Napoleon ingested large quantities of arsenic regularly from roughly the 31st July to the 1st October, 1816. This fits in very well with what we know about the development of his health during that time. From the middle of April 1816 Napoleon no longer went riding long distances. His legs would not support him. At the same time those around him noticed how he became quite changed. From different contemporary portraits we can see how, from 1816, 1817 and 1818 Napoleon began to look more and more like an overweight alcoholist, in spite of the fact that he was very moderate in his consumption of wine and never drank spirits. From the 9th to the 13th September he was more seriously ill, and also for a few days in August 1816.

However, it is not impossible that your strands of hair were cut off at as much as 10 cm. from the scalp. In such a case this should point to an ingestion of arsenic starting at the beginning of January 1816 and going on until the beginning of March of that year. Although this is fairly unlikely, the result of the analyses need not contradict what we know of the development of Napoleon's illness.

When Napoleon ingested arsenic he became fatter and fatter. This could mean that he had to a certain extent become an arsenophagist, that is to say that he could ingest a great deal of arsenic without being immediately sick. After a certain time, however, symptoms of chronic arsenic intoxication appeared.

However, the most probable hypothesis is that your strands of hair were cut off near the scalp, as Santini was concerned mainly in turning out a well-groomed ex-emperor and not in changing the hair style by shortening the hairs on the crown.

In any case your distinguished initiative has led to

definite proof that Napoleon was also subjected to systematic poisoning by arsenic in 1816.

Troubetzkoy was pleased by Forshufvud's report. The accounts he had read of the poison theory and the Glasgow tests had convinced him of the theory's accuracy, and he felt honored that his "distinguished initiative," as Forshufvud called it, had provided an added element in its proof.

CHAPTER TWENTY-SIX

OCTOBER 1820
SANDY BAY, ST. HELENA

══════════════════════ **S**IR WILLIAM Doveton was strolling in his garden when the unexpected visitors came in view. At sixty-seven, Sir William was a retired member of the St. Helena Council and one of the island's leading citizens. His home stood at the head of Sandy Bay, a fertile valley that stretches down to the sea on the opposite side of the island from Jamestown. Above the verdant valley is the barren slope of Diana's Peak. It was midmorning of a beautiful, cloudless day in the austral spring.

Sir William saw a party of men on horseback approaching along the mountain road that zigzagged up from his home to the center of the island and Longwood Plain. Looking through his spyglass, he recognized the short, stocky man in the green coat and cocked hat—Napoleon. One of the group, the Count de Montholon, rode ahead, told Sir William they had set out at dawn from Longwood House—the Governor having dropped most of his regulations concerning Napoleon's movements—and asked if the Emperor might come in and rest.

Sir William invited the party in. Napoleon rode up, accompanied by Bertrand and four servants, and dismounted. When he climbed the steps of the house, Sir William noticed that Napoleon leaned heavily on Bertrand's arm. Napoleon sat on a sofa and, with Bertrand interpreting in his halting English, chatted with his host and the family, his daughter, Mrs. Greentree, and three grandchildren. Napoleon beckoned to one of the grandchildren, a seven-year-old girl, to come to him. He asked her name and age and, fishing out a tortoiseshell box, gave her a piece of the licorice he always carried. Sir William invited them to breakfast, but the exiles in turn invited the family to share the meal they had packed at Longwood.

Breakfast was served in the garden, in the shade of cypress and cedars, by Napoleon's servants. Napoleon got up from the sofa, playfully pinched Sir William's ear, and walked outside with him arm in arm. Sir William was impressed by the lavish repast the French laid out: "Cold pie, potted meat, cold turkey, curried fowl, ham or pork, I could not tell which; coffee, dates, almonds, oranges, and a very fine salad." Napoleon poured champagne and they toasted each other. Then they drank Mrs. Greentree's homemade liqueur called orange shrub. After breakfast, Napoleon questioned the Dovetons on one of his favorite topics: English drinking habits. "Do you ever get drunk?" he asked Sir William, who answered: "I like a glass of wine sometimes." Napoleon turned to Mrs. Greentree and asked: "How often does your husband get drunk? Once a week?"

"No."

"Once a fortnight?"

"No."

"Once a month?"

"No, it is some years since I saw him so."

"Bah!" said Napoleon, and he changed the subject.

Napoleon's party left Sandy Bay soon after breakfast. Sir William recalled that "from every appearance but his pale color, General Bonaparte was in good health. He seemed as fat and round as a China pig."

When the riders reached Hutt's Gate, on the edge of

Longwood Plain, the carriage was waiting. Suddenly tired, Napoleon dismounted. He had to be helped into his carriage. He reached Longwood House exhausted and with a violent headache. A few days later he fainted when getting out of his bath, and in the following days the symptoms of his recurring illness returned: the palpitations of the heart; the weak, irregular pulse; the pain and the icy chill in the legs; the pain in the liver; the pain in the shoulders and back; the dry cough; the loosened teeth and the coated tongue; the severe thirst; the skin rash and yellowed skin; the shivering, the deafness, the sensitivity to light, the difficulty in breathing, the nausea—all these symptoms now returned in force.

CHAPTER TWENTY-SEVEN

SEPTEMBER 1974
MONT GABRIEL, CANADA

===================== **B**EN WEIDER was a man of two
passions. One was health and physical fitness. As founder and
president of a company, based in Montreal, that manufactured
and sold body-building equipment, he had a special interest in
human physiology. The other passion was Napoleon. It had been
his lifelong fascination, and he devoured the major works on the
subject as they came out.

Weider had always been puzzled about the circumstances of
Napoleon's illness and death. He knew that, before St. Helena,
Napoleon was known for his iron constitution. He exercised hard,
ate and drank sparingly, and had the common sense not to take
the drugs, more often than not harmful, prescribed by the physicians of his time. Why, Weider had often wondered, did Napoleon's strong body come apart in exile, when he was only in his
late forties, without any convincing explanation either during his
life or after his autopsy? Weider was not persuaded by any of the
theories he had read. But, given the heavy pressures of his business, the question of Napoleon's death was one that entered his
mind only when he found leisure to browse among his books. It

was not part of his daily life. Only after he met Sten Forshufvud did the question become a major concern for Weider.

He first heard of Forshufvud and his poison theory through an article sent him by a doctor friend. The doctor and Weider knew each other through the Souvenir Napoléonien, the Canadian Napoleonic society to which they both belonged, and of which Weider was president, and the doctor also knew of Weider's professional interest in health and fitness. It was natural for the doctor to send him the article he had come across in a medical journal. It was equally natural—indeed, it was inevitable —that Weider would be fascinated by what he read. He thought this Swedish investigator, whose name was new to him, had put forth the first believable explanation of Napoleon's end. Weider resolved to seek out the author: he wanted to know more about this man and about the theory to which he had dedicated himself.

Forshufvud and Weider started corresponding, but some years passed before they met. In the meantime Weider had the occasion to gather reactions to Forshufvud's thesis among Napoleonists he looked up in his spare time while traveling on business. He spoke with Professor David G. Chandler of the Royal Military Academy at Sandhurst, the foremost authority on the military aspects of Napoleon's career, when they traveled together to tour the battlefield of Waterloo: Professor Chandler told him he found the poison theory convincing. But in Paris the reactions Weider collected from Napoleonists he had known for years, from his membership in the French Souvenir Napoléonien, alerted him to the painful and challenging implications of Forshufvud's theory for French scholars. Whatever they might say in private, and some of them did in fact then tell him the theory made sense, as a group they had to stand united against the interloper with his disturbing idea. This, Weider later learned, was what Forshufvud liked to call the French blockade. One of the French Napoleonists even offered Weider the absurd argument that the evidence of the hairs was valueless because arsenic could have accumulated in the body from the surrounding earth after its burial—though Forshufvud's articles had clearly stated that the hairs were cut before burial under circumstances familiar to any Napoleon specialist. After a few such conversations, Weider realized that Forshufvud was facing opposition that had nothing to do with the merits of his case. Weider's fighting instinct was aroused: he wondered if he could help Forshufvud overcome his opponents and their blockade.

At last Forshufvud and Weider arranged to meet. It was in an evocative location: the little town of Lodi, in northern Italy, scene of one of Napoleon's early triumphs. They strolled on the bridge where the young General Bonaparte rallied his troops and turned impending defeat into a spectacular victory. That evening, at a small restaurant, they ordered chicken Marengo, the dish that Napoleon's cook is said to have invented from what was available at the battle of that name. Weider was impressed by this tall, erect man, then in his late sixties, with the flowing gray hair; his direct, though courtly manner, leavened by occasional flashes of humor, made their conversations easy. They talked about Forshufvud's theory and the help Weider hoped to bring to it. Weider told Forshufvud he wanted to bring his message to a wider audience than the small, inward-looking circle of Napoleon experts. If they did so, Forshufvud said, they would be fulfilling the Emperor's last wish: to make known to the world the cause of his death. The two men realized, as they talked, that there was much work to be done, and, for Weider's part, there were still doubts to be resolved before he could commit himself totally to the project that was taking shape in his mind. They decided they must spend a week together, without distraction, to look over the project, test it from all angles, before they could be sure their collaboration would succeed. And they knew a week would not be easy to find in their two busy professional lives.

Now they had managed it. Forshufvud and Weider were installed in the Mont Gabriel Lodge in the Laurentian Mountains, sixty-five miles north of Weider's home in Montreal. The lodge is almost deserted at this time of the year: people go to the mountains for summer vacation, and in winter for skiing, not so much in fall. Yet September is a lovely season in the Laurentians: the mountain foliage is turning red and yellow and orange, the air is crisp and lively, most of the days are sunny. That first morning the two men strolled in the many-colored woods and talked over what they had undertaken. Their discussion lasted all day and through dinner. Over coffee, in deference to his colleague's seven decades, Weider suggested that he might want to rest. Forshufvud looked at him solemnly, then shook his head. They would work, he said decisively, and then, switching to French, *"travailler c'est la liberté."* Weider laughed at that: the thought that work is freedom was worthy of the superhuman worker who was their subject. Forshufvud filled his pipe and they went on working.

Weider suggested they start by examining the various doubts he had heard expressed about Forshufvud's theory. He wanted to put hard questions and hear Forshufvud's answers: only if those answers were convincing would they have a case to take to the public. Weider pulled out the notes he had made in preparation for the meeting and asked: "The evidence for the poisoning is so clear that I cannot understand why no one before you has made the diagnosis of arsenic. What do you say to that?"

Forshufvud nodded. "I put that very question to Henri Griffon, the great French poison expert at the Paris police laboratory. Professor Griffon said that in no case of arsenic poisoning—and he investigated many of them—did a physician diagnose arsenic correctly and in time. As you know, the symptoms are also characteristic of several diseases more familiar to physicians. One must see the totality of symptoms in order to diagnose the arsenic. And certainly a medical man is more comfortable with disease than with the idea of poison."

"But Antommarchi was on the spot, he was trained in pathology, and certainly poisoning by arsenic was a common enough method of murder in those days. Why didn't Antommarchi suspect poison?"

"True enough, but we must remember the difference

201

between *acute* and *chronic* arsenic poisoning. A chronic poisoning, the slow method to which Napoleon was subjected, causes symptoms that were not at all understood by physicians of that time. In fact, the syndrome of chronic poisoning was not fully understood until a German study made in 1930. So we may perhaps forgive Antommarchi, and also Barry O'Meara."

Weider persisted: "But how about the medical men and historians who have studied the problem in more recent years?"

Forshufvud reminded him that, until Hamilton Smith invented and used his hair-analysis technique, there had been no direct physical evidence that Napoleon was poisoned. The memoirs that added so much detail to the story of Napoleon's last days —those of Bertrand and above all Louis Marchand—had not been published. The question of arsenic was not raised, and so it had not been answered. One hundred and forty years had passed, years during which other theories of Napoleon's death were advanced and won their devoted supporters. Each specialist had taken his position. Forshufvud added: "I have observed that all of those personalities who most strongly attack the arsenic theory have written books or articles arguing other theories—and no tigress defending her little ones can be as ferocious as the scholar defending his publication." Forshufvud stopped to fill his pipe. "What I say applies to the French Napoleonist historians. To my knowledge, no toxicologist or pathologist has disagreed with me, nor has any criminologist or expert in forensic medicine, and several of them have backed me up. But history is owned by the historians, not the scientists, and surely we can understand the reluctance of French specialists to believe that the great man of their nation was assassinated by one of his followers."

"Too bad your evidence did not point to Hudson Lowe as the assassin," Weider suggested.

Forshufvud laughed delightedly: "I would have been the first Swede ever elected president of the Souvenir Napoléonien of France!"

Weider then asked a series of questions concerning the alternative explanations he had heard for the presence of arsenic in Napoleon's hair. Napoleon used a hair cream containing arsenic, was one such theory. Another was that the curtains at Longwood contained arsenic which somehow got into Napoleon's system, and still another was that he took an arsenic-based tonic for his health. Forshufvud had an answer for each of these theories. The hair cream would have produced a constant level of arsenic, not the peaks and valleys that actually appeared in Napoleon's hair. So would the curtains, which also would have made everyone else who lived in Longwood House as sick as Napoleon. The arsenic-based tonic was not used in France until much later, around 1860, and in any event Napoleon consistently refused to take any medication of any kind.

Weider's next question took a different tack: "As you well know, your critics have questioned the origin of the hairs themselves. How can we know the hairs are really those of the Emperor? After all, given its value, there may well be hair in circulation that is falsely attributed to Napoleon. Can we ever be certain?"

Weider could tell, as he listened to Forshufvud's answer, that he had been through this more than once. "What we know for certain, first of all, is that the hairs all came from one person. We know this from the arsenic patterns in the hair, which varies like the fingerprint from one individual to the next. So we have hair that is from a single person who was poisoned with arsenic —hair, I should add, that fits the description of the Emperor's. It is red-brown, and unusually soft and silky, like a baby's hair. But is it Napoleon's? Consider the origin of the hair we received— Lachouque in Paris, Frey in Switzerland, Dame Mabel in Australia, Macauley in England, Troubetzkoy in New York. If the hair is false, then hairs from *one person* would have to have gotten into the hands of each of those people, scattered around the world and all strangers to each other. How? Or did all these strangers conspire to substitute the same false hair? For what purpose? Mind you, one of those supposed conspirators would have been

Commandant Lachouque in Paris, who came to have the usual French view of my theory. Why would Lachouque, of all people, give me a false hair only to support a theory of which the French strongly disapproved? Such possibilities are ridiculous.

"Consider also the provenance, as they say in the world of art. Each of these locks was known from the historical records *before* the present possessor came to us. In two cases, hair came direct from the descendents of those who originally received it from the Emperor—the locks of Betsy Balcombe and Admiral Malcolm. The locks had never been out of the families. Three others came at only one remove from the families. In the last case, the Troubetzkoy hair, the lock came with an authentic page of Napoleon's handwriting and we know that Las Cases collected a lock at St. Helena. No—the only reasonable theory is that the hair is indeed Napoleon's. Any other explanation is impossibly far-fetched. But let us follow the logic. If the hair sent from those people was authentic, and if the analysis was false, what are we to believe? The hair was analyzed by Hamilton Smith, a very well-known specialist in forensic science, and by the Harwell Laboratory, which is famous around the world. Aside from their reputations, what motive would they have to falsify the results? They had nothing to gain—the theory was mine. Would they do such a thing to satisfy some crazy Swede in Göteborg?"

Weider hesitated over his next question. Forshufvud guessed what was on his mind and said: "My dear Ben, you are perhaps thinking that the crazy Swede himself could have substituted false hair in order to prove his theory. You are quite right to explore every doubt! But I did not have the opportunity to do so. With the exception of the Marchand and Noverraz hair, the samples were sent or taken directly to Hamilton Smith in Glasgow without passing through my hands. I did not plan it that way, but now I am glad that is how it happened!"

Weider's next question was of a different nature. It dealt not with the evidence of poison, but with the method of the assassination itself. The question had been put to him by skeptics, and he wanted to hear how Forshufvud would handle it. "Why did the poisoning take so long? Why not kill him at once with one massive dose? After all, every day that Napoleon lived on was another day on which he might escape and return to France and once more overthrow the Bourbons. Why take the risk of delay?"

Forshufvud was ready for that one too. "I also have been asked that question," he began. "To understand what happened, we must look at just what it was that the Bourbons feared. They feared Napoleon himself—of course!—but even more than the man they feared the Bonapartist movement. They had seen the evidence of the support the Bonapartist idea had among the French people. Even while the Emperor was still alive, some of the conspirators against the Bourbons invoked the name of l'Aiglon, his son, rather than Napoleon. At the time of the July Revolution, in 1830, there was a serious effort to give the crown to l'Aiglon, and we know the Bonapartist movement eventually succeeded with Louis Napoleon.

"Suppose, as you suggest, the Count d'Artois had ordered the assassin to kill Napoleon with a single dose. Poison would certainly be suspected, there would be an autopsy, and the visual evidence would prove the presence of arsenic. Imagine what the Bourbons could expect when the news reached France! Surely a popular revolt, led by Napoleon's veterans, that would end their rule forever, and perhaps cost them their lives as well. You recall that, after Waterloo, when the Prussian Blucher and others wanted to shoot Napoleon, King Louis said not a word—he did not dare. That is why it was essential that the poisoning be slow enough to make it seem that Napoleon died a natural death. I might add that the gradual poisoning served the purpose of keeping Napoleon at St. Helena. I am quite certain that a Napoleon possessing his full health and vigor would have tried to escape— and perhaps have succeeded. Finally, there was a personal consideration of great importance to the assassin himself. I would not like to have been at Longwood House when it was discovered I had poisoned the Emperor. No doubt the assassin would have

205

been torn to pieces by Napoleon's loyal followers, instead of sailing away unsuspected, his awful mission accomplished."

That brought the conversation around to the central unanswered question. But it was very late, and Weider's arm was tired from taking down Forshuvfud's explanations. They decided to stop for the night.

After breakfast the two men walked in the woods, Forshufvud as always striding purposefully ahead as if he were catching a train, until they came to a crest overlooking a wooded valley lit by the autumn sun. They settled themselves on a rock, Forshufvud filled his pipe, and Weider pulled out his notebook. He said: "Are you ready now to answer the question you refused to answer when we first met at Lodi?"

Forshufvud was silent for a time. When he spoke, the words came very slowly: "To accuse a person, even a person long dead, of assassinating the greatest man of modern times is a most serious responsibility. I have not wanted to accuse the culprit until I was as certain as I could be of his identity. Now I am certain. We shall go through the list of possible suspects and, when we have finished, I hope you will be as convinced as I am."

They reviewed the cast of characters present during the drama of St. Helena. First they eliminated all those who did not actually live at Longwood on the grounds that, while they could have poisoned the household, they could not target Napoleon alone. That cleared the English—all of them—much as the French might resent the fact. Next they eliminated those who were not present for the entire exile, because the evidence of the hairs was that Napoleon was poisoned in the first, middle, and last stages of those five-and-one-half years. This exonerated those who left: Las Cases, Gourgaud, O'Meara, Albine de Montholon; Cipriani, who died; and those, like Antommarchi, who arrived only in 1819. The list was much shorter now, but it still included two officers, Montholon and Bertrand, and a dozen servants.

"We can also rule out Bertrand," Forshufvud said. "Poor Bertrand was unhappy at St. Helena, and he had every reason to be angry at the way Napoleon treated him. But a slow poisoning is an act of cold calculation, not one of anger. More important, Bertrand did not have the opportunity. He did not live in Longwood House itself, and he had nothing to do with the running of the household."

Weider knew that the standard way of administering arsenic was through food or drink, so he said: "Pierron, the chef, was at Longwood throughout the exile."

"Indeed he was, and he could easily have poisoned Napoleon, but not Napoleon *alone*. Pierron prepared the food, but it was served by the valets—Napoleon would take food from no one else. So Pierron could not know which portion of what he prepared would be eaten by Napoleon, except on the rather rare occasions when food was made for Napoleon to eat alone. These occasions were too few to account for the record of poisoning."

They then discussed the three valets who served Napoleon his food: Louis Marchand, the chief valet; Saint-Denis, known as Ali; and the Swiss Noverraz. Forshufvud said that the latter two could be ruled out because they did not serve the food consistently enough, and that Noverraz was sick in bed during one period when Napoleon was certainly being poisoned.

Weider realized they were now down to only two suspects: Montholon the officer and Marchand the valet. "How ironic!" he said. "Montholon and Marchand—the two most faithful of the Emperor's followers!"

"Ironic surely, but also quite natural," Forshufvud said. "Only the most faithful would have had the constant access to Napoleon required to carry out the assassin's mission." Forshufvud got up and began to pace back and forth in front of the rock on which Weider was still sitting. "Now let us examine the backgrounds of our two suspects and ask ourselves the question: why did this person go to St. Helena? First Louis Marchand. Marchand had served Napoleon for ten years, for all of his adult life. His mother served in the palace. Neither he nor his family had any royalist connections. Napoleon was the only life Marchand had ever known. He was with the Emperor before Elba, at Elba, during the Hundred Days. His mother was in Vienna caring for the son of Napoleon and Marie-Louise, l'Aiglon. It was natural that Louis Marchand would go to St. Helena."

Forshufvud stopped pacing and pointed the stem of his pipe at the other man. "Now Montholon—and what a different man we find! Above all, one question that cries out for an answer— *why did Montholon go to St. Helena?* He was from the old aristocracy. He was an officer who did no fighting—his heroic claims to the contrary. In fact, he had not distinguished himself in any way at all. Napoleon scarcely knew who he was, and certainly Montholon had no cause to be grateful to the Emperor. Napoleon could not view Montholon's military record with anything but contempt. He refused Montholon promotion and denied him permission to marry Albine, then dismissed him when he married her anyway. When Napoleon abdicated and went to Elba, Montholon sought to gain favor with the Bourbons. In any event, he was far better connected in royalist circles than he was with Napoleon. His stepfather, the Count de Semonville, was close to d'Artois. No doubt through that connection, Montholon got a general's commission in the first Bourbon Restoration. At that time a significant event occurs. Montholon is charged with stealing six thousand francs from the pay intended for the men under his command. A very serious accusation, worth many years in prison—but Montholon is never brought to a court-martial. Now Napoleon comes back from Elba. Montholon tells us in his memoirs that he immediately rejoined the Emperor. But there is no evidence of that. Montholon was not in the Belgian campaign, not at Waterloo, when Napoleon needed every man he could get."

Now Forshufvud was pacing again and excitedly waving his pipe. "No—Montholon is not seen in Napoleon's entourage until *after* Waterloo, when he suddenly appears at the Elysée palace in a court chamberlain's uniform. After Waterloo—when Napoleon is finished! Why does this pleasure-loving young aristocrat suddenly want to join a lost cause? And more! He courts Napoleon and is eager to go to St. Helena! Why? Why does this frivolous man, what today we would call a playboy, why does this playboy want to leave the good life in France, where his kind are now in power and his stepfather has access to the king's brother? Why does he want to spend his best years on a remote island in the service of a man to whom he owes nothing? Montholon was thirty-two, only a dozen years younger than Napoleon. The exile could easily last twenty or thirty years, and Montholon would be old when he came home—and for what? What a prospect! Why did Montholon want to go?"

Forshufvud spread his arms wide in a gesture of bewilderment. "And now consider his behavior at St. Helena. Montholon refuses to react to Albine's intimacies with Napoleon, even when Gourgaud taunts him about it. Montholon never complains, never asks to leave. Even Bertrand, the loyal Bertrand, finally asked permission to go—but not the playboy Montholon! When Albine left, Napoleon told Montholon he could leave with her— but Montholon chose to stay. Again I ask—why?"

Forshufvud paused to catch his breath after what for him had been a long speech, and then went on: "I see only one explanation for Montholon's strange behavior. He was sent to join Napoleon and go to St. Helena for the single purpose of killing the Emperor with poison. Surely the man who gave the order was d'Artois, who masterminded so many plots on Napoleon's life. Why did Montholon agree to this awful assignment? I believe that d'Artois, no doubt through Montholon's stepfather, told Montholon that if he did not take on the mission he would be sent to prison for stealing his soldiers' pay. That is my case. Montholon murdered Napoleon!"

With that, Forshufvud stopped and sat down again on the rock. The two men sat in silence for a long time, each occupied with his own thoughts. Weider was trying to sort out what Forshufvud had just told him. In the past he too had noticed Montholon's unlikely background for St. Helena, but he had not given

209

it much thought, and certainly he had not connected his going with the seldom-mentioned episode of the soldiers' pay. Now Weider thought the way Forshufvud had fitted together the pieces made a great deal of sense. At the same time, he knew he was far from being as convinced as the other man. He said so.

Forshufvud said: "Let us turn to the question of method for further evidence. You know that Montholon, along with Cipriani, was in charge of the Longwood household and its supplies. Montholon was the wine steward—he held the key to the closet in which the wine was kept. Now, I believe that the wine was the ideal instrument for the poisoning. Napoleon always drank his own wine, the Vin de Constance, from his own bottle, while those dining with him drank other wines. The wine arrived at Longwood in casks and there it was put in bottles. How simple it would be for the wine steward to put arsenic in the cask itself, before the wine was bottled. And also safe. He was far less likely to be caught doing that than poisoning the food. Food would have to be poisoned each time, but one application of arsenic in the cask of wine would guarantee that Napoleon would be poisoned for weeks or months to come—and, what's more, poisoned with a predictable dose, since Napoleon never drank more than a half bottle at a meal. All this with minimum risk to the poisoner.

"There is more evidence concerning the wine. On rare occasions, Napoleon made a gift of a bottle of his wine—and more than once the person who received the gift fell ill with the same symptoms that afflicted Napoleon. He gave a bottle to the Balcombes, and Mrs. Balcombe was sick. He gave a bottle to Gourgaud, and Gourgaud was sick. Gourgaud warned the Emperor about the wine and even suggested they should all drink the same wine so poison could not be directed at Napoleon alone. Napoleon dismissed the idea. Too bad! It could have saved his life."

Again there was a silence. Weider found the hypothesis of the wine persuasive, and surely it added weight to the case against Montholon. But he felt there was still something lacking. He was not ready to convict Montholon on the basis of what he had heard.

"The jury is still not convinced, I believe?" Forshufvud said with a smile. "And you are quite right, my skeptical friend. There is more to come. The heart of the matter lies in the last phase of the Emperor's life—those first months of the year 1821. That is when the assassin adopted the classical method of killing his victim. That is when he stopped the arsenic and got a physician to prescribe those drugs, otherwise harmless, that finish off the weakened person without leaving a trace of arsenic in the body to be discovered at an autopsy—no trace at least that could be found with the methods available at the time. It is in those last months that we shall find the final proof that Napoleon was murdered, and that Montholon was his assassin." Forshufvud stood up. "But to explain the last phase I need my documents. And now I believe it is time for a bottle of beer and our lunch. Perhaps the chef of our lodge will serve us a chicken Marengo in honor of our first meeting?"

That afternoon Weider joined Forshufvud in his room. The table, the dresser, the bed, were littered with the papers Forshufvud had brought from his study in Göteborg for their meeting: his dog-eared copies of the St. Helena memoirs, scientific books and articles, pages and pages of his handwriting. Spread out on the floor was Forshufvud's time-line. He had described it to Weider, but the latter could hardly believe what he saw. The time-line consisted of perhaps two dozen sheets of paper which Forshufvud had taped together. On this scroll he had plotted the day-by-day evidence of the last days. Here was a graph showing the peaks and valleys of arsenic content revealed by Hamilton Smith's analysis of the hair cut at Napoleon's death. Here were references by date to the testimony of the eyewitnesses, and here were notes in Swedish and French and English. What an extraordinary labor of devotion that scroll represented!

"Well, my friend, what do you think of my work?" Forshufvud asked.

Weider said the first thing that came into his head: "It looks like an Egyptian manuscript."

Forshufvud clapped his hands. "Quite right!" he exclaimed. "It is a Rosetta Stone that explains Napoleon's last days. And with the help of our Rosetta Stone, we shall fulfill the Emperor's last wish. We shall tell the world how he died and who killed him."

For the next week, Sten Forshufvud and Ben Weider were to spend virtually every waking moment in that room—and in Napoleon's sickroom at Longwood House. They pored over the time-line and over the memoirs of those who witnessed those critical last days: Louis Marchand, the chief valet whose memoirs gave Forshufvud the original idea for the theory he was now proving; Bertrand, the quiet, unhappy Grand Marshal whose coded notations were deciphered only in the middle of this century; Saint-Denis, known as Ali, the second valet; Francesco Antommarchi, the handsome young Corsican doctor—and the enigmatic Montholon himself. What appears in the following pages is their reconstruction of Napoleon's end accompanied by Forshufvud's commentary on the evidence of the historic crime committed in those last days.

CHAPTER TWENTY-EIGHT

LONGWOOD HOUSE, ST. HELENA
JANUARY–MAY 1821

January 1

Marchand: That morning, when I entered his room, he was in bed. "Well," he said to me, when his shutters were opened, "what are you giving me for New Year's?" "Sire," I said, "the hope that Your Majesty will soon be better and be able to leave a climate so contrary for the health." "It won't be long, my son, my end is near, I cannot last long."

Forshufvud: According to both the evidence of the hair analysis and Antommarchi's notes, Napoleon has just suffered the latest in a series of attacks in which he showed the symptoms of acute arsenic poisoning. Between these acute periods he continues to show the symptoms of chronic poisoning. Three weeks earlier—on December 5—Montholon wrote to his wife that Napoleon was suffering from a *"maladie de langueur."* This means a wasting illness, and can be interpreted, as it was to be in Napoleon's case, to mean cancer. *Maladie de langueur* was the cause given in the French government communiqué on Napoleon's death.

Bertrand: The weather is bad. The Emperor does not go out; Napoleon has had a seesaw set up in the billiard room. He asks the Grand Marshal if he knows what it is. "It's a war machine. Is it used to lower yourself onto a rampart?" "Not much brains for an engineer, *foutre* . . ." First he says it is a seesaw for the children, finally that it is for himself. It seems it will be good exercise if he can mount it for half an hour a day; it will make him sweat.

Madame Bertrand laughs at the sight of the Emperor on a seesaw and says a caricature will be made out of it: the Emperor on one side and all the sovereigns on the other unable to lift him, with this caption: Remedy for Hepatitis. The fact is that the Emperor is very heavy: he weighs more than Noverraz, who is over six feet tall.

Saint-Denis: This exercise pleased the Emperor for about two weeks, and then he gave it up.

January 27

Montholon to Hudson Lowe: Antommarchi, his surgeon, is not equal to saving him in the present state of his illness. He would like a doctor . . . from Paris. . . . What is necessary can only be done by the intervention of the English or French governments.

Bertrand: General Montholon then spoke of Doctor Arnott [an English military doctor whose services had been offered by Hudson Lowe]: "The Emperor wants a French doctor. It is up to the king to choose one."

Forshufvud: Montholon is trying to get rid of Antommarchi. Why? Antommarchi is dangerous to the assassin in two ways. First, because he is trained in pathology and so can do a better autopsy than most doctors. Second, since he is Italian and owes no loyalty to either government involved, but only to his patient, Antommarchi would not fear to make a finding

214

of poison. A French doctor, chosen by the Bourbons, would know better than to diagnose poison, and so would an English doctor under the authority of Hudson Lowe, given the governor's fear that the English would be blamed for Napoleon's death.

Antommarchi: The night was very bad. The Emperor is extremely weak, his pulse is weak, somewhat nervous—dry cough —somber expression.

January 28

Antommarchi: Extreme weakness; eyes livid, almost sightless. Dry, nervous cough. Mouth dry. Thirst. Feeling of pain in the stomach.

January 29

Antommarchi: Same condition. Profound sadness.

January 30

Antommarchi: The Emperor is in a deplorable state; but the illness only increases his aversion to drugs.

Forshufvud: The sectional analysis of the hair cut at death shows a peak of arsenic content at this period.

January 31

Bertrand: Antommarchi asked the Grand Marshal to come to his room: The Emperor had called the Doctor at one in the morning and told him he had to make up his mind; that he could stay as a surgeon if he wanted; that he, the Emperor, was writing for a doctor and he showed him a passage he was writing; that at the same time he would ask for a surgeon; that their conflicts were not due to [Antommarchi's] medical skill but to his behavior; that he should go see Montholon, that to get along with [Napoleon] he had to get along with Montholon; that he should court him; that he should no longer go to the Grand Marshal's in the evening . . . that the Grand Marshal and his wife were

215

leaving; that [Antommarchi] was crude; that he would do well to speak more politely . . .

February 9

Bertrand [Napoleon's observations on the work of the scholars he took with him to Egypt]: "The Science Commission did nothing in Egypt. . . . It shed light on no question in history or geography. On the island of Mercury and in the Nubian desert we found monuments as well preserved as those of Thebes. They are not mentioned by Herodotus or any historian. How were these cities built that seemed to be religious cities, which presupposes that the arts were developed, that it was a great nation? Were these lands once made fertile by rain? Was there some revolution in nature?

"I believe there was a great nation in the center of Africa. Who destroyed those monuments? Why do we not know Abyssinia and the interior of Africa? That is inconceivable and yet it seems easy to do. One should leave from Egypt. . . . The first thing is to explore Abyssinia and know it well. For that, one must send ten different people, some via Egypt, some via Suakin (why is there no resident agent in Suakin?) where all the caravans from Africa to Arabia pass . . ."

February 11

Montholon to Albine: A few days ago [on January 31] I addressed an official note to the Governor asking for replacements. . . . The Emperor rightly believes that the only way to surmount all the obstacles is to leave the choice of individuals to the king and his ministers . . .

Forshufvud: It is simply impossible to believe that Napoleon, who was afraid of *English* doctors, would put his life in the hands of a physician chosen by the Bourbons, when, as he so often observed, the Count d'Artois had tried again and again to have him assassinated. Montholon is lying because the assassin wants a doctor chosen by the Bourbons in place of Antommarchi.

February 26

Antommarchi: The Emperor, who was feeling fairly well on the 21st, has a sudden relapse. Dry cough. Vomiting. Sensation of heat in intestines. Generally disturbed. Discomfort. Burning feeling that is almost unbearable, accompanied by burning thirst.

February 27

Antommarchi: The Emperor is worse yet than yesterday. The cough has become more violent, and the painful nausea did not stop till seven in the morning.

Forshufvud: The analysis of the hair shows another peak of arsenic content at this period.

March 10

Bertrand: The Emperor believes the English will not want to do away with him; that they will put him in England in a beautiful park; that they will ask him to give his word that he will not leave the area without the permission of the government. . . .

"If the choice were mine, I would go to America. . . . First I would get my health back; then I would spend six months touring the country; seeing five hundred leagues of country will take me some time. I would see Louisiana. It is I who gave it to them. I was criticized for selling Louisiana to the Americans. I would have given it to them for nothing for, when war came, I could not protect it and the English would have taken it. . . .

"On arrival in New York, I would send a messenger to my brother. We would have the English consul come on board; we would ask him to say nothing. A few hours later, Joseph would arrive and then we could go ashore. We would take some of Joseph's people. It seems that his house is located on a river, at Trenton, ten leagues from Philadelphia and twenty from New York. Soon I would have many French families around me . . ."

March 13

Bertrand: At seven, the Governor sends the newspapers: the *Morning Chronicle* for November 27 to December 21. No change in the Cabinet! The elections in France did not go to the liberals. A great disappointment for all of us and especially for the Emperor who was hoping for better news. "We were building castles in Spain," he says.

March 15 or 16

Bertrand [A book Napoleon was reading caused him to reflect on a central issue of his rule]: "One must distinguish between the *interests* and the *theories* of the Revolution. The theories preceded the interests. The interests did not begin until the night of August fourth [1789] after the abolishing of the nobility and their tithes. I preserved all the interests of the Revolution, I had no desire to destroy them. That was what gave me my strength; that is how I was able to put aside the theories of the Revolution. Everyone was content, because they knew the Emperor did not, could not, want a counterrevolution. With me, freedom of the press was unnecessary. . . . The theories of the Revolution are useful only to destroy the theories of the counterrevolution. I preserved the interests of the Revolution and I banned its theories.

March 17

Antommarchi to a colleague in Italy: To clear myself of all responsibility, I declare to you, to the imperial family, to the whole world, that the malady from which the Emperor is suffering is due to the nature of the climate, and that its symptoms are of the utmost gravity.

Marchand: The Emperor took a little aspic I served him, [dressed] and went out leaning on the arm of Count de Montholon. When he arrived at the carriage, he could not step up into it and went back to his room with a glacial chill and shivering throughout his body, and went to bed. I put a second blanket over him while Saint-Denis and Noverraz heated towels in which I wrapped his feet, changing them frequently. "You're bringing me back to life," he said. "I think a crisis is coming, it will save me or kill me."

Forshufvud: The icy chill is a symptom of arsenic poisoning.

March 18

Hudson Lowe to the Colonial Office in London: I yesterday heard of an extraordinary way General Bonaparte has of late contrived to take riding exercise within doors, mounted on a species of hobby.

March 20

Antommarchi: Madame Bertrand appeared. [Napoleon] made an effort and appeared less disheartened. He asked about her health [Fanny Bertrand had recently been very ill after a miscarriage], and after conversing for a few moments with a kind of gaiety: "We must prepare ourselves for the death sentence; you, Hortense [the Bertrand's daughter, also ill], and I are destined to experience it here on this evil rock. I will go first, you second, Hortense will follow, and we shall all three meet in the Elysian Fields," and he recited this verse [from Voltaire's play *Zaïre*]:

I must no longer hope to see Paris again;
You see that I am ready to descend into my tomb.

March 21

Antommarchi: Thinking how useful an emetic would be, I begged Napoleon not to neglect himself, to make a small effort, but his repugnance erupted at the very name of the medication. He answered by exaggerating the uncertainty of medicine. "Can you just tell me of what my illness consists, can you even say where it is located?" I could tell him that the art of healing did not proceed like the exact sciences, that the seat and cause of the afflictions we experience can only be determined by induction; he did not want to admit any such distinction. "In that case," he told me, "keep your medicines, I don't want to have two diseases, the

219

one I have already and the one you'll give me." If I insisted, he would accuse us of working in dark, of administering medications at random, and of causing the death of three-quarters of those who entrust themselves to us. "But how about a slightly emetic drink?" "What! A slightly emetic drink? Isn't that a medication?"

Forshufvud: In the classic method of poisoning, tartar emetic is used to prepare the final blow: the killing of the weakened victim that leaves no trace of arsenic. When the Marquise de Brinvilliers was ready to finish off her father, she served him a glass of wine containing tartar emetic—prescribed by his physician.

There are two reasons for having the emetic prescribed by a physician. First, the emetic, unlike arsenic, has a pronounced unpleasant taste, so the victim knows he is getting something out of the ordinary. Second, the prescription by the victim's physician provides the best possible protection for the poisoner.

In Napoleon's time, as in that of the Marquise, tartar emetic was one of the most common remedies. Physicians hoped the emetic, by inducing vomiting, would rid the body of the ills for which they had no other treatment. A poisoner could therefore feel confident that a patient displaying Napoleon's symptoms would be given an emetic by his physician. Antommarchi is offering the standard treatment of the day.

Tartar emetic is a salt of antimony. For the poisoner, its essential effect is that the antimony, acting on an already weakened body, corrodes the mucous lining of the stomach. This corrosion eventually inhibits the normal vomiting reflex with which the stomach protects itself: the stomach becomes unable to expel poisons. This, as we shall see, is the necessary preparation for the final blow.

March 22
Marchand: The Emperor gave in to the wishes of these gentlemen [Bertrand and Montholon had joined Antommarchi in

220

urging him to take the emetic], took the emetic which was given to him in two doses some time apart; the resulting efforts were most violent . . . he brought up some mucus.

Antommarchi: Increased fever combined with cold; headache and gas in the abdomen. The patient feels an oppressive pressure in the epigastric region, and a feeling of suffocation.

March 23

Antommarchi: Increased fever, icy cold in the lower extremities, gas, yawning, pain in the abdomen, oppressive feeling in stomach, great constipation.

Marchand: He asked me for a small bottle and some anise; he poured some of it, told me to fill it with water and added that in the future he wanted no drink other than this, he even forbade me to offer him any drink that he had not authorized.

Forshufvud: Napoleon's reaction in the days after he was given the emetic are those of a person suffering from antimony rather than arsenic poisoning. To confirm this, Hamilton Smith in Glasgow tested some of Napoleon's hair cut at death for its antimony content. The results, though not as conclusive as the earlier arsenic tests, showed a relatively high content of antimony in those last months. Equally important, analysis of the hair by sections showed that the antimony content varies over time. This is evidence that Napoleon was given enough tartar emetic to accomplish the assassin's purpose: to weaken the victim's stomach in preparation for the final blow.

March 24

Marchand: He shows the Count de Montholon the drink he intends to take: "If it does me no good," he tells him, "it will do me no harm." The doctor, who is present, smiles at these words of the Emperor, but declares that the stomach needs an emetic, that he has to advise it to his Majesty: "Go away," the Emperor says, "and administer it to yourself!" That same day, the doctor tells the Emperor that Noverraz is in bed with a most violent liver attack and that he has just been caring for him. The Emperor fears that [Noverraz's] illness might be prolonged, and that not being fully recovered from my own illness, I may have a relapse because of fatigue; I have in fact spent the nights of the 18th to the 24th seconded by Saint-Denis or Noverraz, who slept in the adjoining room. The Count de Montholon, to whose care the Emperor is accustomed during the day, immediately offers his services for the night; the Emperor decides that [Montholon] will stay with him from nine to two o'clock, at which time I will have my tour of duty with him. Thus the Count de Montholon adds this night service to the daytime hours he spends with the Emperor. . . . The Emperor tells [Bertrand] about the new arrangements he has just made, and the Count Bertrand offers his services. The Emperor answers: "Montholon's care is sufficient, I am used to it. If ever it is lacking I'll accept your services."

March 25 or 26

Marchand: The doctor tells me how worried he is and that day by day the disease is gaining ground because [Napoleon] refuses the help he can be given. "I see only one thing to do," he says, "and that is to put the emetic in the drink he has adopted and in any others he may be offered, without letting him know about it." This proposal was made to me in a low voice in the room of the Emperor, who was sleeping at the time; I answered, in the same low voice, that I refused to give the Emperor an emetic drink because I had been given orders to that effect and the Emperor would find it very wrong for us to treat him so: "Consult General Montholon and the Grand Marshal, but for myself I refuse to participate in any way." The conversation ended, he did not mention it to me again.

March 26

Antommarchi [Antommarchi had been urging Napoleon to let him consult with another doctor]: "A consultation! What good would it be? You're all working in the dark. Another doctor would not see any more than you what is happening in my body;

222

if he claimed to see more, he would be a charlatan who would make me lose what little confidence I still have in the children of Hippocrates. Besides, who would I consult? The English, who get their inspiration from Hudson?" The Emperor was excited, I did not persist; I waited till he was calmer, then tried again. "You're persistent," he said kindly. "Well, all right, I consent. Choose whichever of the doctors on the island you think is the most competent." I spoke to Dr. [Archibald] Arnott, surgeon of the Second Regiment; I described the symptoms, the circumstances of the Emperor's condition; his opinion was that we should:

1) Apply a large vesicatory [a plaster that caused blistering] over the entire abdominal region;

2) Administer a purgative;

3) Apply vinegar frequently to the forehead.

[Napoleon] asked me the result of the consultation. I told him. He shook his head, seemed dissatisfied, and said: "That's English medicine."

March 27

Marchand: On seeing Count Bertrand, the Emperor said: "Well, *Monsieur le grand maréchal*, how are you feeling?" "Perfectly well, sire, I wish the same were true of Your Majesty, how did Your Majesty find the emetic drinks, did they do any good?" The Emperor, knowing nothing of the proposal that had been made to me, called me immediately; I was in the next room. Sudden anger appeared on his face. . . . "Since when, Monsieur, have you allowed yourself to poison me by putting emetic drinks on my table; did I not tell you to offer me nothing I have not authorized? Did I not forbid that? Is this how you justify my confidence in you? You knew it! Get out!" . . . The Emperor had never spoken to me in that way. . . . "Sire," I said, "I can affirm to Your Majesty that to my knowledge those drinks do not contain emetic. It is true that last night the doctor spoke to me of the necessity of putting emetic in the drinks without informing

223

Your Majesty, but I thought I had discouraged him by saying he could not allow himself such an action toward Your Majesty. And for me, I refused to let such a drink be brought in; if the doctor acted on his idea, I was not told about it, it must have been done in the pantry." "Call Antommarchi!" [Antommarchi] tried to excuse himself by saying that if the Emperor continued to refuse help, he was endangering his life. "Well, Monsieur, do I owe you any accounting? Don't you know that death for me would be a gift from heaven?" . . . The incident left the Emperor in a bad mood that lasted for the rest of the day; he made me throw all the drinks on his table out the window and said: "I trust no one put anything in my anise."

Antommarchi: The Emperor needed me frequently. He did not want to make me come and go, wasting time. "You must be overworked, Doctor," he said kindly. "You are constantly being called, you don't have a chance to close your eyes. . . . I'll have a bed set up for you in the next room."

Bertrand: "I am very glad I have no religion. I have no imaginary fears, I do not fear the future."

Montholon: The Emperor persists in not wanting to be treated by Antommarchi and in believing that he will cure himself with diet, orgeat, and *soupe à la reine.*

Forshufvud: Note the reference to orgeat, and note that Montholon tells us Napoleon thought he could cure himself with it. Orgeat—*orzata* in Italian—is a drink that was first brewed from barley (*orge* in French). From the eighteenth century, it was made with sweet almonds. Typically some bitter almonds are added for spice and orange water is added for flavor. Orgeat is the second of the three essential elements of the final blow.

March 29

Thomas Reade, the Governor's aide, to Captain Lutyens, the orderly officer at Longwood: It is your duty to insist, after what has been said to you of General Bonaparte's illness, upon having an opportunity afforded to you of seeing him, if an English medical person is not permitted to him.

Lutyens to Major Gorrequer, the Governor's secretary: I again spoke to the Count [Montholon] about the necessity of my seeing General Bonaparte.

March 30

Bertrand: The Governor came to General Montholon, and told him that the Emperor had not been seen in twelve days; that the other day he had been coming here when he was told that Dr. Arnott had been summoned; but that Arnott had not seen the Emperor; that it was necessary for the duty officer to see him; that the Emperor was said to be ill, but he knew nothing about it. Montholon answered that the Emperor was ill. . . . The Governor answered that [Montholon's] word might mean something to him, Sir Hudson Lowe, but that he was responsible to the Allied Powers, that therefore he needed the testimony of an English officer.

"The Emperor is sick, he cannot go out, he cannot be seen. Would you break down his door?"

"Yes, if necessary, we would break down his door, we would enter by force."

"But that would kill him."

"It doesn't matter, I would do it."

"You would bear the responsibility."

"I am responsible in the eyes of the sovereigns. I am not only the agent of the English government, but the representative of the Allied Powers."

Marchand: For some time the Emperor had been saying: "That *Calabrese* of a Governor has been leaving us in peace! What does it mean? No doubt he knows from the Chinese that I am ill."

Lutyens to Gorrequer: I . . . repaired to the garden, when Count Montholon, who was in the act of shutting the

225

bedroom venetians, came out to me and told me to look through a window, the venetian and curtain of which he had purposely left a little open.

Antommarchi: Napoleon was chronically constipated and had to take enemas; we placed the seat in front of the window, and while General Montholon and I were at the patient's side, Marchand opened the curtain a bit as if he wanted to look out into the garden.

Lutyens to Gorrequer: I looked, as [Montholon] desired, and perceived General Bonaparte, leaning on Dr. Antommarchi, come from the inside room and heard him get into the bed of the room in which I looked.

April 1

Marchand: The Emperor agreed to see Dr. Arnott: "Your English doctor," he told Count Bertrand, "will go tell that executioner about the state I am in; really, it will give him too much pleasure to hear about my agony; besides, what words will he put in my mouth if I see him? *Enfin!* It's more for the satisfaction of those around me than for me, who expect nothing from his insights. Well, Bertrand, tell him to come see you; let him reach an understanding with Antommarchi, tell him about the course of my illness, and bring him to me."

Hudson Lowe to Arnott: Dr. Arnott must ascertain whether he is sent for at the express wish of General Bonaparte himself, or called upon merely by Count Montholon or Count Bertrand; or, if it is at the request and desire of Dr. Antommarchi, he has been sent for. Should it appear that he has been sent for at the desire of General Bonaparte, he will ask to see him in company of his own surgeon, Dr. Antommarchi . . . they will attend upon him together. . . . Should Count Montholon or Count Bertrand endeavor to force Dr. Arnott's attendance on General Bonaparte, without his own surgeon being present, Dr. Arnott will object to the visit, accompanied by them alone, and report forthwith to the Governor . . .

Arnott to the Governor's aide: The wishes of Count

Montholon are directly contrary to the instructions given me in the Governor's private memoranda.

Arnott: I went with [Antommarchi] and was walked into a dark room where General Bonaparte was in bed. The room was dark so that I could not see, but I felt either him or someone else. I examined his pulse and the state of skin. I perceived there was considerable debility, but there was nothing that indicated immediate danger.

Forshufvud: What are those "wishes of Count Montholon" to which the Governor's instructions to Arnott are "directly contrary"? Hudson Lowe ordered Arnott not to visit Napoleon except in the presence of Antommarchi. Presumably Montholon wants Arnott to visit Napoleon without Antommarchi—thus getting Antommarchi out of the case if he cannot get him sent off the island. Why? Arnott is the kind of doctor who does not seem to mind that, at least on this first visit, he cannot even see his patient. Furthermore, Arnott cannot speak either French or Italian. Thus, unlike Antommarchi and O'Meara, he cannot speak directly to Napoleon; their conversation can be only through Bertrand, whose English was far from fluent. Antommarchi, though his conduct often angered Napoleon, could speak to him in his native dialect and had been following his case for more than a year. He would be far more likely to detect—and report—foul play than Arnott.

April 2

Marchand: Dr. Arnott arrived at nine accompanied by Count Bertrand [who interpreted]; the Emperor allowed him to be accompanied by Dr. Antommarchi. . . . After having asked several questions on the organs of the stomach, on the way food entered and then exited through the pylorus, the Emperor said: "I have here a sharp pain that, when I feel it, is like being cut with a razor; do you think the pylorus is affected? My father died of that at thirty-five; is it not hereditary?" Dr. Arnott . . . told him it was an inflammation of the stomach and that the pylorus did not seem to him at all affected; the liver had nothing to do with it; the pain he felt in the intestine was due to gas; if he would not refuse medication, all that would go away; he prescribed poultices and potions to be taken hourly.

Bertrand: Dr. Arnott advises medication, with which Antommarchi disagrees. . . . The Emperor refuses to take it.

April 3

Antommarchi: Profound sadness. Pulse weak and irregular, varying from 74 to 80 per minute. The heat of the body is 96 degrees on Fahrenheit's thermometer. . . . The patient sweats profusely, is thirsty, and says he cannot eat: still he expresses the desire for a little wine, drinks some claret, but obstinately refuses any kind of medication. . . . The fever is worse, accompanied by icy cold in the lower extremities. . . . The Emperor seems to me in imminent danger; I communicate my fears to Dr. Arnott, who, far from sharing them, predicts favorably about his condition. I would like to have the same hope, but I cannot conceal from myself that Napoleon is dying. I so inform Bertrand and Montholon. The latter takes the responsibility of informing the Emperor that his hour is approaching and to put his affairs in order.

April 4

Antommarchi: The fever continued through the night with alternating hot and cold that particularly affected the lower extremities. The patient experienced painful strain in the lower belly, burning thirst, extreme anxiety, general pain. His mind was troubled by nightmares and terrifying dreams. Nausea. Vomiting. Abundant sweating.

April 6

Thomas Reade to Hudson Lowe: Dr. Arnott informed me that he had never found him, during any of his visits, in the state in which he had been described by Dr. Antommarchi. From what I could learn generally, out of Dr. Arnott's conversation, he appears to think that General Bonaparte is not afflicted with any serious complaint, probably more mental than any other. Count

228

Bertrand has asked him his opinion of General Bonaparte; he told him that he saw no danger whatever.

Early April

Marchand: I offered him some orgeat which was on his table. He said, gazing at me: "I trust that no one is putting anything in my drinks?" "Sire," I said, "the lesson was too severe for anyone to do that again."

April 7

Bertrand: The Grand Marshal asks the Emperor for a second time if he may nurse him; he believes he asked with some warmth: "Majesty, zeal and affection make up for many things. . . . I have spent so many nights by you as your aide-de-camp, I would like to spend some as your valet. It doesn't matter in what way I can be useful to you; it's enough for me if I've been good for something." "It's not necessary."

April 9

Bertrand: At seven-thirty Antommarchi comes to the Emperor, who is very angry with him. "He should be here at six o'clock in the morning: he spends all his time with Madame Bertrand."

The Emperor sends for the Grand Marshal, who arrives at 7:45. He repeats what he said. He adds that the doctor is interested only in his sluts: "Well, let him spend all his time with his sluts; let him fuck them in front, in back, in the mouth, in the ears. But rid me of this man who is stupid, ignorant, conceited, without honor. I want you to call Arnott to take care of me in the future. Arrange things with Montholon. I want no more of Antommarchi."

This scene takes place in the presence of Marchand and Antommarchi. He repeats five or six times that Madame Bertrand is a slut. He adds: "I have made a will: I leave Antommarchi twenty francs to buy a rope to hang himself . . ."

After Antommarchi leaves, the Emperor tells the Grand Marshal that the doctor is his wife's lover. He adds, in front of Marchand and Ali, that he is countenancing something

229

dishonorable for himself as well as for Madame Bertrand; that the doctor destroyed himself when he stopped being close to Montholon and got close to Madame Bertrand; that this was easy to foresee; that Madame Bertrand destroyed Antommarchi just as she had destroyed Gourgaud. . . . The Grand Marshal continues to listen without saying anything.

Antommarchi told the Governor he wanted to go back to Europe; that unfortunately for the Emperor he could no longer be of any use to him; that he had finished his textbook and wanted to go to Europe to publish it.

Antommarchi: [No entry for this date.]

Forshufvud: Obviously Napoleon's mind is unhinged at this time. Who is planting those ideas about Antommarchi in his disordered thoughts? Certainly not Bertrand, whose own very proper wife is being slandered. But Montholon, as we know, has been conducting a campaign to get rid of Antommarchi.

April 10 or 11

Marchand: The Emperor . . . works with Count Montholon during the day on his bequests; and he asks him in front of me whether two million will be enough to buy back his family's properties in Burgundy; is the Emperor planning to make another will? Yet I know there already is a will, that I took to Count Bertrand one evening.

April 11

Antommarchi: During the previous night, the vomiting became alarming; I tried to stop it, and proposed an antiemetic mixture, anodine, with opiate. He refused impatiently; I did not insist. I went to my apartment; he sent for me. "Doctor," he said when I appeared, "your patient wants henceforth to be obedient; he has resolved to take your remedies." Then looking with a slight smile at those of his servants who were around his bed: "First drug all these scoundrels for me, drug yourself, you all need it." Hoping to challenge his pride, we all tasted the potion. "Well, all right,

I don't want to be the only one who is afraid of a drug. Come on, quick!" I gave it to him: he seized it and drank it at one gulp. Unfortunately it had little effect and the vomiting continued.

Bertrand: He dismissed Antommarchi, then Bertrand, saying to him: "Since I was willing to see Antommarchi, let him show his gratitude through his care."

April 13

Marchand: His Majesty continues to dictate; Count de Montholon is alone with the Emperor, who until three o'clock dictates his wishes to him.

Bertrand: At half-past four, the two doctors enter. . . . The Emperor spends an hour giving a diatribe against the English oligarchy: ". . . one day John Bull will rebel against the oligarchs and hang them all. I will be gone, but you will see it. You will have a revolution more terrible than ours. The oligarchs are the same everywhere: self-important and insolent when they are in command, cowards when there is any danger." The Emperor wants to give Arnott his volume on the campaign of their greatest captain, Marlborough, for the regiment's library: "They will see that I honor brave men of all nations." Doctor Arnott asks the Grand Marshal to express his thanks.

Marchand: The Emperor sent me to get the book from his library: it was a beautiful volume, with plates and a luxurious binding.

April 15

Bertrand: The Grand Marshal told the Emperor that he did not like to speak of his own troubles when the Emperor was suffering, but that the Emperor's harsh treatment of him made him most unhappy.

"I don't know what you mean. Explain. I'm sick, in my bed, I say little. You have nothing to complain about."

"Your Majesty no longer has any confidence in me. I have lost almost without regret the high rank, the fortune, and the honors to which you raised me. But this new misfortune is too much to bear. I gave up those honors as I would a borrowed suit of clothes, but I thought I had some right to your esteem and your friendship. I cannot lose that without feeling great pain. Not long ago Your Majesty told me my conduct had been perfect. . . . How in such a short time have I lost your good grace?"

"But I don't know what you mean. I treat you very well. I have nothing against you. Marchand is the one whose care is most agreeable because I am most accustomed to him. That is all there is to it."

"My poor wife, if the climate doesn't kill her, she will die of grief. You have forgiven so many enemies—will you not forgive an old friend? No doubt she has her faults, but hasn't she suffered enough for them: isn't she very unhappy? Has she not been exposed to the most dreadful slanders?"

"But I have nothing to reproach Madame Bertrand. She is an excellent woman. I am not in the habit of seeing her."

"She would have nursed you with so much affection. She is sincerely attached to you, a lot more than you think. See her tomorrow, even if it is only for a moment."

"I will see Madame Bertrand before I die."

The Grand Marshal could not hold back his tears. He stayed for a half-hour longer with the Emperor, who said no more.

Hudson Lowe to Arnott [ordering him not to deliver the book from Napoleon to the regimental library]: The attempt to make you the channel of communication in such matters, they well know, is foreign to your professional duties, and it will probably, therefore, not have been made without some ulterior design in view.

April 16

Marchand: The Emperor tells me to give him some of the wine sent by Las Cases; I take the liberty of expressing my fears about the result. . . . The Emperor insists on taking it, soaks a biscuit in it, and goes on writing . . .

April 17

Bertrand: Montholon tells Antommarchi that the Emperor has taken care of all his dispositions, but that he has

not yet made a will, that if he dies no one will get anything.
Antommarchi: The Emperor took his usual dose of quinine solution.

April 17 and 18

Marchand: The Emperor spends several hours on the days of the 17th and 18th alone with Count de Montholon; tired of his anise water, he tries some of the refreshments placed on his table, such as lemonade, currant, and orgeat . . .

April 18

Antommarchi: The Emperor has one of his worst nights. He feels pain and an unbearable burning sensation in the abdomen. He is icy, covered with sweat; he has continual nausea and vomiting that lasts until 4:30 in the morning. He is sad, defeated, speaks with difficulty. He attributes his condition to the tonic he took the night before.

Bertrand: At 5:30, the Emperor sends for the Grand Marshal. He hands him three packages tied with ribbon and sealed with his coat of arms, and says: "I have made my will, everything is in my handwriting; put your signature and your seal there. Montholon will sign here, Vignali there, Marchand there. You will also put your seals on the three packages. Do this without asking questions."

Napoleon gets up from his bed. The Grand Marshal goes to help him as he has done for the last ten or fifteen days—"No." He walks with a firm step to his armchair. . . . The doctors enter. Napoleon is quite cheerful, speaks easily, does not lean too much on the chair, asks for his dinner. He eats some hash. . . . He asks if there is a leg of lamb, to bring him a slice that is easy to chew. . . . At 8:30, he takes his quinine and soon after vomits a large part of what he had eaten at six o'clock, but not the quinine.

April 19

Arnott: "Tell me, Dr. Arnott, is this quinine solution made here or in the town?"

"In the town, sire."

233

"Did the apothecary come at the same time as the Governor?"

"No, sire."

"Did Thomas Reade [aide to the Governor] get hold of him?"

"No, sire, the man was here before the Governor came. He is employed by the East India Company and is most trustworthy."

April 21

Bertrand: He has the arrival of Julius Caesar in Greece, before the battle of Pharsala, read to him, mainly by Bertrand. He then dictates to Marchand a note to add to his commentary on Caesar's campaigns.

Marchand: When I was alone with him, standing by his bed, he told me that he was naming me one of his executors jointly with Count de Montholon and Bertrand; my surprise was as great as the honor he was according me; I stammered that I would be worthy of his trust and of the position to which he was elevating me. He told me: "I have a will at the Grand Marshal's to be opened by him after my death, tell him to give it to you and bring it to me." When I made this request to the Grand Marshal, on behalf of the Emperor, he seemed quite surprised, but he got it from his writing table and gave it to me without showing any sign that he was thinking that the Emperor was making new dispositions. The Emperor took the envelope, tore it open, scanned its pages, tore it in half and told me to burn it in the fireplace. Beautiful pages to save, written in the Emperor's hand! I held them in my hands, but the Emperor wanted them destroyed! . . . soon they were devoured by the flames, without my knowing their provisions.

Antommarchi: At 1:30 he called Vignali: "Do you know what a *chapelle ardente* is [a mortuary chapel lit with tapers]? "Yes, sire." "Have you ever officiated at one?" "Never." "Well, you will officiate at mine." He went into great detail, and gave the priest long instructions. "You will conduct all the usual ceremonies, you will stop only when I am underground."

Marchand: That day was certainly one of the most fatiguing the Emperor had experienced as yet during his illness. . . . The morning had been spent writing his codicils: although very tired, he made me sit by his bed and dictated to me the official instructions for his executors, instructions which I copied and he signed on the 26th, after rereading them.

During this week, he suffered several fits of vomiting that forced him to stop dictating for a few moments. Nothing I could say would make him stop this work that had such grave consequences: "I am very tired," he said, "but I have little time left and I must finish; give me a little bit of the Vin de Constance from Las Cases." I dared to remind him of the effect the wine had produced a few days earlier. "Bah," he said, "a drop can't hurt me." . . . The Vin de Constance soon produced vomiting, which did not prevent him from continuing to work until the Grand Marshal and the doctors entered.

Bertrand: The Emperor told the Grand Marshal he had made three wills: the first was to be opened only in Paris; it should be said that it had been taken to Europe by Buonavita, so that the English would not find it; the second was a codicil to be opened here and shown to the English; in it he disposed of all his possessions here so the English could not seize them; the third will was for the Empress.

In the will he declares that he is dying in the Catholic faith in which he was born . . . because this is acceptable to public opinion.

He would prefer to be buried in the Père-Lachaise cemetery [in Paris].

He stated in his will some facts and principles of his government, for example the judgment of the Duke d'Enghien: he had him executed . . . because there was in Paris a conspiracy of sixty assassins sent by the Bourbons. He had him arrested out of a feeling of justice and national dignity; he had the right to do it, and today, on the edge of the grave, he does not repent and would do it again.

Montholon owes him nothing and lost 300,000 francs of his fortune by coming here; he hopes the Grand Marshal will stay close to Montholon.

He wants to elevate Marchand . . . he must not dissipate what he is giving him, but must establish a solid fortune . . . he hopes that [Bertrand] will protect Marchand, that we will help him with our advice.

He is leaving one million to the Grand Marshal, the same to Montholon . . . there is only the poor doctor to whom he is leaving nothing; he had wanted to leave him 200,000 francs, but did not, less through lack of confidence in his skill than because [Antommarchi] did not show dedication to him . . . but he could still share in his bequests; a codicil could be added.

[Bertrand] must spend some time in Paris to conclude the business of the will; then he should stay quietly in his [home] department for a year, get himself named a deputy. . . . he must not leave Berry, he should buy farms and properties ten leagues from Chateauroux and a nice property five or six miles away, if possible.

The Emperor then searched a great deal in his memory and often asked if he had not forgotten one of his former servants. He did this with a kind of anxiety, wanting not to overlook any of those who had served him well: "I am examining my conscience, I want to pay all my debts, all those of my childhood."

April 23

Bertrand: "It is probable that Montholon, who had no previous credit, had worked to gain it. . . . I am well aware that Montholon is courting me for an inheritance, but in order to get money from people, one must not beat them with a stick."

April 24

Bertrand: "[Napoleon's] family must establish itself in Rome by allying itself to the princely families, those who have produced Popes. . . . They can kiss the Pope's ass, that is not kissing the ass of any individual or any family; but they must not kiss the ass of the King of England or Sweden or Naples."

Bertrand: He asks if there are any bitter almonds at Longwood. They are rare here; they were only obtained once, three years ago.

Antommarchi: He was feeling better; I had some medications to prepare, so I took advantage of the time to go to my pharmacy. As soon as he was alone, some cruel whim about eating took hold of him. He ordered fruits, wine, tried a biscuit, then champagne, asked for a prune, took a grape, and burst into gales of laughter when he saw me.

Lutyens to Gorrequer: Count Montholon has requested me to ask if any bitter almonds could be got from Plantation House, as they could not find any for sale in Jamestown.

Bertrand: The Governor sent a case of bitter almonds.

Forshufvud: Bitter almonds are used to make the true orgeat. They can also, in the right combination, be a deadly poison. The orgeat that now sits by Napoleon's bedside is harmless. Add the bitter almonds and it can kill.

April 26

Bertrand: Today he often seems to have lost his memory. For the last ten days, he has been asking the same questions, sometimes two or three times, and forgetting that it has been answered; sometimes he talks nonsense, but not often.

Madame Bertrand . . . asked to see the Emperor. Montholon told the Emperor, who answered [according to what Montholon told Madame Bertrand]: "I will not see her; I fear my emotions. I am angry with her for not being my mistress. I want to teach her a lesson."

Seven P.M. The Emperor moved to the salon, supported on one side by the Grand Marshal and on the other by Marchand, and when he was lying down he said to the Grand Marshal: "The Empress . . . must watch over the education of his son and his security; she must be careful of the Bourbons who will surely want to get rid of him."

Marchand: He sent for Dr. Antommarchi and was affectionate with him . . . he asked him if he would want to enter the service of the Empress, to whom he would write a letter of recommendation: "You will be pleased with what I am doing for you." I heard with pleasure this renewed kindness toward Dr. Antommarchi.

Antommarchi: Napoleon at last agreed to leave his small, inconvenient, and poorly ventilated room and stay in the salon.

April 28

Antommarchi: The Emperor gave me the following instructions: "After my death, which cannot be far off, I want you to open my body; I also want, I demand, that you promise me that no English doctor will lay a hand on me. But if someone's help is indispensable, you will employ only Dr. Arnott. I want you to remove my heart, which you will put in spirits of wine and take to Parma, to my dear Marie-Louise. . . . I recommend that you examine my stomach particularly carefully, make a precise, detailed report on it and give it to my son. . . . I charge you to overlook nothing in this examination. . . . When I am gone, you will go to Rome, to my mother, my family . . . tell them I bequeath to all the ruling families the horror and shame of my last moments."

Forshufvud: Despite Napoleon's resentment of Antommarchi's overly independent behavior, and despite the slanders of him that he has evidently heard and in his deranged moments believed, still it is obvious that the Emperor trusts Antommarchi, and only Antommarchi, to perform the autopsy that is so important to him. He is, after all, a fellow Corsican.

April 29

Bertrand: The Emperor summons Pierron, to ask if he had been in town, if the schooner that arrived the day before had brought oranges. Pierron said it had.

"Did it bring limes?"
"No."
"Almonds?"
"No."
"Grapes?"
"No."
"Wine?"
"No, not in bottles."
"So it didn't bring anything?"
"Cattle."
"How many oxen?"
"Forty."
"How many goats?"
"None."
"How many hens?"
"None."
"So it didn't bring anything? Did it bring nuts?"
"No."
"I believe nuts come from cold countries, almonds from hot countries. Are the limes good here?"
"I have seen no good ones."
"Did it bring limes . . . pomegranates . . . almonds?"

Three times he called Pierron to repeat the same thing, like a man who has completely lost his memory. One could recognize the Emperor only in the continual, uninterrupted flow of questions.

His deafness has worsened since yesterday to an extraordinary extent. One has to speak very loud, shout at him like a deaf person, which I had never seen in the Emperor, though for many years I had known him to be rather hard of hearing.

At noon, the Emperor was given soup, an egg, a biscuit, a spoonful of wine. Antommarchi also gave him three spoonfuls of coffee. It seems that Montholon said to him: "Stuff the Emperor and try to give him strength. I have something I want to get him to sign": the letter to the Empress recommending the doctor.

That morning he had asked twenty times if he was allowed

to have coffee. "No, sire." . . . The tears came to my eyes at the sight of this man who had been so awesome, who had commanded so proudly, so absolutely, begging for a spoonful of coffee, obeying like a child, asking again if he was denied permission, all without anger. . . . Such was the great Napoleon: miserable, humble.

From one o'clock to three o'clock, he kept repeating the same question every minute: "What is the best syrup? Lemonade or orgeat?"

Marchand: Before he left, [Montholon] took me aside and gave me drafts of two letters the Emperor had told him to write for me to make clean copies which, on his return, he would get the Emperor to sign, for if he did not sign today, he might not be able to tomorrow. . . . I gave the copies to Count de Montholon, saying that I had dated them the 25th, as they were in the draft, although today was the 29th. If I have lingered over these two letters it is because Count de Montholon, in the two volumes he has published on St. Helena, in which his memory is often at fault, says that these letters were dictated to me by the Emperor, which is not true. These letters are the work of Count de Montholon . . .

Bertrand: Montholon told the Grand Marshal he had been unable to get the Emperor to sign anything. . . . Montholon said the Emperor was out of his mind; that one could say that it was not the Emperor who had made his will, but he, Montholon, who dictated it to him . . .

April 30

Antommarchi: Nine A.M. The patient has almost no fever; he is quite calm; the pulse is weak and varies from 85 to 91. . . . The vesicatories placed on the thighs have had no effect; the one placed in the area of the epigastrium causes no pain to the patient, who is not aware it is there. Noon: Burning sensation in the pharynx. Three P.M. The fever increases . . .

Bertrand: "Where is Gourgaud?"

"In Paris."

"Why did he leave?"

"Because he was sick."

"With my permission?"

"Yes, sire, you even wrote him a letter."

May 1

Marchand: At eleven o'clock, Countess Bertrand was admitted to the Emperor's bedside. . . . The Emperor spoke with her for a few minutes, then asked her to return later. She left in order not to tire him; I accompanied her as far as the garden, where she burst into sobs: "What a change in the Emperor since I last saw him! . . . The Emperor has been cruel to me in not allowing me to see him. I am glad to have his friendship again, but I would be happier if he let me take care of him." Doctors Arnott and Antommarchi are both sleeping in the library.

Antommarchi: The pulse is weak and rapid, up to 100 a minute. . . . Little by little the worst symptoms diminish, and the morning is quite calm. Noon: hiccuping is worse than ever.

Bertrand: "Is O'Meara here?"

"He is gone."

"Ah! I didn't see him. Did you see him?"

"Yes."

"Did he say goodbye to you?"

"Yes."

"Who made him leave?"

"The Governor."

"Why? Because he was too linked to us?"

"Yes."

"So he won't come back?"

"No."

"Do we have any news about him? Do we know what he is doing in London?"

"No."

"And Balcombe, where is he?"

"He is gone."

"What, gone? When?"

241

"A few months ago."

"And his wife also? Oh, how strange that is. What, she is gone." [The Emperor repeated this ten times.]

May 2

Antommarchi: Two A.M. Fever increases. Delirium. . . . Suddenly Napoleon gets up and wants to go out to walk in the garden; I go to catch him in my arms, but his legs give way, and I am unable to prevent him from falling. Noon: The patient regains his senses. . . . Frequent hiccup of an alarming nature. . . . Potion of orange water with a few drops of tincture of opium and ether. . . . Napoleon could no longer stand light; we were forced to lift him, change him, give him the care his condition required, all in pitch darkness. . . . The Grand Marshal was worn out, so was Montholon, I was not much better: we gave in to the repeated requests of the French people living at Longwood and allowed them to share in our melancholy duties. . . . The Emperor was touched by the zeal they displayed, he recommended them to his officers, told them not to forget them: "And my poor Chinese! Don't forget them either, give them a few dozen napoleons: I have to make my farewell to them also."

Bertrand: About seven o'clock he is offered orange water with sugar: "My phalanx! What is that?" "Orange water." "Ah! I understand." A little bit later: "It is a lost cause."

Forshufvud: The "orange water" that Napoleon is now drinking every day is undoubtedly orgeat with bitter almonds. Two of the three elements of the final, killing blow—the treatment with tartar emetic and the bitter almonds in the diet—are now in place.

May 3

Antommarchi: 8:45 A.M. The Emperor takes two biscuits, wine, and an egg yolk with some pleasure: still he continues to get weaker. Somnolence. Hiccup. Frequent nausea. Vomiting similar to preceding days. The usual anodine potion is administered. Hudson, suddenly seized with humanity, gets the idea that cow's milk could relieve this cruel agony, and offers some. Doctor Arnott admires his chief's inspiration and wants to try it. I oppose it wholeheartedly . . . we have a lively discussion . . . I succeed in preventing the giving of milk.

Marchand: The Emperor wants nothing but sugared water with a little wine; every time I give it to him, he says with a look of satisfaction: "It's good, it's so good!"

Bertrand: All during the day, when he was given wine or orange water with sugar, he said the same thing.

Antommarchi: Noon: The pulse is up to 110; temperature is much higher than normal. Napoleon drinks a great deal of water with sugar.

Marchand: That same day, at two o'clock, I was alone with the Emperor when Saint-Denis came to tell me the priest Vignali was asking for me. "The Emperor sent word through Count de Montholon that he wanted to see me," he said, "but I must be alone with him." The priest was wearing civilian clothes, and under his clothing he was holding something he was trying to hide. I did not try to guess what it was, assuming he had come to perform some religious duty.

Antommarchi: Three P.M. Hiccup is strong and almost constant. Napoleon has all his faculties. He tells his executors: "I am going to die; you will return to Europe; I will give you some advice on how you must behave. You have shared my exile; you will be faithful to my memory; you will do nothing to injure it. . . . Be faithful to the beliefs we defended, the glory we won; otherwise there is only shame and confusion."

Bertrand: Arnott said medical men would not understand how they could let the Emperor go three days without a bowel movement, that one must be induced either by enema or medication. . . . Antommarchi refused and [said] he would take the responsibility. . . . Arnott persisted.

Marchand: I returned to the Emperor whom I found with eyes closed, his arm stretched out to the side of the bed; I got down on one knee and brought my lips to his hand without his opening his eyes. . . .I remained alone, standing by the Emperor's bedside, holding back my sobs but allowing my tears to flow . . .

Bertrand: About two-thirty, the Governor comes to see General Montholon. He says his government instructed him, in case of danger to the Emperor's life, to send the leading doctor of the island and the admiral's doctor. . . . [Drs. Shortt and Mitchell] ask to see General Montholon, who receives them in his apartments.

Antommarchi: I described the symptoms of the illness to [Shortt and Mitchell]; they are not satisfied and want to see Napoleon's condition for themselves; I assure them that is impossible; they side with Doctor Arnott, who proposes a purgative made up of ten grains of calomel; I cry out against that prescription; the patient is too weak; it will fatigue him for no purpose; but I am alone, they are three, and numbers prevail.

Marquis de Montchenu, the French commissioner: The discussion was referred to Montholon, who sided with the English doctors, and the medicine was consequently administered.

Forshufvud: This is it, the final blow, and Montchenu tells us it was engineered by Montholon over the determined opposition of the doctor he had tried to drive away from his victim's bedside—Antommarchi. By a vote of three to one, the doctors have signed Napoleon's death warrant.

Calomel was the miracle drug of the time, much like penicillin today. Physicians prescribed it, as they did tartar emetic, for many kinds of illnesses they could not otherwise treat, and especially as a cathartic for the constipation from which Arnott believed Napoleon to be suffering.

By itself, calomel is rather harmless. But it is deadly in combination with the bitter almonds in the orgeat Napoleon was now drinking every day. This is what happens: the almonds contain hydrocyanic acid (prussic acid) which releases poisonous mercurial salts or mercurous cynanide from the otherwise inert mercury in the calomel. The victim loses consciousness soon after drinking the lethal mixture. The voluntary muscles become paralyzed; the victim loses sight and hearing. The autonomous sympathetic nervous system will go on functioning for a brief while. The corrosive effect of the poison on the stomach would explain the "ulcer" found there at the autopsy of Napoleon's body.

But the victim's stomach can protect itself against the calomel-orgeat poison if it promptly expels it by vomiting. That is the purpose of the earlier administration of tartar emetic, to weaken the stomach's natural protective reaction. If the body does not quickly rid itself of the poison, death can be expected within a day or two.

The lethal combination of calomel and orgeat, preceded by tartar emetic, was known to professional poisoners of Napoleon's time. In fact, in 1814, just seven years before the final blow at St. Helena, a doctor in Paris had tested the method on dogs and found that it worked.

The dosage of calomel given to Napoleon—ten grains—can only be called heroic, or insane. Normal English practice at the time was two grains divided into several doses; German and Swedish doctors gave only one grain. Did Montholon help talk the doctors into this enormous and unusual dosage? There is no direct evidence, but it *is* known that Montholon, in his memoirs, refers to an earlier occasion, undated, on which Napoleon was ill with dysentery and: "For three days, we were extremely anxious. Although the illness did not become worse, his life was still in danger as long as calomel had not achieved that which the doctors called its effect." This is a strange tale. No other memoirs report that Napoleon had ever taken calomel before the last days. Antommarchi never prescribed it. In any event, we can be quite sure that Napoleon would have refused to take it just as he refused other medication.

Marchand: As a result of the consultation, I was called on to give calomel to the Emperor. I told the Grand Marshal and Count de Montholon, who spoke to me about it, that the Emperor had positively told me he wanted no drink or potion that he had not approved and that they must remember the Emperor's anger with Doctor Antommarchi under similar circumstances. "Yes, no doubt," the Grand Marshal said to me with his usual kindness, "This is a last resort; we must not have it on our consciences that we did not do everything humanly possible to save him." Encouraged by these words of the Grand Marshal, I mixed the powder in water with a little sugar and when the Emperor asked me for something to drink, I presented it to him as sugared water. He opened his mouth, swallowed with difficulty, tried unsuccessfully to reject it; turning to me, he said, in a tone of reproach that was so affectionate and is so difficult to convey: "You too are deceiving me?"

Bertrand: Bertrand told Monsieur Vignali to come see the Emperor when he wished, but not to stay constantly with him, so that slanderers and the enemies of the Emperor could not say—as Bertrand knew had already been said on the island—that the Emperor, this man who was so strong, was dying like a Capuchin monk and wanted a priest always with him—which [Vignali] understood.

Antommarchi: Ten P.M. The ten grains of calomel still having produced no result, another dose [of ten grains] is suggested. I do not measure my words, I am formally opposed to such a proposal.

Bertrand: Arnott and Antommarchi were both heated in their opinions, when, at eleven-thirty, the Emperor had a bowel movement. It was black, enormous, larger alone than all those he had for a month.

Saint-Denis: The potion had an effect: it produced a large evacuation of a blackish substance, thick and in part solid, resembling pitch or tar. As the Emperor was extremely weak, it was impossible to move him from the bed, as we had done two days earlier. Then he had been able to sit on his toilet; but this time the best we could do was to change his sheet. This was not done without difficulty. . . . I stood on the two sides of the bed, put my arms under the Emperor's back, clasped my hands and lifted him enough for Marchand to remove the sheet filled with everything that had come out of the patient's body. This was all the more difficult because the Emperor was still very heavy and I had no place to brace myself.

Bertrand: Perhaps this will save the Emperor.

Forshufvud: Stools from a stomach that is corroded and therefore bleeding will be very dark brown. The metallic mercury, from the calomel-orgeat reaction, is black as ink.

May 4

Antommarchi: 1:30 A.M. Complete collapse. Cold sweat. Pulse irregular, can hardly be felt. Constant desire to urinate. These symptoms lasted through the night. The Emperor took orange water in small quantities at considerable intervals. The weather was terrible, rain fell without interruption, the wind seemed about to destroy everything. The willow under which Napoleon used to sit had given way; our gardens were all torn up; a single gum tree held out till a gust seized it, uprooted it, laid it down in the mud. Nothing that the Emperor loved was to survive him. . . . His debility is general and gets constantly worse.

Arnott to Thomas Reade: Calomel had the desired effect. The patient does not appear to be worse but rather better. After thorough consideration I have decided that there is more hope today than yesterday and the day before. Tell the Governor this.

Marchand: The Emperor refuses all the remedies that are offered to him; he continues drinking sugared water with wine or with orange, it is the only drink that he finds agreeable; each time I offer it to him, he answers with these words: "That's very good, my son."

Antommarchi: 7:30 A.M.: Hiccup is strong and continuous. The patient refuses to take any medication. . . . Later he drinks a great deal of orange water, mixed with ordinary water and sugar. . . . Sardonic laughter. Eyes staring.

Bertrand: At 6:30, bowel movement . . . very weak. . . . At 10:45: "Well, Bertrand, my friend." At noon, another bowel movement. At 1:30, he stares at everybody. Faints seven or eight times during a bowel movement. At 2:30, faints twice, five minutes apart. Bowel movement. . . . Montholon and Bertrand receive the two doctors [Shortt and Mitchell], who say the Governor demands that they see the Emperor that evening, when the darkness will permit them to approach him, take his pulse, feel his stomach, etc. . . . At eight, quite large bowel movement.

Arnott to Hudson Lowe: Nine P.M.: I have just left our patient fast asleep. He appears better than he was two hours ago. He had no hiccup, his respiration is easy, and in the course of the day he has taken a considerable quantity of nourishment for a person in his state.

Bertrand: At 9:30, Antommarchi thinks he will not last past midnight. . . . Until the last moment, that is until the day he was motionless, he was very sensitive to flies: they made him moan twice on the last day.

Marchand: About ten P.M., he seems drowsy beneath his mosquito net, which has been lowered. By his bedside, I watch his slightest movements, while the two doctors, Count de Montholon, and the Grand Marshal speak softly to each other by the fireplace. The Emperor makes an effort to vomit, I immediately lift the mosquito net to hold out a small silver basin in which he throws up some blackish substance, after which his head falls back on the pillow.

Forshufvud: Again, the blackish color is characteristic of bleeding plus the metallic mercury. Napoleon's stomach is trying to save the body, but it is far too late: the poison has done its work.

Antommarchi: The night is extremely uncomfortable. The pain is general, breathing difficult. . . . 5:30 A.M.: Napoleon is still delirious, he speaks with effort, inarticulate words: *"Tête . . . armée."*

Bertrand: Some words we could not hear, and *"qui recule";* and certainly: *"à la tête de l'armée."*

Montholon: *"France, l'armée, tête d'armée, Josephine."*

Marchand: *"France, mon fils, armée."* These were the last words we were to hear.

Bertrand: All through the night, not so much hiccups as groans, sometimes loud enough to awaken those who were dozing in the room.

Marchand: At six o'clock, the blinds were opened, and the Grand Marshal sent word to Countess Bertrand of the Emperor's condition; she arrived at seven, and an armchair was put at the foot of the bed where she sat for the entire day.

Arnott to Hudson Lowe: Seven A.M.: He is dying. Montholon prays I will not leave the bedside. He wishes I should see him breathe his last.

Antommarchi: I thought the essence of life had gone, but little by little the pulse revived. . . . Deep sighs: Napoleon is still alive. . . . Then took place what was perhaps the most excruciating scene of his long agony. Madame Bertrand, who despite her own illness did not want to leave the side of the august patient for a moment, sent first for her daughter Hortense, then for her three sons, for them to see for the last time the person who had been their benefactor. It was about fifty days since they had been admitted to Napoleon, and their tear-filled eyes searched with horror in his pale and disfigured face for the expression of grandeur and kindness that they used to find there. All at once they dashed to the bed, seized both the Emperor's hands, kissed them, sobbing, covering them with their tears. Young Napoléon Bertrand could not long endure this cruel scene; he gave in to his emotions; he fainted. We had to pull the children away from the bedside and take them to the garden.

Marchand: The French people in the Emperor's service whose duties did not give them access to the interior came in at eight . . . and joined us gathered around the bed.

Bertrand: Sixteen people were present, of whom a dozen were French.

Antommarchi: 10:30 A.M. I was following the pulse with anxiety when I saw Noverraz enter; he was pale, disheveled, beside himself. This unfortunate man, weakened by forty-eight days of acute hepatitis accompanied by fever, was just beginning to convalesce, but he had learned of the Emperor's state and he wanted once more to see the person he had so long served. I tried to send him away, but his excitement grew as I was speaking; he thought the Emperor was in danger, that he had been called to the rescue; he will not abandon him, he wants to fight, to die for him. He was out of his mind; I complimented his zeal, calmed him, and came back to my post.

Marchand: Our eyes were fixed on that august head, looking away only to try to read in Dr. Antommarchi's expression whether there was any hope. In vain; merciless death is there.

Bertrand: From eleven to noon, Arnott placed two mustard plasters on the feet, and Antommarchi two vesicatories, one on the chest, the other on the calf. The Emperor sighed several times. At 2:30 Arnott ordered a hot-water bottle placed on the stomach.

Arnott to Hudson Lowe: Three P.M.: The pulse cannot be felt at the wrist now, and the heat is departing from the surface.

Antommarchi: I bring water mixed with orange water and sugar to his lips, but the passage is closed, none of it is swallowed; all is in vain.

Arnott to Hudson Lowe: 5:15 P.M. He is worse. The respiration has become more hurried and difficult.

Marchand: At 5:50 in the evening, we hear the cannon

250

sound retreat, and the sun vanishes in a burst of light. Doctor Arnott, his eyes on his watch, counts the time from one sigh to the next: fifteen seconds, then thirty, then a minute passes; we wait, but in vain. The eyes open suddenly. Doctor Antommarchi, standing by the Emperor's head feeling the last heartbeats at the neck, immediately closes the eyes.

Antommarchi: The eyes roll up under the upper lids, the pulse vanishes. It is eleven minutes before six. Napoleon is no more.

Arnott to Hudson Lowe: 5:49: He has this moment expired.

CHAPTER TWENTY-NINE

JUNE 1975
GERANIUM VALLEY, ST. HELENA

=================================== **S** TEN FORSHUFVUD stood alone
at the empty grave. All was silence here, at the spring where
Napoleon had gotten his drinking water, in the valley where,
under the three weeping willows, the Emperor's poisoned body
had lain for nineteen years. The willows were gone, replaced by
cypress and pine planted over the years by both French and
English. The grave was an unmarked cement slab surrounded by
a simple metal fence. Forshufvud was the only visitor that day;
the only sound was the cry of an occasional bird. The sun was
warm, but here, in the deep shade, the silence was cool.

Forshufvud had arrived at St. Helena a week before and was
due to depart the next day. The voyage had not been easy to
arrange, for St. Helena is in some ways less accessible in the late
twentieth century than it was in Napoleon's time. In the 1860s,
with the opening of the Suez Canal, the little island lost its
function as a stopping place on the sea route to the Orient. Its
population of about five thousand, most of them supported by the
British government, was a little more than it was when Napoleon
was there, less than it was in the 1860s. It had no airport; other

than a rare cruise ship, the only way to reach St. Helena was by one of the two English freighters that shuttled between Southampton and Capetown, and their twelve cabins were usually reserved months or years in advance.

The tiny port of Jamestown, as Forshufvud had first glimpsed it a week ago, seemed hardly changed from the place Napoleon saw a century and a half earlier. It still consisted mainly of a single street along the water, and a handful of shops. Most of the buildings dated from the nineteenth century, some from Napoleon's time. Ships still could not dock at Jamestown. Forshufvud had come ashore on a lighter and landed on stone steps a hundred feet or so from the similar steps on which Napoleon, and his assassin, first set foot on that October evening while Betsy Balcombe and the other islanders strained for a glimpse of him.

Though Longwood House, now restored by Gilbert Martineau, the French consul and author, was much as Forshufvud had pictured it, St. Helena had one notable surprise for him: the climate. From the exiles' endless complaints about the weather and the "climatic disease," Forshufvud had expected the worst, but now, though it was winter in the Southern Hemisphere, he found the island positively balmy. When he made this observation in Jamestown to Martineau, who lived in Longwood House, the Frenchman admitted the coast was all right but said Longwood plain was another story. But at Longwood, when he asked Martineau's eighty-five-year-old mother, she said the climate was "delicious" and added: *"Ici, monsieur, c'est le paradis."* Forshufvud decided that the exiles, hating the fact of exile and seeking to blame the English for Napoleon's illness, were determined to find fault with everything about St. Helena. Later French writers had followed their example: so history is written.

Now, as he stood gazing in silence at the unmarked cement slab, Forshufvud's thoughts turned to the scene in October of 1840 when, at this place, Napoleon's body had provided the last piece of evidence in his case. Earlier that year, King Louis-Philippe, under pressure from the Bonapartist tide then rising in

France, had decided to send a delegation to St. Helena to fulfill the dying Emperor's wish by bringing his remains back to lie in glory on the banks of the Seine. All the surviving companions of the captivity were invited to accompany their master's body on its journey home. Most of the central figures of the exile had accepted and were now at the grave. Bertrand, sixty-seven, gray and weary, was there with one of his sons, now grown; Fanny Bertrand had died four years earlier. Las Cases was over eighty and blind, and his son Emmanuel went in his place. Gourgaud, hot-tempered as ever, quarreled with Emmanuel instead of his father. Louis Marchand was now middle-aged and, thanks to Napoleon's legacy, a comfortable member of the bourgeoisie. He was there, and so were his two assistant valets, Saint-Denis and Noverraz, the Swiss bear. Pierron the chef and Archambault the groom were there. The two doctors, O'Meara and Antommarchi, were both dead by then, O'Meara in England, Antommarchi in Santiago de Cuba.

Montholon was not there. He was, in fact, in jail while the others were at the grave, though he was free and available in July when the expedition set sail from France on board *La Belle Poule.*

Montholon's life after the return from exile had been as ambiguous and puzzling as his career before St. Helena. He had collected 1.5 million francs of his legacy, a huge amount, but managed to lose it all, and by 1829 he was bankrupt. He was in and out of the army, always on the fringe, never seeming to belong anywhere. It was known that in 1827 he was received in secret by King Charles X, the former Count d'Artois and the man, Forshufvud was certain, who had sent Montholon to St. Helena to poison the fallen Emperor. Charles never rewarded Montholon, at least not in public, but then governments seldom reward those who do their dirty work for them. Charles had so mismanaged his rule, so misjudged the French, that he was ousted in 1830, this proving once more the old French saying, often quoted by Napoleon, that the Bourbons learned nothing and forgot nothing. When an American ship took Charles into his third and final exile—surely some sort of record, Forshufvud thought—a member of the royal party asked where the ship was going. "To St. Helena," a sailor said. Charles died near Trieste four years before his great enemy's remains were brought back with spectacular honors to France.

Earlier in that year of 1840, Montholon had attached himself to Louis Napoleon, the son of Louis Bonaparte's wife, Hortense, and the future Emperor Napoleon III. (Louis Napoleon had become the Bonaparte heir on the death eight years earlier, at twenty-one, of Napoleon's son. In his brief life, l'Aiglon had been known as the King of Rome, Napoleon II, the Duke of Reichstadt, and the Prince of Parma, Piacenza, and Guastella— but had never exercised any of the powers that those titles implied.) In August, Montholon headed a harebrained expedition from England to conquer France for Louis Napoleon. French troops, evidently forewarned, were waiting on the beach at Boulogne, and the invaders were quickly captured. Montholon was sentenced to twenty years but would be released after six years.

He would die thirteen years later, without having said a recorded word about his role in the most monstrous crime of his time. Did he even tell his wife Albine that he poisoned the man whose mistress she had—in all likelihood—been? Did he tell her why he had never objected to her dallying with Napoleon—so that he would be allowed to stay close to the Emperor and accomplish his mission? Probably not, Forshufvud thought, it was too dangerous. Had word gotten out that he assassinated the Emperor, one of Napoleon's loyal veterans would no doubt have put a quick end to Montholon's own life. Was he just a weakling submitting to the blackmail of the Count d'Artois? Or did he justify his betrayal of the man who trusted him by telling himself he was an officer carrying out a dangerous and disagreeable mission on behalf of the legitimate rulers of France? Was his sleep ever troubled by memories of himself standing at Napoleon's bedside watching the dying agonies of the man he had poisoned? There were no answers to these and many other questions: much of the Montholon story was lost forever in the past.

It was just as well for Montholon, Forshufvud reflected, that he was not at this spot on that rainy, foggy day when the companions of the exile watched workmen open the Emperor's grave. The assassin might have feared that the witnesses would understand the meaning of the startling sight they saw in that grave. Napoleon's body had not been embalmed, but merely buried as it was after the autopsy. It was enclosed in four coffins, two of them of metal, but none of these was airtight. The witnesses expected, given the normal decay of nineteen years, that when the innermost coffin was opened they would see a skeleton.

Napoleon's body was perfectly preserved. He looked as if he were asleep. His face had changed less in those nineteen years than the faces of those who were now gazing down into the grave. Napoleon's clothing, the uniform in which he was buried, was decayed, but not the body itself. Forshufvud knew the explanation for this seeming miracle—arsenic. Arsenic the destroyer is also a preservative of living tissue: museums often use it to preserve specimens, and a human corpse will decay much more slowly if the person was exposed to chronic arsenic poisoning. And so Napoleon's body was mutely testifying to the fact of his assassination. It could still testify today if the French would only agree to open the great tomb at Les Invalides and the six coffins within which the Emperor's remains were sealed.

But that would have to be someone else's job. Forshufvud had completed the mission he had undertaken twenty years ago, after reading Louis Marchand's memoirs. He had earned the Napoleonic bee that hung in the third-floor study where he solved the riddle of the Emperor's death. He had come on a pilgrimage to this remote site, this empty grave, to mark the end of an extraordinary period in his life. And now it was time to go home. With a last glance at the cement slab behind its metal fence, Forshufvud turned and strode rapidly off toward the road to Jamestown and home to Göteborg.

POSTSCRIPT

In the years that followed their week-long meeting at Mont Gabriel in the Laurentian Mountains, Sten Forshufvud and Ben Weider produced a scholarly work titled *Assassination at St. Helena,* which was published in 1978 by Mitchell Press Ltd. of Vancouver, Canada. Sten Forshufvud, who still lives in Göteborg, cooperated with the authors in the writing of *The Murder of Napoleon.*

INDEX

261

ABOUT THE AUTHORS

BEN WEIDER is president of the Napoleonic Society of Canada and a member of the council of the Napoleonic Society in Paris. He lives in Montreal. He was recently awarded membership in the Order of Canada.

DAVID HAPGOOD is editor of *Focus,* the magazine of the American Geographical Society. He has been a writer and editor for the *News of the Week in Review* section of *The New York Times,* and among his books are *Africa from Independence to Tomorrow; The Screwing of the Average Man;* and *No Easy Harvest* (with Max F. Millikan). He has been an evaluator for the Peace Corps and held a fellowship from the Institute of Current World Affairs, for study in French-speaking Africa. He is a trustee of the Katherine Dalglish Foundation. His translation of Jean-François Revel's *The Totalitarian Temptation* won the Scott-Moncrieff Prize in 1978.